Practical JRuby on Rails Web 2.0 Projects

Bringing Ruby on Rails to the Java™ Platform

Ola Bini

Practical JRuby on Rails Web 2.0 Projects: Bringing Ruby on Rails to the Java™ Platform

Copyright © 2007 by Ola Bini

ISBN-13 (pbk): 978-1-59059-881-8

ISBN-10 (pbk) 1-59059-881-4

Printed and bound in the United States of America 9 8 7 6 5 4 3 2 1

Lead Editor: Steve Anglin
Technical Reviewer: Pat Eyler
Editorial Board: Steve Anglin, Ewan Buckingham, Gary Cornell, Jonathan Gennick, Jason Gilmore,
    Jonathan Hassell, Matthew Moodie, Jeffrey Pepper, Ben Renow-Clarke, Dominic Shakeshaft,
    Matt Wade, Tom Welsh
Project Manager: Sofia Marchant
Copy Editor: Susannah Pfalzer
Assistant Production Director: Kari Brooks-Copony
Production Editor: Laura Cheu
Compositor: Gina Rexrode
Proofreader: Lisa Hamilton
Indexer: Julie Grady
Cover Designer: Kurt Krames
Manufacturing Director: Tom Debolski

Distributed to the book trade worldwide by Springer-Verlag New York, Inc., 233 Spring Street, 6th Floor, New York, NY 10013. Phone 1-800-SPRINGER, fax 201-348-4505, e-mail orders-ny@springer-sbm.com, or visit http://www.springeronline.com.

For information on translations, please contact Apress directly at 2855 Telegraph Avenue, Suite 600, Berkeley, CA 94705. Phone 510-549-5930, fax 510-549-5939, e-mail info@apress.com, or visit http://www.apress.com.

The source code for this book is available to readers at http://www.apress.com in the Source Code/ Download section. You will need to answer questions pertaining to this book in order to successfully download the code.

This book is dedicated to Hans Nordlöf for believing in me and always being my mentor.

Contents at a Glance

PROJECT 1 ■■■ The Store (Shoplet)

PROJECT 2 ■■■ A Content Management System (CoMpoSe)

PROJECT 3 ■■■ An Administration System (Big Brother)

PROJECT 4 ■■■ A Library System (LibLib)

Contents

PROJECT 1 ■■■ **The Store (Shoplet)**

PROJECT 2 ■■■ A Content Management System (CoMpoSe)

PROJECT 3 ■ ■ ■ An Administration System (Big Brother)

PROJECT 4 ■ ■ ■ A Library System (LibLib)

Foreword by Pat Eyler

"Hey, you got your Ruby in my Java!"

"You got your Java on my Ruby!"

I'm not going to claim that JRuby is as delicious as a Reese's Peanut Butter Cup, but it sure has been a real treat watching Ola and his codevelopers work on JRuby. They've taken an incomplete, niche Ruby environment (and subcommunity) and turned it into something that is pushing the whole Ruby community in a number of different ways.

Some time ago, Tim Bray was lamenting the lack of solid programmer tools (things like a powerful IDE, a refactoring browser, etc.) in the Ruby world. At the time, I took the stance that they hadn't really been developed because the Ruby community was able to do without them. With the advent of JRuby, though, NetBeans and Eclipse have really begun to gain momentum and are starting to produce the kinds of tools Tim was pining for into the Ruby space. I think a lot of this came to pass because JRuby drew Java developers with Tim's same desire for tools into the Ruby world.

The JRuby team's commitment to testing their implementation has been quietly filtering back into the other development teams. These days, it's common to see JRuby developers hanging out on the rubinius IRC channel (#rubinius on freenode), the YARV developers are making appearances on both the rubinius and JRuby IRC channels, and so on. The discussions between these different development groups have been great to sit in on. I think you could even build a case that JRuby has helped spur Microsoft's IronRuby.

With JRuby running on the JVM, Ruby is better able to get into some enterprise environments. Even at my day job, where I've been pushing Ruby from day one, JRuby is making Ruby solutions possible in places it wouldn't have gone on its own. Pretty soon, JRuby will be our common gateway between the infrastructure world of quick Ruby scripting and the application world of large-scale Java apps. It's a future I'm looking forward to.

JRuby has been driving changes in the Java/JVM world too. JRuby's success and acceptance is helping make the JVM a better place for languages like Groovy, Jython, and their cousins. Common requirements are being pushed by a new, more dynamic voice inside of Sun, and over the next couple of years it will make quite a difference.

Whether you're a Java hacker who's new to Ruby or a Rubyist taking your first steps into Java, this is a great guidebook to help you navigate the gray area between the new languages. I hope you'll enjoy Ola's efforts to help you see not only how great JRuby is on its own, but also how great Java and Ruby taste together.

This book is really about bringing you into an expanding new community. With each new JRuby user, the potential for exciting change grows. I hope you'll take up the torch as you read this book, and that you'll soon be out there finding (and sharing) new ways to use JRuby to make your life better.

Happy JRuby hacking! I'll look forward to seeing you on the JRuby IRC channel and mailing lists soon.

Foreword by Martin Fowler

The world of web application development has been given quite the shake in the past couple of years by the rise of Ruby on Rails. Many famous names (or incessant loudmouths) who are well known in the Java world have become strong advocates of Ruby and Rails—even to the point of leaving the Java world for good.

I've been using Ruby for many years, and I'm a big advocate of the language. It focuses on a clear but simple syntax that I find captures my intentions much more clearly than the mainstream curly brace languages. It's fully object oriented and has powerful language features such as closures. In particular, it offers a wide range of tools for metaprogramming and creating domain-specific languages. These features underpin Rails—making it much easier to create such an influential web framework.

Since Rails has appeared, I've talked to many colleagues who've given it a spin. These are people with track records of delivery with various Java and .NET web platforms. Overwhelmingly, what I hear is that they feel their work is significantly more effective with Rails. I don't take statements like "50% more productive" seriously, not least because software productivity is not something we can clearly measure. Lacking that, a clear majority of qualitative approval is the strongest sign of a good technology that we are likely to find.

Thus far, most books and articles have focused on using Ruby on Rails in its original C implementation. This volume is different because it works with the same Rails on a different platform—Java. I view the JRuby effort to create a fully effective Ruby implementation on the Java JVM to be an important project both for Ruby and Java. For Ruby developers, it offers a deployment platform that is well understood, particularly in corporations. We've already found that doors that were once closed to Rails now open when we start talking about a Java deployment.

For the Java community, JRuby is important because it offers a chance to experience a powerful language and framework while still taking advantage of Java's excellent libraries and the ability to work in both Ruby and Java. I see a polyglot future for the JVM, one where there is a choice of languages you can use on it—languages that can interoperate cleanly so you can choose the right language for a particular project. JRuby is an important step in this direction because it brings not only a language to the JVM, but also an important framework. This book is an important tool to understanding Rails in its new caffeinated home.

About the Author

OLA BINI, a longtime developer from Sweden, started programming at the age of 9 with Basic on an Apple IIc; from there he learned C, C++, Assembler, Lisp, Java, Ruby, and various other languages. He has no formal education except for a few Sun Java certifications. He worked as system developer and architect at Karolinska Institutet between 2001 and 2007. Ola is now a developer for ThoughtWorks Studios, the product development division of ThoughtWorks, Ltd. He has contributed to various open-source projects, and is one of the core developers for the JRuby project.

About the Technical Reviewer

PAT EYLER has been involved in the Ruby community since 2000 and has organized the first two semiannual Ruby Implementors Summits. He's lucky enough to work for the Church of Jesus Christ of Latter-day Saints on a project that he loves and to be able to use Ruby there (and maybe JRuby soon). When he's not working with Ruby or writing about it, he can be found outdoors serving as a scoutmaster for a small Boy Scouts troop in Utah or hanging out at home with his family, dog, cat, fish, and books.

Acknowledgments

As all people who set out to write a book inevitably discover, it is always harder than you expect. Even if you expect it to be hard, it will be even harder. (This is an instance of Hofstadter's Law, which says that something of complexity will always take more time than you expect, even if you take into account this law.) I find this very true. I have spent enormous amounts of time on it, and many people have helped me out during that time. I would like to thank them here.

First of all, thanks to Charles O Nutter and Thomas Enebo of the JRuby core team for giving me the chance to contribute to JRuby in the way I've done, and for always putting up with last-minute changes I've pushed into JRuby to correct information in this book and my insistent ranting on many and varied topics. Charles and Tom have also provided much-valued feedback on ideas while preparing the book.

A big thank-you to Steve Anglin, who initially proposed that I should do this book and has provided much editing help during the process. The rest of the Apress team has transformed this book into something that is actually readable (it wasn't at the first draft). Sofia Marchant, Susannah Davidson Pfalzer, Stephanie Parker, and Laura Cheu have definitely made this into a totally different book, and I'm eternally grateful to them. Pat Eyler's very good technical reviewing has also improved the book several times.

It is worth mentioning my coworkers at Karolinska Institutet, who spent over two years listening to me talk about everything related to Ruby, JRuby, Rails, and programming languages in general. Without their discussion and encouragement, I would probably never have had the nerve to get started on this project. So a huge thanks to Pop Qvarnström, Lars Westergren, and Eva Ragnar.

That brings me neatly to the point of family. I would never have started, would never be where I am today, without the support from my family: Dag, Görel, Kim, and Mikael. I'll always have the comfort of your support.

I would be remiss to not mention my second family in Stockholm, who have always taken care of me. Lena, Hans, Sandra, Julia, and Oliver, thank you.

And finally, the one who has suffered the most for this book: Stella, you have given me the courage, the inspiration, and the energy to bring this to fruition. You are the light of my life.

CHAPTER 1

■ ■ ■

Introduction

JRuby on Rails is an exciting technology. If you've picked up this book, you've probably realized the same thing. You might not have much experience with either Ruby or Rails, or you've tried both of them out and want to see why the combination of JRuby on Rails is so spectacular. Regardless of the reason, I hope this book will teach you something about some of the technologies involved, introduce you to new ways to look at problems, and help you see solutions in the intersection of languages where each one isn't perfectly suited for a problem.

I've been using Java for a long time, but my heart has never been in it. I've always been a programming language nerd, trying out new languages like my girlfriend tries new shoes. I knew what was out there, and that Java wasn't the end-all solution for all the problems in the world. However, the fact remained that Java was the main language used for implementing systems during most of my employment. I compensated by continuing to have fun with other languages in my spare time. About three and a half years ago, I found Ruby. I can't exactly remember how I did that, but I started using it and liked it very much. It combined some of the more useful parts of Lisp metaprogrammability, with a Smalltalky sensibility and cleanliness, while still retaining much of Perl's pragmatism of doing whatever works.

It took me more than two years to convince my employer to start using Ruby. As much as I'd like to attribute that to the growth of my persuasion capabilities, the real reason was much more about the rise of Rails. At the time we decided to do a Rails spike, we faced a situation with resource and time limitations and needed to create a fairly simple database-backed web application. We finally convinced everyone to do this using Rails, which proved to be a clear win. Since then, more and more development is done in Rails, and right now about half the projects developed are Ruby on Rails projects instead of Java.

However, I still felt that something was wrong. As much as I liked Ruby and Rails, there were situations in which I felt it wasn't enough. In Java, I always felt constrained by the language. With Ruby, the situation was the inverse: the language was lovely, but important things were missing in the platform and ecosystem. In most cases this was caused by the relative newness of Ruby and Rails, but some of it came from features that make Java code more robust and well-performing.

That's when I started looking for a combination of the features I liked best from Ruby, while still retaining some of the good parts of the Java platform. I spent some time with different Lisp implementations on Java, ending up as a committer on the Jatha project (a Common Lisp implementation), but the Lisp implementations all shared the same problem: they didn't have Ruby's killer apps. I liked Jatha very much, but there wasn't enough community behind it, and not enough pressure to support major libraries.

So I continued my search, and I found JRuby. That was in fall 2005. At that time I really wanted to start using JRuby, and also to contribute to it, but I didn't have time. Cue three months later; Charles O. Nutter and Thomas Enebo had done some great work during that time, and it seemed obvious that JRuby would be able to run Rails sometime in the future. At that point I started helping out, contributing some smaller things, and later creating some of the more important extensions that JRuby absolutely needed to run major applications. YAML (standing for YAML Ain't Markup Language) was the key one that finally enabled us to start working on RubyGems and Rails support in earnest. Around that time I realized how powerful Rails and JRuby could be together. Now, one year later, we're successfully running almost any pure Ruby application. Rails applications usually work perfectly, and the full power of Java is also available to these applications. These applications can take full advantage of Java while retaining everything about the Ruby language.

It seems I've finally found a solution I can work with. The culmination is this book, describing what you can achieve by harnessing Ruby and Java together, creating useful Rails applications, and deploying them with tools that just aren't available when using the regular Ruby implementation.

In this first chapter, the focus will be on looking at the background behind Ruby, Rails, and JRuby; where they come from; and briefly what they are. I'll describe in more depth why JRuby on Rails is such a sweet match, and finally give a quick overview of the rest of the book, so you know what awaits you.

Ruby, JRuby, and Rails are exciting technologies. I love working with them; being involved with JRuby for the last 18 months has been the best choice I ever made. I hope I can share some of my enthusiasm—and the reasons for it—with this book, and that by the end of it you will feel some of it too. To me there's a profound difference in working in Ruby compared to Java. If you're a Java programmer, you might be skeptical about this proposition right now. However, the nice thing about JRuby is that it can act like a security blanket. You can do fun stuff with Ruby, but you'll also have Java available when you need it.

Let's get started with a quick introduction to the technologies we'll cover in this book.

Background

This book focuses on four technologies: Ruby, Rails, JRuby, and Java. The point of including Java on this list is that Java is what differentiates JRuby from Ruby. In fact, we won't look at much Java code in this book. The presence of Java should be felt, but it won't be obvious. The importance of Java is as a platform, enabling other technologies running on top of it.

I assume that you know enough about Java already. I'll quickly introduce Ruby, Rails, and JRuby, though, mostly from a historical perspective. The descriptions won't contain any direct language or API information; for that, refer to Appendix A for Ruby and Chapter 3 for Rails.

Both Ruby and JRuby have been around for much longer than you would expect. Ruby matches Java in age, and JRuby is more than six years old. In both cases their importance is fairly new, particularly because Ruby recently got a killer application in Rails, and JRuby hasn't been able to serve as a general interpreter for that long.

A Brief History of Ruby

Ruby was created in 1993 by Yukihiro "Matz" Matsumoto. It was first released to the public in 1995. The main implementation is an interpreter written in C, usually called Matz Ruby Implementation (MRI) when there's a need to distinguish between the Ruby language and the Ruby implementation.

Matz has repeatedly said that Ruby is designed for programmer productivity and fun. In many cases this is obvious from the Ruby code. Matz has also emphasized that Ruby tries hard to follow the principle of least surprise, meaning that the language should minimize confusion for experienced users. A nice side effect of this is that the basics of Ruby are easy to pick up. It's important to realize that the language design is focused on the human, not the machine. This means that features that don't perform well are a part of the language, just because it's worth more to give this capability to the programmer, rather than excluding it because it's hard to implement.

If you're interested in computer language terminology, it might interest you to know that Ruby is a reflective, dynamically and strongly typed, object-oriented, garbage collected language with support for many interesting language features such as continuations, green threads, coroutines, iterators, generators, closures, and metaprogramming. It draws primarily on features from Perl, Smalltalk, Python, Lisp, Dylan, and CLU.

A Brief History of Rails

Ruby on Rails is a web application framework that was first released in 2004. It was originally extracted from the application Basecamp, created by the company 37signals. The main creator of the language is David Heinemeier Hansson (usually called DHH). After its initial release it started to gain traction, and in time attracted a large following. In retrospect, Rails can be seen as the killer application for Ruby, spreading knowledge about Ruby and making it more popular to the masses.

Rails as a framework doesn't really contain anything new; what makes it special is that it combines several usage patterns and implementations of libraries in a productive way guided by some core philosophies. One of these is "Don't Repeat Yourself" (DRY)—meaning that information should be located in a single, obvious place. Even more important is "Convention over Configuration," which means that you need to do extremely small amounts of configuration and coding if your application follows the conventions of Rails. It also helps that the implementation extensively uses many of Ruby's metaprogramming features in a way that makes web development with Rails a pleasant thing.

Rails offers scaffolding and skeleton code created by code generators to speed up application development. That means that you're usually up and running with simple create, read, update, delete (CRUD) applications within minutes of first installing Rails. This gives you an opportunity to use a different and more agile structure for developing a system, because the feedback loop is short enough that the customer usually can take part from the beginning.

You can find more information about Rails in Chapter 3, which aims to tell you all you need to know about Rails before starting to develop with it.

A Brief History of JRuby

JRuby was originally a direct port of the Ruby 1.6 C code. It was created in 2001 by Jan Arne Petersen, and for a long time it only supported 1.6 semantics. After 1.8 was released, the maintainers introduced 1.8 features piecemeal over the course of two years. The final turning point came in the beginning of 2006, when the goal by project leads Thomas Enebo and Charles O. Nutter was set to be full compliance with Ruby; the acid test of this compliance would be running Rails unmodified. To set out on this project, many hours were devoted to creating better test suites and reworking large parts of the system.

It was obvious from early on in this endeavor that it wouldn't be a good solution to just port the C code straight off. There are large differences in the execution model of Java and C programs, which means that it would be hard to duplicate the C structures when better solutions were available in Java, and also that performance would be bad if trying to use an execution model that looked like MRIs.

After porting several important extensions to Java (YAML, ZLib, and other important parts of a Ruby system), both RubyGems and Rails started working. There were problems, but the support improved by leaps and bounds. The story got even better when Tom and Charles got hired by Sun Microsystems in September 2006 to work full time on JRuby.

Due to the great amount of tests that JRuby had, it was possible to do massive refactoring of the code base, change much of the internals, and be confident that if the test suite ran, the interpreter was good. The JRuby team has also been including test suites from other projects into JRuby. The more notable of these tests are many of the regular Ruby implementation tests, most of the tests from rubinius (another alternative implementation), and several application suites. JRuby runs a continuous integration server where the full Rails test suite is run, as well as RubyGems and Rake tests.

During much of this time, the core developers spent time looking at ways to compile Ruby code to Java bytecode. When 1.0 was released in June 2007, the runtime system by default ran in mixed mode, doing Just In Time (JIT) compilation of methods. The compiler wasn't completed at that point, handling about half of the syntactic construct of Ruby, but it gave a perceivable boost. At the time of the 1.0 release, JRuby performed close to MRI, being much closer in some cases, and slower in others.

Several things separate JRuby from MRI. The threading model is different, because JRuby uses real operating system threads, where MRI uses green threads (implemented by the Ruby interpreter and running within the same process).

JRuby doesn't support continuations. Continuations are one of those features that are incredibly hard to implement on a system running on a virtual machine, such as Java. Another reason for this decision is that it would be impossible to mix Java integration features with continuations. If this debate interests you, there are many posts in the archives of both the Jruby-dev and Ruby-core mailing lists.

There are also incompatibilities with how file system operations work, but in most cases these parts don't work well on Windows systems with MRI either.

There are currently plans to support an execution model that mimics the next big version of Ruby, called YARV (Yet Another Ruby VM). There is also talk of supporting rubinius execution.

Why JRuby on Rails?

Now you know why Ruby and Rails are interesting and exciting technologies. What's left to tell is why JRuby on Rails is different enough to warrant a book about it. I didn't mention in the introduction to Ruby that there are several problems with MRI. Many of these problems are caused by the flexibility of the language, and the fact that Matz has always focused on the language itself, not on its implementation.

The first problem is performance. In many cases, Ruby is fast enough and it works very well for many of its tasks. On the other hand, Ruby routinely finishes last in all language performance benchmarks. There's a common attitude that if you have performance problems in Ruby, you can always drop down to C and implement the critical parts there. Now, I love the Ruby language. That's why I want to use it. I don't want to drop down to C, and I especially don't want to drop down to C for the critical areas of my application. In fact, it should be the case that the critical parts are where I'll gain the most by using Ruby. However, that's not always possible today.

JRuby aims to fix that by focusing heavily on performance. The 1.0 release didn't have much performance work in it, and that shows. It's hard to measure general performance, but in most cases JRuby 1.0 seems to be about 1.5 to 2 times slower than Ruby 1.8.6. The raison d'être for 1.0 was compatibility. However, while working on the interpreter and compiler, the core team laid down the foundations to build on and improve performance. So, there seems to be no reason why JRuby can't be much faster than it currently is, and also much faster than the C implementation.

The second problem with the current Ruby implementation is that the support for Unicode and UTF-8 is spotty at best. To create applications connected to the Internet in 2007, you need to have fast, reliable, omnipresent Unicode support at the language level. Without it, you're lost. MRI does have some support for it, through something called KCode. However, this isn't at all pervasive; many string methods aren't KCode aware, and there are many problems with it. Application developers have resorted to creating libraries to handle these deficiencies; Rails has it in something called `Multibyte`.

Because JRuby runs on the Java platform, you can technically have access to all support Java offers for Unicode. At the moment you need to work with real Java `Strings` to do this, but adding better language-level support for JRuby is one of the major priorities. It's also something that will be easy to put there, because it's already available natively. The first step towards this will be to implement a native back end to `Multibyte` and other similar libraries. When you read this, that should already have happened.

The fact that a Ruby program will never be able to take advantage of more than one core in your processor, due to it using green threads, is unacceptable in certain applications and merely inconvenient in others. JRuby solves this by having Ruby threads be based on real operating system threads instead. This causes some incompatibilities with MRI, but the general consensus is that it's worth it.

These are the major poster children for using JRuby instead of Ruby, and they apply equally well for running Rails on the platform. However, with regard to Rails there are a few more interesting opportunities and capabilities that the Java platform provides. First of all, Rails development is generally considered pleasant; Rails deployment isn't. There are many tools to help with this, but what it comes down to is that Rails development doesn't have the maturity that Java has. So, deploying Rails applications in JRuby is one selling point. (You'll see how to do so in Chapter 11.)

In many situations, an application needs to use several libraries for functionality. Ruby has been around for a long time, but the maturity of its libraries can't be compared to that of the Java platform. In some cases you'll have to write your own libraries for Ruby because no one has done what you've tried to do yet. That never happens with Java anymore. With Java, you usually have a good amount of libraries to use, and usually also commercial offerings. So, when developing a new application it can be highly useful to do it with JRuby on Rails, but it's also helpful to be able to fall back and use Java libraries from inside the application for certain functionality. JRuby makes it easy to do so.

There are more reasons to consider JRuby on Rails, and I'll touch on most of them in several places in the book.

Overview of the Book

This book is divided into four different parts, with some information before and after, and three appendixes. To help you get a feeling for how the book is laid out, I'll give a quick introduction to each chapter here. If you need specific information about a subject, please feel free to jump around. Keep in mind that most chapters use an overarching project for that part, which means that in some cases important context can be found in preceding chapters.

The four project parts are relatively separate from each other, but they each depend on things you learned in earlier chapters.

Chapter 1: Introduction

This is the introduction to the book, giving you information about the technologies covered, why they should interest you, and an overview of the book. You should be reading it right now.

Chapter 2: Getting Started

This chapter is aimed at getting you up to speed by helping you to install everything you need for the rest of the book, including all RubyGems you'll be using. The chapter also gives a small introduction to each of them, and tells you how to do basic tasks with the gem command.

Project 1: The Store (Shoplet)

The store application is the first Rails project you create, and as such won't differ much from what you would have done if you were developing the application with MRI. The big difference is that the system is backed by Java Database Connectivity (JDBC).

Chapter 3: Introduction to Rails

This chapter is a gentle, mostly non-coding introduction to Rails; it describes what parts it contains and things that are good to know when doing Rails development.

Chapter 4: Store Administration

Here you build the first half of the Shoplet application. The chapter introduces many of the more practical details of Rails in the process.

Chapter 5: A Database-Driven Shop

The Shoplet application gets finished and you take a look at the databases that JRuby on Rails supports.

Project 2: A Content Management System (CoMpoSe)

The second application isn't much larger than the first one; the difference is that it makes heavy use of some Java libraries to process Extensible Markup Language (XML) and handle content rendering.

Chapter 6: Java Integration

In this chapter we take our first detour and focus exclusively on the syntax and usage of JRuby's Java integration features.

Chapter 7: A Rails CMS

Using what we learned from the first project, we proceed to create most of the Rails code needed for the CMS application, but stub out all rendering functionality.

Chapter 8: Content Rendering

Using some of the Java integration features displayed in Chapter 6, this chapter completes the CMS application by adding all the rendering functionality and also taking a look at a few alternative approaches.

Project 3: An Administration System (BigBrother)

The BigBrother system is based on separating the Rails front end from an enterprise back end. It also has some features allowing it to be managed by Java Management Extensions (JMX).

Chapter 9: A JRuby Enterprise Bean

We look at how to use JRuby from inside a J2EE Enterprise Bean, implementing the functionality of this bean in Ruby.

Chapter 10: An EJB-Backed Rails Application

Most of the BigBrother application is completed by implementing a Rails front end that talks to an Enterprise JavaBean and also uses JMX to manage itself.

Chapter 11: Deployment

The next detour details deployment options for a JRuby on Rails application, how regular Rails deployment usually works, and how to make the situation much better with JRuby.

Project 4: A Library System (LibLib)

The final project is a distributed library system that shares a centralized data storage inside of the boundaries of a legacy system. The application uses messaging services to interact with other instances of the application, and also the legacy system.

Chapter 12: Web Services with JRuby

This chapter looks at the options available to consume web services with JRuby, and implements a library to search for books at Amazon.com.

Chapter 13: JRuby and Message-Oriented Systems

We take a deep dive into message-oriented middleware, looking at implementing both ends of such a system using JRuby and JMS. The chapter culminates in creating two different libraries for JMS interaction.

Chapter 14: The LibLib Rails Application

We create the final project application, using the libraries developed in Chapter 12 and 13 to provide some interesting library services.

Chapter 15: Coda: Next Steps

This chapter contains a few pointers as to what to do next and how to contribute to JRuby or its surrounding projects.

Appendix A: Ruby for Java Programmers

This appendix offers a short introduction to the Ruby language; it's aimed at Java programmers, but it should be digestible by anyone with programming experience.

Appendix B: JRuby Syntax

This appendix has a table detailing the Java integration features and other JRuby-specific APIs.

Appendix C: Resources

This appendix contains pointers to web pages, blogs, and posts that might be of further interest to you.

Summary

It's time to get started. I've talked in depth about what the book will cover and why these technologies are interesting, and might just transform your life. What's missing is the *how* of it; before we get into that, a short chapter will tell you how to install everything needed, and then it's time to start learning JRuby and Rails.

CHAPTER 2

■ ■ ■

Getting Started

After reading through the first chapter, you should know *why* JRuby and Rails are interesting for you. In this chapter we'll walk through *what* needs to be done to get started using these technologies. I'll talk you through how to install JRuby, using both the source and binary distribution; how to test your resulting JRuby installation; and how to install all the software you'll need in the rest of the book.

I'll briefly introduce RubyGems (the main Ruby package installation tool) and walk through installing all the Gems used in the book. We'll do this right now so you won't have to begin each chapter reading instructions on how to install the required Gems. I'll give a small introduction to each package we install too, so you know what you get.

After that we'll look at how to get and install MySQL, and how to create new databases for it. After that we're ready to begin creating our first project!

Installing JRuby

It's easy to install JRuby, but there are also some gotchas to be aware of. We'll take a look at what's needed and what we need to do to install both on Unix-like environments and on Windows. Most of the problems that surface are the same, regardless of which platform you're running on; this is both one of the good and bad characteristics of running on Java.

At the time of writing, the current JRuby version is 1.0, and work on 1.0.1 and 1.1 is starting up. Regardless of which version has been released when reading this, these instructions should be almost exactly the same. If something has substantially changed, the JRuby documentation will highlight that information.

There are several ways of installing JRuby. The first step is to choose if you want to use a precompiled binary distribution, if you want to compile a source distribution of a specific release, or if you want to use the bleeding edge of JRuby and use the latest trunk version from Subversion.

Java

Regardless of which JRuby version you choose to use, you'll need to have the Java SDK installed. If you're on Mac OS X, you already have a good Java installation that will work perfectly for JRuby. If you're running Windows or Linux, you'll need to install the Java SDK. It doesn't matter how you do this; download it from the Java home page and manually install it or use your operating system's package management software (such as Debian's APT). The only thing you need to make sure of is that you have Java on your path, and that JAVA_HOME has been set. The easiest way to check if Java is on your path is to execute this command:

```
java -version
```

This has the added benefit of displaying your current Java version. JRuby is compatible with all Java versions beginning with Java 1.4.2, but there is a definite improvement in functionality and speed when using later versions. If you can do so, running with Java 6 is the best choice. To make sure you have JAVA_HOME set correctly, on Linux or Mac open up a terminal and write this:

```
echo $JAVA_HOME
```

If you're running Windows, you should do this instead:

```
echo %JAVA_HOME%
```

The output should be the path to your Java installation. If it isn't set, you need to do that before continuing.

If you're planning on building JRuby from source, you'll also need to install Ant. This is easy to do; go to http://ant.apache.org, download the latest version, unpack somewhere, and add the bin directory to your PATH. You can also install Ant from package management tools if you want.

Binary JRuby

The binary JRuby distribution is built using Java 1.4.2, and works well on any platform that supports 1.4.2. To install it, you just need to download it from http://jruby.org and unpack it. It's almost always useful to add JRuby's bin directory to the path, but it isn't entirely necessary. You can write the full path to it instead and everything will work fine. In fact, you can run the jruby script in almost any way, except for one special case.

The special case that you can't do, and that won't work at all, is to try to run the jruby script while you're in the bin directory. All kinds of strange problems result from doing this, and the easy solution is to just avoid it. (The JRuby team has a reported bug in this issue, and will fix it at some point, but currently other things are taking precedence.)

JRuby from Source

You can either download the JRuby source from one of the distributions at http://jruby.org, or check out the latest version from JRuby's Subversion trunk. Either way works fine and depends on why you want to build JRuby yourself. If you just want the latest released version and you'll compile it with some other compiler than the one that comes with the Sun JDK, you should download the source distribution. If you want to stay current with more recent bug fixes and new functionality, trunk is the place to be. JRuby trunk is usually very stable, and developers have an extensive test suite that gets run before checking in new code, so there's usually no problem running with bleeding edge JRuby. However, there's still a remote possibility that errors can be introduced. It's also important to keep in mind that some of the features in trunk might be removed at any point. We generally try to retain backward compatibility to earlier versions, but this isn't true for features that have only appeared in trunk.

If you have a Subversion client installed, it's easy to check out the latest version:

```
svn co http://svn.codehaus.org/jruby/trunk/jruby jruby
```

This creates a new directory called `jruby` in the current directory, containing the latest source of JRuby. To build it, enter the directory and run Ant without any target. You use the same technique to compile the source distribution; just unpack it, enter the directory, and run Ant. After you've seen that everything compiles correctly, it might be prudent to run the test suite. You can do this by running `ant test`. This takes some time, because it tests many features of the JRuby system. It also runs most tests twice to make sure both compilation and interpretation work as expected. When it's finished (which might take as long as ten to fifteen minutes, depending on your computer), the Ant output will say `BUILD SUCCESSFUL`. If it doesn't, please report what happened to the JRuby community. (You can find more information about how to do this in Chapter 15.)

When JRuby has been built, you can use the scripts in the `bin` directory just as if you had a binary distribution. In fact, it's not a large difference at all. If you want to, you can also put parts of the JRuby distribution in a more convenient place. For example, if you're on Linux, you might want to keep JRuby in `/usr/local`:

```
cp -r bin/* /usr/local/bin
cp -r lib/* /usr/local/lib
```

Rehash, and JRuby is available from that directory. If you decide to upgrade, make sure not to forget upgrading this location, though. Mixing old and new versions of libraries might cause interesting problems. The best bet when upgrading is to search your system for `jruby.jar` and `jruby-complete.jar` and remove them or make sure they're replaced with new, fresh versions.

Testing the Installation

Once you've installed JRuby, it's time to make sure it works correctly. The first step is usually to run one of the test scripts that the JRuby distribution and source ships with. I'll use `$JRUBY_HOME` to refer to JRuby's home directory. You usually don't need to set this environment variable explicitly, though.

To run a test script, just execute this command:

```
jruby $JRUBY_HOME/samples/fib.rb
```

If everything works all right, JRuby should print the 20th Fibonacci value—6765—and quit. The script looks like this:

```
def fib(n)
  if n<2
    n
  else
    fib(n-2)+fib(n-1)
  end
end
puts fib(20)
```

After you're sure that JRuby works, it can be prudent to make sure that the Java integration features work correctly. To do so, run this:

```
jruby $JRUBY_HOME/samples/swing2.rb
```

You should see a Java window with a button pop up. Click the button and a new window should open up. That script looks like this:

```
# Import Java packages
include Java

import javax.swing.JFrame

frame = JFrame.new("Hello Swing")
button = javax.swing.JButton.new("Klick Me!")

class ClickAction
  include java.awt.event.ActionListener
  def actionPerformed(evt)
    javax.swing.JOptionPane.showMessageDialog(nil, <<EOS)
<html>Hello from <b><u>JRuby</u></b>.<br>
Button '#{evt.getActionCommand()}' clicked.
EOS
  end
end
button.add_action_listener(ClickAction.new)

# Add the button to the frame
frame.get_content_pane.add(button)

# Show frame
frame.set_default_close_operation(JFrame::EXIT_ON_CLOSE)
frame.pack
frame.visible = true
```

We'll look at more of the Java integration features in Chapter 6, but this script uses some fairly advanced features to display the Swing window.

If this example works too, you can be fairly certain that your JRuby installation is correctly set up. Now it's time to play with JRuby. Do that by starting the Interactive Ruby console, JRuby version:

```
jirb
```

Enter any Ruby code you like. You may use the Ruby tutorial in Appendix A as a starting point and try some of that out. To exit, write exit. If you want something more fancy, try the JRuby Swing console by running jirb_swing. This is almost exactly like jirb, but with nice colors and code completion (try pressing the Tab key halfway into a statement).

Now that your environment is all set up, it's time to install some software you'll need in the rest of the book. However, before that, let's say a quick word about running JRuby versions of the regular commands. Now, jirb and jruby won't clash with an installation of regular Ruby. However, installed programs, such as gem, rake, and rails will clash. If you have both on your

PATH, you can't be certain which will get run (it depends on which is found first in your PATH list, and if your operating system searches from the front or back). The best way to ensure that you'll always run the version of a Ruby command that you expect is to use the -S flag to the interpreter. This works on both Ruby and JRuby, so if you want to run the JRuby version of rake, you should run this:

```
jruby -S rake
```

The logic behind the -S argument is easy. In fact, the interpreter will just start searching for the command named in the same directory as the script is located, so if you have JRuby installed in /usr/local, and have Ruby installed there too, your two installations will clash and you can expect some funny behavior in some cases.

RubyGems

JRuby comes with a fairly loaded standard library from scratch, but that doesn't mean there aren't other things you'll need. Almost all of them are installable as Gems. RubyGems is the premier package management tool for Ruby. It works fine with JRuby, and JRuby ships with it. You use it through the gem command. You can extend RubyGems, but Table 2-1 shows the base operations you can do with the gem command.

Table 2-1. *RubyGems Commands*

Command	Description
build	Create a new Gem.
cert	Adjust certificate settings.
check	Check installed Gems.
cleanup	Clean old installed versions in the local repository.
contents	Display the contents of installed Gems.
dependency	Show the dependencies of installed Gems.
environment	Display information about the RubyGems environment.
help	Provide help with the gem command.
install	Install a Gem into the local repository.
list	Display all Gems that start with a specified string.
outdated	List all local Gems that need to be updated.
pristine	Restore Gem installation directories.
query	Find Gem information in local or remote locations.
rdoc	Generate RDoc for Gems.
search	Search for Gems.
sources	Manage the places RubyGems searches for Gems.
specification	Display the YAML Gem specification.
uninstall	Remove an installed Gem.
unpack	Unpack an installed Gem to the local directory.
update	Update the named Gem into the local repository.

Of all these commands, the most important ones are install, search, and uninstall. RubyGems by default installs Gems from a central repository hosted by RubyForge, one of the largest places for Ruby code on the Internet. In most cases Gems will be available from there, but in some cases you'll need to specify an alternate source. That's most often the case when installing prerelease Gems or specially built versions.

Rake

The most important Gem to install, and the first one you should always have on your system, is called Rake. Rake is a build tool, like Make, but allows the Rakefiles (the definitions of how to build something) to be written in Ruby using a specialized domain-specific language (DSL) that makes them very readable, while still retaining the power of Ruby.

Most projects use Rake for several purposes, and Rails itself provides most of the things you can do through Rake tasks.

To install, just run this:

```
jruby -S gem install -y rake
```

The -y parameter tells the gem command to answer "yes" to all questions it wants to ask. In most cases, these questions are whether Rake should install a dependency or not. When using -y, all dependencies are automatically installed, which is almost always what you want.

Be patient when the gem command generates RDoc and Ruby Interactive (RI). These operations take some time because they are data intensive; when installing Rails and all its dependencies you'll need to wait a good five minutes for it to finish, but it's worth it to have the documentation readily available locally.

Rails

Rails is in fact composed of several smaller Gems that are heavily interdependent. We'll take a closer look at these in the next chapter, but suffice it to say that currently, installing the Gem rails with dependencies also installs actionmailer, actionpack, actionwebservice, activerecord, and activesupport. You should see that in your output when you install Rails. The version of Rails used to write this book is 1.2.3. It's probable that a new version will have been released by the time you read this. Make sure that you use a version in the 1.2 branch, and everything here should work. If you try the new 2.0 instead, many things are bound to break. The online errata contain information about what is different between Rails 1.2 and 2.0 as pertains to this book.

```
jruby -S gem install -y rails
```

Make sure to test that Rails works by typing this command in any directory:

```
jruby -S rails foo
```

You should see about a page of output detailing new directories and files. After you get the console back, you should see that the rails command has created a directory named foo. If this doesn't happen, something is wrong.

ActiveRecord-JDBC

After Rake and Rails, ActiveRecord-JDBC (AR-JDBC) is also incredibly important. You need to have AR-JDBC installed so that your JRuby code can use JDBC drivers to connect to databases. Because most of Rails uses extensions written in C to communicate with databases, these database drivers won't work on JRuby. There's a MySQL library written for talking to MySQL that's pure Ruby. It works well with JRuby but isn't well-performing enough for doing real applications with. So, you need to install AR-JDBC.

The current version is 0.4, but development happens all the time. AR-JDBC aims to be fully compatible with the rest of the drivers in ActiveRecord, which means that you should never see any problems using the latest version of AR-JDBC with the latest released version of Rails. There are a few bits of AR-JDBC that aren't available in regular ActiveRecord; for example, you can use the `insert_bind` and `update_bind` commands to make use of prepared statement caching if your database performs better by doing that. These features are more variable and subject to change.

As with the other Gems, it's incredibly simple to install AR-JDBC:

```
jruby -S gem install -y ActiveRecord-JDBC
```

To use a database driver, you need to make sure that the JAR file for that driver is on your classpath before trying to use AR-JDBC, though.

BlueCloth and RedCloth

BlueCloth and RedCloth are Gems that implement Textile and Markdown, respectively. These are formats for text markup that make it easy to write good-looking text without resorting to HTML. We'll look more closely at both of them in Chapter 8.

Installation is done in the same way as other Gems:

```
jruby -S gem install -y BlueCloth
jruby -S gem install -y RedCloth
```

Facets

Rails has added many small, convenient utilities to the standard library. They usually reside in ActiveSupport, in the parts named core extensions. Among these you can find the highly useful `Symbol#to_proc` trick (you can read more about that in Appendix A), and some nice ways to make your Ruby code much more readable, such as writing `4.hours + 20.minutes` instead of `4*3600 + 20*60`. You can find most of the utilities in ActiveSupport, and you can find many things that haven't been added to Rails in Facets. Facets is a collection of useful utilities; some are small and some are larger, and everything can be used separately.

To install, use this:

```
jruby -S gem install -y facets
```

To get hold of the methods for handling time units in a nice way, just do this:

```
require 'facets/more/times'
```

The best way to discover new, useful ways of using Facets is by looking at the home page. The front page randomizes new, useful features of Facets each day, so just visit the home page every day and you'll learn to use the full set of Facets sooner or later.

Mongrel

The Mongrel web server is good to have installed, and it's easy to get it on JRuby. When installing Mongrel on the regular Ruby distribution, you need to compile it during the installation process, but when running on JRuby everything will work just as a regular Gem installation. Run this:

```
jruby -S gem install -y mongrel
```

You get a list with lots of versions of Mongrel. You should choose the latest version, which has "jruby" or "java" within parentheses after the version.

Mongrel JCluster

Using Mongrel is incredibly nice, but when you want to deploy ten Mongrels, it soon gets inconvenient. That's where the mongrel_jcluster plugin is interesting; it allows you to run several Mongrel processes inside the same Java Virtual Machine (JVM) and control all of them with the same command. I'll go further into mongrel_jcluster in Chapter 11. You can install it by running this:

```
jruby -S gem install -y mongrel_jcluster
```

Setting Up a Database

You can choose any database you like to run JRuby on Rails applications with, but in practice you get some benefits from using the more mainstream ones. In this book I'll be exclusively using MySQL, except for Chapter 5 where we'll take a brief look at other databases. This chapter will only introduce you to what's needed to get a MySQL server up and running.

If you're on Windows, this is easy to do. You first need to download MySQL from http://www.mysql.com. Choose the Community Edition, version 5, and make sure also to download the JDBC drivers. (They're called Connector/J.) You should put the JDBC drivers on your CLASSPATH, and you should run the installer and start MySQL up. After you've done this, you can move on to configuring MySQL.

If you're on Mac OS X, you can either use the Unix instructions, you can use Mac Ports, or you can download an installer from MySQL's home page. I use the installer, and that's been working well for me. The process is almost entirely automatic. You also need to configure the installation, though.

Finally, the best way to install MySQL on Unix systems, in my opinion, is to compile it yourself. I've been running MySQL extensively in Unix environments, and I usually find that the precompiled binaries aren't as stable or well-performing as what I can achieve by compiling myself. The first step towards compiling MySQL is to download the source distribution. You also need to create a user and a group so MySQL won't run as root. Compilation follows the pattern ./configure && make && sudo make install, and you shouldn't have any difficulties.

MySQL is installed in /usr/local/mysql by default. If you want to run MySQL as a service you need to make sure that it starts on system boot, by using appropriate start scripts for your operating system. Finally, there's usually some more initializing to do on a MySQL installation. You can find what else needs to be done in the manual.

When you finally have MySQL running, you also need to configure it and set up some initial accounts. The first step towards doing this is to run the mysql client program:

```
mysql -u root
```

This depends on you having the bin directory of MySQL on your path. You're greeted by a prompt where you can execute SQL and change permissions. Because there's usually a test account, and the root user doesn't have a password, you'll want to change this by writing this on the prompt:

```
DROP DATABASE test;
USE mysql;
DELETE FROM user WHERE User='test';

UPDATE user SET Password=PASSWORD('your secret root password');
FLUSH PRIVILEGES;
```

You can exit by writing exit. From now on, you'll need to use the command

```
mysql -u root -p
```

and write the root password you provided earlier to connect to and do administration with MySQL.

When we create new Rails applications in this book, the first step will usually be to create the databases and users needed for them. For example, when you create the application called foobar, you'll usually need to create a user with username "foobar" and password "foobar". You'll also need to create three databases called foobar_dev, foobar_test, and foobar_prod. The way to do that from the MySQL prompt looks like this:

```
CREATE DATABASE foobar_dev;
CREATE DATABASE foobar_test;
CREATE DATABASE foobar_prod;

GRANT ALL ON foobar_dev.* TO 'foobar'@'%' IDENTIFIED BY 'foobar';
GRANT ALL ON foobar_test.* TO 'foobar'@'%' IDENTIFIED BY 'foobar';
GRANT ALL ON foobar_prod.* TO 'foobar'@'%' IDENTIFIED BY 'foobar';

FLUSH PRIVILEGES;
```

It's important that this database isn't exposed to the Internet. If it will be exposed, make sure that you use other passwords to make them less obvious to guess.

This is all the knowledge about MySQL administration that you'll need for this book. In most cases, ActiveRecord migrations will take care of the rest for you.

Summary

We've installed Java and JRuby, we've installed all needed Gems, and we've installed and configured a MySQL database engine. We now have everything we need to have in our environment to be able to start creating JRuby on Rails applications from scratch. One thing I haven't mentioned is the question of where to write your code. I won't give you a recommendation about this, because it's a highly inflamed topic. Suffice it to say, everyone chooses different solutions. What's important is that you write your code yourself right now—don't use code generators that write code for you that you won't understand. I usually use Emacs for writing Ruby code; I know many people love TextMate for Rails development. NetBeans, Eclipse, IntelliJ, and JBuilder all have solutions for writing Ruby code. In the end, you'll have to choose for yourself, but for most of the book, Notepad or vi will work fine.

It's now time to look at Rails, and see what parts are in it and what purpose they serve. The first project won't use many Java resources at all; the focus will be on introducing Rails.

The Store (Shoplet)

CHAPTER 3

■■■

Introduction to Rails

This chapter will serve as an introduction to the various parts of the Rails framework. Because Rails is loosely coupled, it makes sense to introduce the parts by themselves, and then describe how to fit them together.

On July 24, 2004 the first public version (0.5) of Rails was released. David Heinemeier Hansson extracted and generalized it from Basecamp, 37signals' first commercial web application. This first release immediately created a huge buzz in the developer community, partly because of the rapid development made possible by the Rails application architecture. Fifteen months later, after much progress and many new features, version 1.0 was released on December 13, 2005. This release solidified everything that made Rails successful and fixed most bugs and problems discovered before going final.

The next major milestone came on March 28, 2006, when David and company released version 1.1 with lots of new, interesting support for various JavaScript and Ajax features, better handling when returning different document formats, polymorphic database associations, and integration tests.

The last year has seen more than 20 books published about Ruby and Rails. Adoption among American companies is seriously getting started, and in the summer of 2006 the first-ever International Rails Conference was held in Chicago. It was a major success, and a few months later a European RailsConf was held in London.

Let's get started with the different parts of Rails.

The Structure of a Rails Application

When creating a new Rails application with the `rails` script, the Rails application generator will create it following certain conventions. The output directory structure will be deep and will have support for many different things. Contrary to what you might expect, this makes development easier within Rails. These constraints free you from lots of decisions that otherwise would have to be made. Of course, many of the Rails helper scripts also depend on this structure being there, so you deviate from it at your own risk.

These directories are automatically created when generating a new Rails application:

- `app`: This is where most of the application code resides. It has subdirectories for models, views, and controllers, and also for helpers.

- `components`: Before the plug-in system was finished, components were the main way to extend a Rails application. They're now mildly deprecated, and I won't cover them at all in this book.

- `config`: The `config` directory contains some pretty important files, including the one for database configuration. It also contains the different configuration parts for separate environments.

- `db`: The `db` directory houses all migration information for the databases.

- `doc`: You can generate an RDoc for your application. If you choose to do that, it will reside in this directory.

- `lib`: If you create code that doesn't fit neatly into the categories of model or controller, you can place it in the `lib` directory. The `lib` directory is on the load path, but you need to `require` the parts you need. Also, when adding new Rake tasks to your build system, you should put the file containing the tasks in the `tasks` subdirectory in the `lib` directory, so Rake will automatically recognize it.

- `log`: When your application is running, all the logs will end up in this directory.

- `public`: Some parts of your web application need to be directly accessible without going through the Rails call stack; for example, images and style sheets. You should put these things in the `public` directory. You should also set this directory as the application root if you're using Apache to deploy your application. When caching is configured in your Rails application, the cached files will end up here too.

- `script`: Rails depends on some helper scripts for different purposes. You can find all of these in this directory. I'll describe these scripts further in the section "Rails Helper Scripts."

- `test`: You can test Rails applications in many different ways. What is common for all methods is that you should place the actual tests in this directory. The Rails Rake file already supports much of the directory structure within, so try to make your testing fit within the existing architecture.

- `tmp`: During runtime, Rails needs to create numerous temporary files. By default, these are placed in this directory. You should never place anything you need to keep here.

- `vendor`: When installing plug-ins, they'll end up in `vendor/plugins`. Also, if you decide to freeze the current Rails version, all the Rails Gems will be copied to this directory.

Of all these directories, the most important ones are the `app`, `config`, `test`, and `db` directories. This is where most of the work on a Rails application takes place. Try to take a few minutes with a newly generated application to walk through all subdirectories and see what they contain.

Models

In Rails, the models are where the data resides. The model classes correspond more or less directly to a database table (if you use ActiveRecord, that is). You can find all models in the directory `app/models`, where each file corresponds to one model. It can be easy to create a model. In fact, the easiest possible model could look like this, in a file named `order_item.rb`:

```
class OrderItem < ActiveRecord::Base
end
```

In this case, the only thing necessary is to create a class that inherits from `ActiveRecord::Base`. If you have configured a working database, and that database contains a table named `order_items`, then this model will work fine. The next step would be to add some references to other parts of your model:

```
class OrderItem < ActiveRecord::Base
  belongs_to :order
end
```

`belongs_to` is one of the more common references that can be used. In this case, the agreement is that the `order_items` table has a foreign key field called `order_id` that you can use to find the `Order` that this `OrderItem` is part of. Correspondingly, the `Order` model could look like this:

```
class Order < ActiveRecord::Base
  has_many :order_items
  has_one :shipping_address, :class_name => 'Address'
end
```

As you can see, in this way you can use one model object (`Address`) with a different name in a model. This allows you to use a generic model object such as `Address` in several different parts of your application, if need be.

Models also contain validation information. For example, take the `Address` model referenced earlier:

```
class Address < ActiveRecord::Base
  belongs_to :order
  validates_presence_of :country, :zip
  validates_numericality_of :zip
end
```

This simply says that an `Address` needs to contain country and ZIP code information, and a ZIP code needs to be only digits to be a valid ZIP code. There are many kinds of validators, and you can also write your own.

Defining models is one thing, but you also need to know how to use them. Mostly, it's intuitive. For example, say you want to find all orders:

```
Order.find :all
```

Or, say you have an ID for an order and want to get that instance:

```
Order.find 123
```

Or, say you have an order instance called o and you want to create a new address that references this order:

```
Address.create :order => o, :country => 'Sweden',
        :zip => '12559'
```

This was a small introduction to models with ActiveRecord. I'll expand on most of this information in later chapters.

Controllers

The controller is the part of your application that first sees a request. The controller decides which models to use, how to use them, and also which view to render. Controller code is usually simple to write when following the Rails conventions. If you have to do something different, things can get more complicated, though.

A Rails controller is a class that can be found in app/controllers, and controllers follow a specific naming scheme. Specifically, a controller should be called SomethingController and exist in a file called something_controller.rb. If you follow this convention, that controller's actions will by default be available under the /something/action URL. You can change this by editing the file config/routes.rb, but it's a useful convention to stick to. If there is no action named in the URL, the default action name will be index. This is a neat thing in Rails: all public methods in a controller are an action. So, you could create a simple controller that displays the view named index.rhtml like this:

```
class FooController < ApplicationController
  def index
  end
end
```

If you don't specify a view to render, by default Rails will use one with the same name as the action. However, you can also specify one explicitly:

```
class FooController < ApplicationController
  def index
    render :action => 'bar'
  end
end
```

The ApplicationController class is something Rails provides for free. You can find it in the app/controllers/application.rb file, and it's useful to change this file to add things to all controllers.

There isn't much to tell about controllers. Except for specifying which view should be rendered, you can also provide data to the view. This is best done by setting instance variables to the values you want the view to have. With some trickery, Rails copies all instance variables from the current controller to the view that should be rendered. So, you can give a view some much-needed data by doing it like this:

```
class FooController < ApplicationController
  def index
    @products = Product.find :all
    @title = "All the Products in the World"
  end
end
```

Another useful thing you can do with controllers is to use filters. You can specify that some code should be executed before, after, or around every action. This allows you to achieve authentication and authorization quite easily, but you can also add encryption, compression, or many other things to your application in this way. Filters will be covered later in the book, when we look at implementing authentication for Rails applications.

Views

The view is the part that generates HTML (or XML, or JavaScript, or anything else really). In Rails, the standard way of doing this templating is called ERb, and the standard file extension is RHTML. There are also a few other ways of doing this, but ERb is the method I'll use in this book.

The Rails view templates live in the app/views/{controllername}/ directory. That means, if our controller is named FooController, the index view will be found in app/views/foo/index.rhtml. Most of an RHTML file is regular HTML, but parts enclosed in <% %> and <%= %> blocks are evaluated as Ruby code. As I mentioned in the section on controllers, all instance variables from the controller will be available in the view too. So, say this fragment is in the index.rhtml file for the FooController specified earlier:

```
<head>
  <title><%= @title %></title>
</head>
```

Then, this would be what was returned to the browser:

```
<head>
  <title>All the Products in the World</title>
</head>
```

That's more or less it for the views. They aren't complicated. In the basic case it's simple to generate the dynamic code you need inside the confines of regular HTML. Rails does give you helpers for many tasks. For example, you should never write your own <FORM> tag, because there are many things to keep in mind, and you'll have lots of pieces to change if you switch URL schemes or something like that. For example, say you want to have a button that posts some information to your server. You could use the helper button_to like this:

```
Press this button:
<%= button_to "Press Me", :action => 'button_press' %>
```

This generates a small form with a button that when pressed does a POST to the URL corresponding to the current controller, but with the action button_press. There are many helpers in Rails; I'll introduce them as we go.

Layouts

If you want to have a common style on more than one page of your application it can be a good idea to consider creating a layout. By default, a layout is found in app/views/layouts/, and it should have the same name as the controller under execution for it to be loaded automatically. For example, you should call the layout for FooController app/views/layouts/foo.rb. This file could contain the HTML header and footer, a menu, and everything else that should be shared in many views. You mark the place where Rails should insert the real view by calling yield inside an output block, like this:

```
<%= yield %>
```

This outputs the dynamically generated data from the real view at that place. If, for some reason, you would like to have the content duplicated, you shouldn't call yield twice. Instead, save the output from the first yield and print it two times:

```
<% content = yield %>
ABC:
<%= content %>
CDE:
<%= content %>
```

If you want to have the same layout for more than one controller, you can specify a specific layout inside your controller:

```
class FooController < ApplicationController
  layout "bar"
end
```

For all actions in FooController, the file bar.rhtml is used as a layout, instead of the default foo.rhtml.

Partials

You'll often find yourself needing certain blocks of code over and over again. For example, say you always want to print product details the same way. You could copy and paste this in all the places you need it, but that wouldn't be DRY. So, for these cases you have access to partials. A partial should be in the same directory as the view using it (but you can use partials from other controllers too). You should name it with an underscore (_) before the name to differentiate it from real views. So, you could have a partial that's named _product.rhtml and looks like this:

```
<p><b><%= product.name %></b> $<%= product.price %></p>
```

You could use it from a view in this manner:

```
Your choice: <%= render :partial => 'product', :locals =>
                {:product => @prod} %>
```

We need to explicitly import the product to use by giving the locals parameter to the call. This gives us some flexibility, though. For example, say that we had several products in a list called @products and we wanted these rendered the same way. We could do that with the same partial:

```
Products:<br/>
<%= render :partial => 'product', :collection => @products %>
```

The partial is called once for each item in the collection, and the current object is set to a local variable with the same name as the partial itself.

Partials are incredibly useful for allowing great code reuse. You should use them as much as possible, especially later, when we start talking about how to use Ajax to re-render only parts of a page.

THE MVC PATTERN

Rails is a pure implementation of the Model-View-Controller (MVC) design pattern. This pattern first originated in the Smalltalk world but is now widespread (and is known under the name Model-2 in the Sun parlance). The pattern has been implemented hundreds of times in several different kinds of applications, but it shines most in those situations where you can cleanly delineate the user interface from the data back end, and the main purpose of the interface is to present massive amounts of data to the user.

The pattern was first described in 1979 by Trygve Reenskaug, then working on Smalltalk at Xerox labs. His implementation of the pattern is described in depth in a well-read paper called "Applications Programming in Smalltalk-80: How to use Model-View-Controller" by Steve Burbeck. Many other systems have been inspired by this original implementation, including parts of Cocoa for Mac OS X, Java Swing, Microsoft Foundation Classes (MFC), and the Qt toolkit. Apart from these, the pattern is heavily used in many web systems.

The basic idea in MVC is that you divide the responsibility into three parts: the model, the view, and the controller. Each part should be more or less self contained, meaning that a change in the view system should not have any impact on the model or controller logic. As a typical benefit, if you code a Java Swing application in a typical MVC architecture, you would only need to change the view logic to port this functionality to a web interface. Of course, this ideal will almost never be purely realized, but it's still useful to design your application with this separation of concerns in mind.

The model is where the domain-specific representation of data resides. This layer is also known as the domain layer. The model objects should be composed of all raw data the application needs, with domain logic added to this. A typical example of model objects can be Product, Order, and Customer. If the application needs persistence of some kind, this will also be a part of the model layer. The view and controller should ideally not need to know anything about databases or other forms of persistence.

The controller is responsible for providing the view with all data that should be available for the current event. The controller reacts to events by evaluating them and then updating the view as a response. Controllers are commonly divided into separate actions, where any one action corresponds to a specific event. For example, in the Java framework Struts, you never write a controller; you just provide different actions for different URLs. The real controller is one big class that dispatches to the different actions and provides different services to the system.

The view renders the model information and the data provided by the controller in a suitable form for the current request. The view displays user interaction elements, and in a typical web application it corresponds neatly to the code that directly generates HTML. The ideal view doesn't contain any logic at all, but only displays the information that is available to it.

The MVC pattern is easy to see in the Rails framework. Most of the components are named in such a way that they correspond directly to the different parts of the pattern. For example, model objects in Rails map neatly to the M in MVC, by handling database communication, validation, and internal logic. Controller classes map to the C in MVC, and each public method in a controller corresponds to a separate action. Finally, there is one separate view—which is an RHTML file—for each distinct action, unless you override the rendering logic. All pieces are there.

When coding an application with Rails it is important to follow this separation of concerns in your own code too. If you don't, many of the benefits you can get from Rails will be void. In real terms, this is simple: never write any code in the view templates that contains business logic in any way. If you find yourself using much code in RHTML, be suspicious. It's not always a sign that something is bad, but it could be. If you need lots of presentation logic, try to abstract it and put it into helper methods. By the same token, try to refactor all logic that concerns the model into the model classes. Make your controllers as clean as possible. Look at the code generated for scaffolds for examples of how to write controller logic that only contains what's necessary for the controller. Finally, any view information should not be found in the model objects. This is probably one of the few things I object to in the Rails framework. Validation messages are usually placed inside the model objects, together with the rest of the validation rules. However, because this is view information, it's certainly not the right place for it. Keep this in mind, especially when trying to create something that should be used in more than one language.

Much of the power of Rails comes from MVC and the relentless use of it. Don't let that get wasted.

The Other Parts of Rails

Rails is divided into several smaller packages, each more or less self sufficient. ActiveRecord is the component used for the models; ActionPack contains ActionController and ActionView, which are the controller and view parts, respectively. The package Rails (previously called Railties) contains the code that pulls all these parts together. That isn't everything, though— Rails contains several more packages.

ActiveSupport

ActiveSupport's main purpose is to add several helpful extensions to different parts of the Ruby core. It contains core extensions and new utility classes that aren't Rails specific, but that Rails needs to make life easier for the developer. For example, it contains the class `HashWithIndifferentAccess`, which lets you index into a hash with a symbol or a string, and you'll get the "right" value back regardless of which you choose.

ActiveSupport adds many methods to the core classes. The time and date utilities are especially helpful. When ActiveSupport is loaded, you can write things such as `2.days.ago` or `Time.today + 2.hours + 14.minutes`, and get something back that does what you want.

Probably the best thing that ActiveSupport provides is called the `to_proc` hack. It adds a `to_proc` method to the `Symbol` class. The utility of this is that some common iteration scenarios in Ruby will be much more succinct. Thanks to this, instead of writing

```
%w(abc cde efg).map {|v| v.inspect}
```

you can write

```
%w(abc cde efg).map &:inspect
```

This makes code much easier to read. Refer to Appendix A for a small explanation of how this works.

ActionMailer

The ActionMailer package makes it simple to create templates for sending mail, by using much the same view techniques that regular Rails views provide. If you need to send mail with a predetermined format, ActionMailer is probably the best way to do it.

ActionWebService

The new rage in Rails and web applications with regard to web services is called Representational State Transfer (REST). The base idea is that you use regular HTTP calls with human-readable URLs to provide the most common operations. You use the different HTTP methods (such as GET, POST, PUT, DELETE, and so on) to provide different operations on the same address, and in the request you provide just the information needed, in a simple XML or YAML format. This makes web services much less painful than they currently are with Simple Object Access Protocol (SOAP) and Web Services Description Language (WSDL). ActionWebService helps you develop clients for such services easily in Rails. Because Rails already has good support for easy URLs, and also makes it easy to do different things depending on which HTTP method is used, Rails has become one of the best ways available with which to implement REST services.

ActiveResource

ActiveResource is not a part of Rails at the time of writing, but will probably be released when you're reading this. The purpose is to take the REST architecture of Rails one step further by providing easy ways to expose web services transparently. This is accomplished by using the same MVC code that regular Rails uses. Because Service Oriented Architecture (SOA) is hailed as the future of application development, this could well provide another sweet spot for Rails applications.

Rails Helper Scripts

Ruby's first major philosophy point is DRY: Don't Repeat Yourself. This shines through the Rails framework in many ways. One of the ways Rails makes your life simpler as a developer is by providing several scripts that help you with different tasks in the development of an application. I'll guide you through the scripts that can be found in the script directory of a newly generated Rails application. Some of these you won't use often; some will be totally indispensable. I won't describe Rake tasks used for different tasks here, though, because they have a slightly different purpose.

about

If you create a new Rails application, start a WEBrick instance, and point your browser to http://localhost:3000/, you'll see a page describing your application. The about script provides exactly the same information. It prints the versions of Ruby, RubyGems, and Rails (and all dependent packages). It also prints which environment is used, the database, and which migration version number the application is currently at. As such, it can be useful debug information.

breakpointer

The breakpoint library in Ruby allows you to call a method at an arbitrary point of your code. If you run this program locally, outside of Rails, this will open up an Interactive Ruby (IRB) instance that lets you debug the application at the point of the breakpoint. But if you use such a breakpoint in a Rails application, something else happens. Because most Rails applications don't have a natural place to dump you into an IRB, the application won't do that. Instead, Rails will provide a breakpoint server. The `breakpointer` script lets you attach to such a breakpoint server (it works remotely too), and when the application hits a breakpoint you get an IRB session into it. Quite neat, and very useful.

console

This script lets you start up an IRB console with the current Rails application loaded. You have access to your model objects, all Rails helpers, and much more. You can use this script to test how you think some method in ActiveRecord will work, or almost anything else you can think of. When I create a new Rails application, I usually make sure always to have a console started, because it's so easy to test things out. You can also use it to check on the data in the database. Because you can execute arbitrary SQL through a model object, this means you can do mostly anything you want.

destroy

The `destroy` script is the negative counterpart of the `generate` script, described next. It's generic and uses a generator class to remove something that has been created by the `generate` script. It won't remove things you have changed, only unchanged files and code. However, it can be handy to have, because the `generate` script creates many files in different places.

generate

The `generate` script is one of the most important scripts for DRY in Rails. The purpose is to allow you to autogenerate as much code as possible. As such, it doesn't do anything you couldn't do by hand, but remembering everything you should add when creating a new model quickly becomes tedious. The `generate` script is also generic, which means you can install new generators that can generate your own custom code. The most-used generators are probably the model, the controller, and the scaffold generators.

The model generator creates a new empty model file, a new migration file for this model, and several test files where you can add your own test code. The controller creates a simple controller file and corresponding tests. Scaffolding creates a new controller and views that give access to CRUD operations for an existing model. It's useful as a base for further code, especially for administrative interfaces. You'll use this approach with the Shoplet application in the next chapter.

plugin

Rails' plug-in mechanism is very powerful (and one of the main methods the core Rails team uses to test new features). This script is the portal to all plug-in goodness. You use it to install new plug-ins and remove old ones. You can also use the script to extract parts of an existing code base into a plug-in. The most common usage is to install a new plug-in, possibly through the `-x` flag (that only works if you store your Rails application in a Subversion repository—which you should), which links directly to the version control repository for the plug-in you want to install. Very handy.

runner

Sometimes you need to run a bit of code within the context of a Rails application without having to start an IRB console. In those cases, the runner allows you to execute an arbitrary piece of Ruby code, written on the command line. One of the more regular uses of this mechanism is to add a `crontab` entry to clean old sessions from the ActiveRecord store by running a command with `runner`.

server

You most commonly use the `server` script to start up your application and try it out. It starts up a standalone Rails instance listening on port 3000. The default is to start WEBrick, but if you have Mongrel or lighttpd installed, the script will use one of them instead. In production, the `server` script isn't usually used, because there are better ways to deploy a Rails application. However, the `server` script works fine for development, especially when you need to restart your application often.

RAILS VS. OTHER WEB FRAMEWORKS

There are hundreds, if not thousands of web frameworks in different languages. Some people consider it a good task to learn a programming language better so you can implement your own framework. In that respect it would be hard to compare Rails to other frameworks. However, I'll still try to describe the most popular frameworks in several different languages and also contrast them against Rails. Some would say that such a comparison will always be subjective. I won't argue with that; these are my personal thoughts about the closest competitors to Rails.

Struts (Java)

Struts is arguably the number one web framework used with Java. It doesn't usually sit alone, though. The most common situation is probably Struts combined with Tiles and Hibernate. That's the scenario I'll consider here, because the different parts neatly match against the letters in MVC. This is also the first major difference between Struts and Rails. Struts doesn't provide MVC functionality at all; it just gives you the controller part. Tiles is easy to get going with Struts, but it's not part of the framework and also needs separate configuration. Configuration is also the part of Struts that can be quite painful. You gain lots of flexibility, but at the same time you need to keep numerous XML files up to date.

Rails configuration is basically guesswork unless you want to provide something substantial to it. Only one configuration item is needed to get Rails working, and that is the database parameters.

The model is the big difference between Struts and Rails, though. The only part of the model that is available within Struts is validation, and this also requires some configuration to get going. Using Hibernate gives you much flexibility, and you can do some things with Hibernate that are hard to achieve with ActiveRecord in Rails. This flexibility comes at the cost of another configuration file. You also need to create model classes (or autogenerate them once and work from there), which contain getters and setters for attributes. It is in the model that the cost of a statically typed, compiled language gets in the way of rapidly getting something working.

In summary, Struts gives you much flexibility, but the cost of getting started is much higher. Maintenance also suffers, because there is just much more code and configuration.

Django (Python)

Django is, on many levels, very similar to Rails. The big difference between the two frameworks is first and foremost one of philosophy, and this difference hails more from the respective languages than from any explicit design choice the creators have made in the software.

There is also a difference in feel. Django seems more aimed at web publishing applications, while Rails is well suited for generic web application development. Django ships with some things out of the box that Rails doesn't contain. For example, a built-in authentication system comes with Django, but not with Rails.

Another difference is how Django places all information about models in one place. Python code defines the database tables, and this is generated from the same place that defines the attributes on a model object. In Rails you define migrations for your models in Ruby, and then the attributes in the database are available to your model object without you having to specify them. These are two slightly different approaches, but in the end which one you choose doesn't matter much.

In summary, the big difference between the frameworks is in style and feeling, rather than functionality. They are both perfectly satisfactory for most web tasks. However, if you want Ajax, Rails will probably give you a big head start. Also, Rails runs on the JVM, but Django does not.

Seaside (Smalltalk)

It's hard to compare Seaside with Rails, because they embody completely different design and architectural decisions. Seaside is a web framework based on continuations. Now, the thing that makes Seaside such an interesting framework is that it inverts the usual way of writing a web application. Instead of having small separate parts of functionality that trigger at different points in the life cycle of a web interaction, and maintaining state by saving away small nuggets of information indexed by data in client cookies, Seaside lets you write your web application more or less in the same style as you would write a regular command-line application. You start up, initiating everything, then loop and let the customers specify products they want to order. Then, when that part is finished you go ahead by asking which delivery address they want the order sent to, and so on.

In reality, Seaside works the same way as all other web applications, under the covers. However, this part of the system is hidden from the person using the framework. Most of the complexity of maintaining state is managed by saving continuations at strategic points of the execution that can be resumed at any time, or discarded.

Seaside doesn't contain explicit support for a database or model layer. The developer has to add this. In the same manner, Seaside doesn't contain a separate templating system for easily creating HTML views. Instead, you write Smalltalk code that generates HTML. In some situations this flexibility can be good, but in other cases—especially when creating larger applications—this makes it hard to let a designer generate the HTML design for you and then integrate it into the application.

So, Seaside is good at several things that almost no other framework handles well, but other detriments make Rails a more widely useful full-stack solution for web applications.

PHP

There are certainly many frameworks for PHP that I could compare Rails against, but Ruby on Rails sits more or less in the exact same spot that PHP has traditionally occupied. The big difference is that Rails scales better and provides more benefits. With PHP, you first need to choose a framework that gives you some kind of

Object-Relational mapping. For small sites, you could use SQL directly, but that would be far from MVC, and as I said earlier, not scalable. Zend (the company behind PHP) has announced the Zend Framework, aimed at competing with Rails and providing some of the features that are missing (or hard to use) in a regular PHP installation.

PHP is good for a few reasons, though. It's widely available. It's easy to learn and many people know it already. It's designed specifically to be a web language. However, this is also a weakness, because it isn't a general-purpose language like Ruby. Sometimes PHP doesn't feel object-oriented enough, and it can be hard to abstract functionality.

The big problem compared to Rails is that there is no difference between the view and the other places. There's never an overarching controller. Everything is file based. This makes a PHP project simple to start but hard to continue working with.

So, in summary, if you want one or two pages that fetch data from a database, you can probably do it faster with PHP than Rails, but that's about it.

Testing

One of the strengths of Rails is that it makes testing easy and natural. You can run your tests often, and the testing is an integral part of the application. I won't talk specifically about how to write the tests here, but instead will describe the different kinds of tests available to you, and where they live.

First, to start testing, just run `rake` in your application directory. That runs all unit tests you've written. That's the first and best way to test.

As you can see, if you check in the `test` directory of a new application, Rails comes with several versions of tests. The directories found here are `fixtures`, `functional`, `integration`, `mocks`, and `unit`. However, only the `functional`, `integration`, and `unit` directories contain tests. In the `fixtures` directory, you'll define data fixtures for your models, so that the tests you write can have a consistent and dependable basis for testing. In the same way, the `mocks` directory contains fake implementations of real parts of your application. The canonical example is the credit card payment service. You don't want to talk with a payment gateway each time you run tests, so instead you create a mock of this service code, which generates implementations of the interesting methods that return predetermined values.

In Rails, unit tests have the explicit responsibility to test the model. There should be one file in the `unit` directory for each model you've created, and if you've used the generators to create them (as you should), these files will have been created automatically.

A typical unit test looks much like a regular `Test::Unit` test case, except that Rails unit tests can specify a fixture to use. You can use more than one fixture in the same test case, but the way Rails generates your test files, you'll get one separate fixture for each test case file.

Functional tests—in contrast to unit tests—should test controllers. They're usually written at a higher level than unit tests, because the functionality of models is a part of the functioning of the controllers. The best way to see how to write simple functional tests is to generate a scaffold controller and read the code for the generated functional test. As you can see in Listing 3-1, the language is high level, and looks more like a DSL for testing than regular Ruby code.

Listing 3-1. *Parts of Functional Test Code for a User Controller*

```ruby
class UsersControllerTest < Test::Unit::TestCase
  fixtures :users

  def setup
    @controller = UsersController.new
    @request    = ActionController::TestRequest.new
    @response   = ActionController::TestResponse.new
  end

  def test_index
    get :index
    assert_response :success
    assert_template 'list'
  end

  def test_list
    get :list

    assert_response :success
    assert_template 'list'

    assert_not_nil assigns(:users)
  end

  def test_show
    get :show, :id => 1

    assert_response :success
    assert_template 'show'

    assert_not_nil assigns(:user)
    assert assigns(:user).valid?
  end

  def test_new
    get :new

    assert_response :success
    assert_template 'new'

    assert_not_nil assigns(:user)
  end
end
```

Integration tests, finally, are even higher than functional tests. The purpose is to test the flow through an application. As such, this kind of testing uses operations that resemble the actions that a user will execute while using the application, rather than going behind the covers, on the bare metal, like functional and unit tests. In the integration test, you send in requests, check the response, follow redirects, fill in form information, and so on.

All in all, these three versions of testing let you have good control over your application's behavior, and it also makes it easy to test against regression. As such, testing should always be written concurrently while writing the implementation code. Alas, due to space constraints, this book won't contain much testing information. This will be part of the downloadable complete code, and I'll also show you how to test your first application with unit and functional tests. However, the rest of the projects won't have tests written for them in this book.

Plug-Ins

Rails sports an easy-to-use plug-in system. It allows you to extend and replace functionality in any part of the core system, or add completely new capabilities. There's some debate going on as to whether there should be a separate plug-in mechanism from RubyGems. That's because you can do almost everything with RubyGems that you can do with plug-ins, and Gems also gives you some extra features. My own opinion is that it can be useful to associate plug-ins with a specific Rails application. If you install a Gem, it will be available to all Ruby applications in the system. It's also easier to develop a plug-in without some of the overhead that a Gem requires.

The way to work with plug-ins is through the `script/plugin` script. With it, you can list all available plug-ins, and install, update, and remove plug-ins. To get more information about how the script works, just run it without parameters.

Some plug-ins are more useful than others. These are my picks of a few that have proven handy from time to time.

Acts As Taggable

This simple plug-in adds the class method `acts_as_taggable` to ActiveRecord. If you mark a model class with this method, each instance of that model can be associated with tags. The plug-in also gives you ways to search on tags.

CAS Filter

If your organization uses Central Authentication Server (CAS), which is a common protocol for centralized authentication and single sign-on, this filter allows you to add authentication easily to your application. You have the choice to protect only parts of the application, or everything.

Globalize Plug-In

This plug-in adds transparent translation of both models and views. Because Rails currently doesn't handle internationalization that well, something like this plug-in is much needed if you want to do development outside the United States. Globalize provides localization of numbers, dates, and currencies, and helps with translation.

Rails Engines

This plug-in is a little bit different, in that it doesn't add anything by itself. Instead, it adds more specialized plug-in functionality. In the parlance of engines, you can install a Login Engine, or a User Engine, or something else, and these engines provide a full chunk of more-or-less finished functionality that you can use or modify. The idea is that these engines won't affect the existing code at all, and they are aimed at being fully featured, vertical, MVC solutions.

Summary

As you can see, Rails is a fairly complex beast, comprised of several interacting parts. As such, this chapter has given you a cursory introduction to all the important parts. However, there's still much to learn. Instead of taking the components on separately, in the next chapter we'll start building an application, using most of the parts of a typical Rails application. In this way it will be easier to see how all the parts fit together.

The creators of Rails often say that Rails is "opinionated software." This is manifest in many ways, but the most important way is that you should follow specific paths when creating an application. You can deviate from them, but the framework benefits you most while following the rails. The purpose of the next few chapters is foremost to show you how a Rails application should be developed. The only differences here are that the application will be backed by a database accessed through JDBC, rather than through a native database driver, and that we'll run it with JRuby instead of Ruby.

CHAPTER 4

■■■

Store Administration

This chapter will walk you through the first part of the Shoplet application. It will be a fairly detailed look at most of the code necessary, and as such will give you a good overview of what's required to create a Rails application from scratch.

The Shoplet application is a basic web shop. It lets customers look through different products in an inventory, partitioned by type and categorized. Customers can add products to their shopping cart and later check out, and order the products in question. Payment is by billing address, because implementing the handling for a payment gateway is out of this chapter's scope.

The second part of the Shoplet application is the administrative user interface. This part is protected by username and password, and it's possible for currently authenticated users to add new ones. The administrative tasks that we'll create include adding, removing, and editing products, and handling orders.

Because most of the administrative user interface is easy to create from the basis of scaffolding, that's what I'll show you first. The customer part of the Shoplet system is covered in the first part of the next chapter.

As mentioned in the last chapter, I'll show some test code, but not nearly as much as would be necessary in a real application. The same thing is true with regards to validation in models. I'll add enough of these to show how it works, but not all parts of the model will be validated in a way that would be necessary in a deployed application.

Also note that the instructions from here on require that you have set up your environment in the way described in Chapter 2. The commands will be shown in a Linux environment, but should be trivial to translate into the Windows or Mac OS counterparts.

Creating a New Rails Application

The first step to create a new Rails application is to go to the directory where the new application will live, and then execute the `rails` command with the name of the application to create as a single argument. In this case, you'll do it like this:

```
jruby -S rails shoplet
```

This command generates 20 to 30 lines of output, telling you what files and directories it created. On my system the first few lines look like this:

```
create
create  app/controllers
create  app/helpers
create  app/models
create  app/views/layouts
create  config/environments
create  components
create  db
```

What has happened is that the rails script has created a new subdirectory called shoplet in the current directory, which contains the standard structure of a Rails application (described further in Chapter 3). With just one small adjustment, this will be a functional (but not very useful) Rails application that can be run with a web server and executed by visiting the correct address with a browser.

The next step requires that you have set up a database, as described in Chapter 2. For our purposes, I'll assume it's a MySQL database on localhost. If this isn't the way you've done it, you'll have to translate the instructions into your circumstances.

First of all, you need to create some databases in your MySQL installation. You also need to add users with the correct privileges to access and create tables in the database. The script in Listing 4-1 works fine on any MySQL installation.

Listing 4-1. *create_shoplet_db.sql*

```
CREATE DATABASE shoplet_dev;
CREATE DATABASE shoplet_test;
CREATE DATABASE shoplet_prod;
GRANT ALL PRIVILEGES ON shoplet_dev.* TO shoplet_dev@'%'
        IDENTIFIED BY 'shoplet';
GRANT ALL PRIVILEGES ON shoplet_test.* TO shoplet_test@'%'
        IDENTIFIED BY 'shoplet';
GRANT ALL PRIVILEGES ON shoplet_prod.* TO shoplet_prod@'%'
        IDENTIFIED BY 'shoplet';
FLUSH PRIVILEGES;
```

This creates three new databases, with three corresponding users who all have the same password. Of course, you should modify this script for your own needs, but the three databases named dev, test, and prod should exist in some form, because this is one of the things that makes Rails a joy to work with.

After you've created the databases, all you need to do is to configure the file config/database.yml. There are three top-level entries in this file, called development, test, and production. When you write in this file, you need to make sure that you don't accidentally get a tab character in. Try to indent using spaces instead. With the preceding settings, and the comments removed (lines that begin with # are comments), the new Shoplet database.yml should look like this:

Listing 4-2. *config/database.yml*

```
development:
  adapter: jdbc
  driver: com.mysql.jdbc.Driver
  url: jdbc:mysql://localhost/shoplet_dev
  username: shoplet_dev
  password: shoplet

test:
  adapter: jdbc
  driver: com.mysql.jdbc.Driver
  url: jdbc:mysql://localhost/shoplet_test
  username: shoplet_test
  password: shoplet

production:
  adapter: jdbc
  driver: com.mysql.jdbc.Driver
  url: jdbc:mysql://localhost/shoplet_prod
  username: shoplet_prod
  password: shoplet
```

Now you've configured the database, which means you're just about set to test your Rails application for the first time. The only thing missing is a small change to the file `config/environment.rb`. Just before the line that begins with `Rails::Initializer`, you need to add this line:

```
require 'jdbc_adapter'
```

This makes sure that Rails will be able to use AR-JDBC as the database provider.

RAILS ENVIRONMENTS

The Rails framework consistently uses the concept of environments to control various configuration options. These decide which runtime parameters are set, how they interact, and a few other things. There are three different runtime environments in standard Rails. These are called development, test, and production. It's important to keep in mind that the three environments have separate databases and don't share session information.

development

The development runtime environment is the default environment where you run migrations and start a web server. This is where you'll most likely spend your time. This environment tries to make the development process as easy as possible. It does this in a number of different ways. The most important one is that it reloads most of your code on each request. This means you can change the validators in your model, and the next time you hit the browser, the changes will be there, without having to restart the web server or Rails. In the same way, you can change controllers and views and never have to restart.

Another difference from what you might expect is that caching isn't turned on. The error messages are also informative, and tell things that you should never let a user see. A third thing is that the development environment enables the breakpoint server automatically. See Chapter 3 for more information about the breakpointer.

test

The most important thing to remember about the test environment is that you never use it explicitly. Whenever you run any tests in Rails, the test environment is used, but you shouldn't specify it explicitly when starting a Rails console or web server. To make sure everything is as Rails expects it to be when running tests, the database in question is always re-created before each test run. So, don't store any important data here.

Information is cached when testing, but error messages are still on the more talkative side.

production

The production environment is where your application should run in production, simply. Caching happens, the production database is used, and error messages are specifically written for users, not developers.

staging

The staging runtime environment doesn't come with Rails. It's something that many in the community wish were there, though. Simply enough, in a real customer-developer relationship, you often find yourself in the situation that you want to show the customer what the web site will look like, but you don't want it to run against the production database. There might also be other things you don't want to have it using in this situation. So, what you do is simply add a new environment, copied from the production one. This is simple to do; you just copy the file `config/environments/production.rb` to `config/environments/staging.rb`, and add a new entry in `config/databases.yml` called `staging`, which describes the database settings for this environment.

The staging environment should be as close as possible to the real production environment, without using the same resources. In some situations there is no production database to clobber, and in that case you won't need the staging environment. However, in most real deployment scenarios there are always things going wrong, and this solution works well.

Running with Mongrel

When the time comes to test your application, you'll need to start it up in some way. For now, we won't look at the more advanced deployment options available, but instead I'll show you the simplest way possible to get something started. As you might have guessed, the support for this is already available within Rails. In Chapter 3 I mentioned the server script, and you can use that to start a number of different web servers. By default, Rails starts WEBrick, but if you have installed Mongrel, Rails will use it instead. To just run everything, execute this command:

```
jruby script/server
```

If you have configured the database correctly, and there are no exceptional errors in your code that would make everything crash during startup, you'll see some startup messages from Mongrel, telling you that it has started and is listening on port 3000. So, just point your web browser at `http://localhost:3000/` and you should see be able to see the Rails status page.

The `server` script takes several parameters. The two most interesting are `-e` and `-p`. With `-p` you can set which port Mongrel should listen on, and with `-e` you can specify that Mongrel should start with another runtime environment than the default (which is development).

From now on you should just leave Mongrel running in the background so you can check your results easily, whenever you have changed anything.

Of course, if you'd like to try running with WEBrick, or any other web server, you can do that by naming it on the command line like this:

```
jruby script/server webrick
```

If Rails can find the web server, it will start using that instead.

A First Model

After you've generated the new application and tested that your database configuration is sound by starting up the web server, it's time to create the first parts of your model. You'll create three different model classes here, define their relationship, and then create the migrations for them. You'll generate the models associated with products first, because that's the first part of the administrative user interface you'll create. I've decided to name the models `Product`, `ProductType`, and `ProductCategory`. These names are important to remember, because Rails has some guidelines regarding how to translate a model name into a database table.

Product Type

First of all, you'll create the model called `ProductType`, because it doesn't have any dependencies on other models. Each `Product` will have one type, and each `ProductCategory` will also have one type, so these depend on the type being there.

To create a new model, you use the model generator, like this (in the root directory of the Shoplet application):

```
jruby script/generate model ProductType
```

This creates several files and also prints some output. It should look like this:

```
exists  app/models/
exists  test/unit/
exists  test/fixtures/
create  app/models/product_type.rb
create  test/unit/product_type_test.rb
create  test/fixtures/product_types.yml
create  db/migrate
create  db/migrate/001_create_product_types.rb
```

Now, as mentioned before, all model code resides in the directory `app/models`. A file called `product_type.rb` now exists in that directory. However, because the `ProductType` is a simple model object, you won't add anything to it right now. It's fine as it is. You do need to define the migration for ProductType, and decide which fields it should contain. The way to do that is to open the file called db/migrate/001_create_product_types.rb in a text editor. Right now that file is quite sparse, because you haven't added any content to it. So, right now it will create a table with one column called id in it, and that's it. A ProductType should probably contain some information, at least. Right now, you only need a name, and that's easy to add because Rails has added a name definition in a comment. So, remove the pound sign and you have all the table definitions you need for a ProductType.

But that's not all; you also need some initial data. There will never be many types in the system, and you know already what types those should be. Further, this is part of the definition of the product types, so you should also add some code that adds three new rows to the product_types table. The easiest way to do this is to use ActiveRecord. The final code for the file 001_create_product_types.rb should look like this:

```
class CreateProductTypes < ActiveRecord::Migration
  class ProductType < ActiveRecord::Base; end

  def self.up
    create_table :product_types do |t|
      t.column :name, :string
    end

    data
  end

  def self.data
    ProductType.create :name => 'Book'
    ProductType.create :name => 'Music'
    ProductType.create :name => 'Movie'
  end

  def self.down
    drop_table :product_types
  end
end
```

There are three differences from the code that Rails generated. First, the line defining the name column isn't commented out any more. Second, an inner class called ProductType is defined that inherits from ActiveRecord::Base. The class definition is empty, but it still allows us to access the ActiveRecord helpers later on. Third, you've defined a method called data, and you call that method last in the up method. The data method creates three ProductType objects with different names. The create method saves these directly to the database. That's all there is to it right now. Before showing how to make the migrations go into the database, we'll go through the Product and ProductCategory models and define these.

Product

The next step is to create the Product model. As with the ProductType, you'll do it with the generate script:

```
jruby script/generate model Product
```

The output from this command looks almost exactly like the one for ProductType, so I won't repeat it. The migration file for products is called db/migrate/002_create_products.rb, and you need to add some more changes to this one. A Product should have a name, a description, a product type, and a price. It also has zero or more categories associated with it, but we'll take care of those next. For the moment you'll save the price in cents, because Rails 1.1.6 doesn't handle decimal types in databases that well. (Also, you should never store a price as a float or double, due to the problems with representing real numbers exactly in binary.) So, open up the file db/migrate/002_create_products.rb and uncomment the name entry. You should also add some new columns. The final version of the file should look like this:

```ruby
class CreateProducts < ActiveRecord::Migration
  def self.up
    create_table :products do |t|
      t.column :name, :string
      t.column :description, :text
      t.column :product_type_id, :integer
      # This price will be in cents to make it easier
      # It might be better to implement this using Decimal
      t.column :price, :integer
    end
  end

  def self.down
    drop_table :products
  end
end
```

As you can see, you just added entries for description, product_type_id, and price. A comment is also in place to make it obvious why the price is an integer. After adding the database information, you need to change some parts in the model definition. That file is called app/models/product.rb. After the current changes it should look like this:

```ruby
class Product < ActiveRecord::Base
  has_and_belongs_to_many :product_categories
  belongs_to :product_type
end
```

The directives simply say what it looks like they say. Having belongs_to means that for every ProductType there are zero or more Products for it. Using has_and_belongs_to_many requires us to have a join table for product_categories, and that's what we'll look at next.

Product Categories

As for the other model objects, you generate the base with the generator script:

```
jruby script/generate model ProductCategory
```

The migration code for product categories is slightly more involved than the other two, because you need to do a fair number of things in it. First of all, a product category belongs to a product type, and has a name. That means the part that defines the product_categories table looks like this (in db/migrate/003_create_product_categories.rb):

```
create_table :product_categories do |t|
  t.column :product_type_id, :integer
  t.column :name, :string
end
```

You also need a data method, like the one you used for ProductType. Because ProductCategory references ProductType, you first need to fetch those. Second, you create some categories for each type. The data method looks like this:

```
def self.data
  book = ProductType.find_by_name 'Book'
  music = ProductType.find_by_name 'Music'
  movie = ProductType.find_by_name 'Movie'

  %w(Computers Mysteries
     Science\ Fiction Crime).each do |v|
    ProductCategory.create :product_type => book, :name => v
  end

  %w(Jazz World\ Music Electronic
    Rock Indie Country).each do |v|
    ProductCategory.create :product_type => music, :name => v
  end

  %w(Action Science\ Fiction Drama
     Comedy Thriller).each do |v|
    ProductCategory.create :product_type => movie, :name => v
  end
end
```

However, this won't work unless you define ProductType and ProductCategory, so that's what you'll do first, before the up method:

```
class ProductType < ActiveRecord::Base; end
class ProductCategory < ActiveRecord::Base
  belongs_to :product_type
end
```

Last, you also need to create the join table that connects Product and ProductCategory. Rails has a specific naming scheme for such tables. The two tables to join should be in the name, ordered alphabetically, and joined with an underscore. In our case, the join table should be named product_categories_products, and the definition looks like this:

```
#join table for products and product_categories
create_table :product_categories_products, :id => false do |t|
  t.column :product_id, :integer
  t.column :product_category_id, :integer
end
```

Because a join table should only contain the IDs for the two entries to join, you need to tell Rails that no id column should be generated for the table. The final file for defining ProductCategories should look like this:

```
class CreateProductCategories < ActiveRecord::Migration
 class ProductType < ActiveRecord::Base; end
 class ProductCategory < ActiveRecord::Base
   belongs_to :product_type
 end

 def self.up
   create_table :product_categories do |t|
     t.column :product_type_id, :integer
     t.column :name, :string
   end

   data

   #join table for products and product_categories
   create_table :product_categories_products, :id => false do |t|
     t.column :product_id, :integer
     t.column :product_category_id, :integer
   end
 end

 def self.data
   book = ProductType.find_by_name 'Book'
   music = ProductType.find_by_name 'Music'
   movie = ProductType.find_by_name 'Movie'

   %w(Computers Mysteries
      Science\ Fiction Crime).each do |v|
     ProductCategory.create :product_type => book, :name => v
   end

   %w(Jazz World\ Music Electronic
      Rock Indie Country).each do |v|
     ProductCategory.create :product_type => music, :name => v
   end
```

```
   %w(Action Science\ Fiction Drama
      Comedy Thriller).each do |v|
     ProductCategory.create :product_type => movie, :name => v
   end
 end

 def self.down
   drop_table :product_categories_products rescue nil
   drop_table :product_categories
 end
end
```

When this migration runs, you'll have a few different categories to choose from in every type. The model file for `ProductCategory` is comparatively simple. You just define the same relationship to `ProductType` and `Product` as you've already done in the corresponding models:

```
class ProductCategory < ActiveRecord::Base
  has_and_belongs_to_many :products
  belongs_to :product_type
end
```

Notice that you could have put a `has_many :product_categories` inside of `product_type.rb`, if you ever were interested in going from `ProductType` to all product categories for that type.

Running the Migrations

You've defined three different migration files, mostly automatically generated by the Rails scripts. You might have noticed that the file naming follows a simple pattern. That's because a database used with migrations always has a version number associated with it. From scratch, that version number is 0. For each migration file run, the version is incremented by one. Because migration files are run alphabetically from the `db/migrate` directory, it's a good custom to name each file with the version number it will result in, even though it isn't necessary.

So, how to go about creating the database tables for your model? It's simple. You run `rake` on the target `db:migrate`, and Rails takes care of the rest:

```
jruby -S rake db:migrate
```

By default, this migrates your database to the latest version present in your files. If you want a specific version, you can specify that:

```
jruby -S rake rake db:migrate VERSION=2
```

The environment this runs in is `development`. At some point you should run your migrations for `test` and `production` too, and that's equally easy:

```
jruby -S rake db:migrate RAILS_ENV=production
```

That's about it for migrations at the moment. There's more to it, but right now this will get you started.

Validations

Normally the values that can be accepted on an attribute are constrained in one or several ways that won't show up in the database schema. For example, a price for a `Product` shouldn't be negative. These model constraints exist in the model class, and you'll add a few to show how Rails validations typically look. Validations are important, because they stop invalid data from entering the database.

The first model is `ProductType`. There's only one invariant, and that is that there should always be a name for it. (Rails automatically caters for the `id` field, so you won't have to ensure that it exists.) Validating the presence of an attribute, where *presence* means it should be there, and not be empty, is easy. You just add the `validates_presence_of` method to the model class. After adding that, the file `app/models/product_type.rb` looks like this:

```
class ProductType < ActiveRecord::Base
  has_many :products

  validates_presence_of :name
end
```

You'll also add a few validations to the `Product` model. First, there are a few required attributes. These are `price`, `name`, and `product_type`. A `Product` isn't valid without this information. On the other hand, a `Product` doesn't need a description. So, you add the validation to the `app/models/product.rb` file:

```
validates_presence_of :price, :name, :product_type
```

The next part is price. Because you represent price as cents, it should be an integer, and nothing else. You ensure that with the `validates_numericality_of` validator:

```
validates_numericality_of :price, :only_integer => true
```

Note the `only_integer` attribute. If you didn't write that part, `numericality` includes real numbers too, which you don't want.

The next two validations are slightly more involved. You first want to check that the price isn't `0` and that the price isn't negative. You should use `validate_each` to achieve that:

```
validates_each :price do |m,attr,value|
  if value == 0
    m.errors.add(attr,"Price can't be 0")
  elsif !value.nil? && value < 0
    m.errors.add(attr, "Price can't be negative")
  end
end
```

In this validator you need to check the attribute value specifically, and also add the error conditions by hand. The `m` parameter is the model object in question, so you can validate by comparing different attributes if you want. That is also useful in the next validation, which is a bit more complex. You want to make sure all the `product_categories` have the same type as the current model object:

```
validates_each :product_categories do |m,attr,value|
  if !value.nil? && value.any? {|v| m.product_type != v.product_type }
    m.errors.add(attr, "Category can't be of another type")
  end
end
```

You do this by using the `Enumerable` method `any?`. If any objects match the condition, you add an error condition.

These kinds of validations are useful, and can include many important preconditions and postconditions. Whenever you create models, you should think long and hard about what the invariants and contracts for that object should be, and add validations that take care of the exceptions from these contracts. As the next section talks about, you should also test that the validations you've written say what you think they say.

Unit Testing Products

As mentioned in the section about testing in Chapter 3, unit tests are used to test models. I'll show a few tests for `ProductType` and `Product` here, but as mentioned earlier there won't be space enough to test everything as it should be tested. First of all, there is only one interesting fact to test about `ProductType`: that `name` must be provided. So, open up the file `test/unit/product_type_test.rb`, remove the `test_truth` method, and add this method instead:

```
def test_invalid_name
  p = ProductType.new
  assert !p.valid?
  assert p.errors.invalid?(:name)
end
```

This method first creates a new `ProductType`, and because you don't specify a name, it shouldn't be valid. The method `assert`, and all methods beginning with `assert_`, are used to check a certain invariant. In this method, you just check that the model object is not valid, and that the errors provided include at least one for `name`.

There are more things to test for `Product`, though. First of all, go ahead and open the file `test/unit/product_test.rb` and remove the `test_truth` method. The next step demands a slight deviation into the territory of fixtures. A fixture is a YAML file that contains data for test fixtures, which means your tests will always use the same data, instead of relying on whatever can be found in the database at the moment. Because `Products` needs product types to work, you'll first change those fixtures. Open the file `test/fixtures/product_types.yml` and replace the contents with this:

```
book:
  id: 1
  name: Book
music:
  id: 2
```

```
  name: Music
movie:
  id: 3
  name: Movie
```

■**Caution** The indentation here must be done with spaces, not tabs. You'll see errors when running the tests otherwise.

As you might notice, this is the same type as the migrations added, but adding them here means you can get at the objects much more easily later on. Next, you add two fixtures for Product by replacing the contents of the file test/fixtures/products.yml with this:

```
first:
  id: 1
  product_type_id: 1
  name: Abc
  price: 1440
another:
  id: 2
  product_type_id: 2
  name: Cde
  price: 2990
```

Now you're almost ready to add some Product testing. You just need to tell Rails that it should use the fixtures for product types, in addition to the fixtures for Product. You can achieve this by adding this line after the corresponding line for products, in the file product_test.rb:

```
fixtures :product_types
```

The first test is the same as for product type, just checking that an invalid name can't get in:

```
def test_invalid_name
  p = Product.new
  assert !p.valid?
  assert p.errors.invalid?(:name)
end
```

You do the exact same thing for type:

```
def test_invalid_type
  p = Product.new
  assert !p.valid?
  assert p.errors.invalid?(:product_type)
end
```

The next step is to check that invalid categories will be noticed, and that your validation for that works:

```
def test_invalid_category
  p = Product.new
  p.product_type = product_types('book')
  c = ProductCategory.create :name => 'ABC',
            :product_type => product_types('music')
  p.product_categories << c
  assert !p.valid?
  assert p.errors.invalid?(:product_categories)
end
```

Here you use the product type fixtures, by calling the method product_types with the name of the fixture to fetch. In this way you conveniently create a new Product with a specific type and add a newly created category from another type.

You need also to make absolutely sure that invalid prices can't be set:

```
def test_invalid_price
  p = Product.new
  p.price = nil
  assert !p.valid?
  assert p.errors.invalid?(:price)
  p = Product.new
  p.price = 1.0
  assert !p.valid?
  assert p.errors.invalid?(:price)
  p = Product.new
  p.price = 0
  assert !p.valid?
  assert p.errors.invalid?(:price)
  p = Product.new
  p.price = -17
  assert !p.valid?
  assert p.errors.invalid?(:price)
end
```

This test is slightly longer because you want to try a few different invalid prices, to see that all corner cases are covered.

These tests are all well and good, but they only test the negative side. For what it's worth, each of these tests would pass if something was really wrong with the system. So, what you do is add a positive test too, where everything works as it should. If that test fails, you know something is iffy:

```
def test_valid_product
  p = Product.new
  p.price = 122
  p.name = "Hello Goodbye"
  p.product_type = product_types('book')
```

```
    assert p.valid?
end
```

That concludes the testing of the product family of model objects. Do add more tests if you come up with something suitable. You can never have too many tests.

To run these tests, just execute this command:

```
jruby -S rake
```

The standard rake task runs all unit and functional tests by default. Make sure that you've migrated everything in the test environment before doing this, though.

Creating a Scaffold for Products

Now that we've created the basis for our model, added some validations, and also made sure that those validations work, it's finally time to create a web interface to handle products. The first step in such an endeavor is to create a scaffold. In Rails, a scaffold means generated code to support the basic CRUD operations for a specific model object. We'll begin from such a scaffold and then change it to fit our needs. This will be the most important part of our administrative user interface.

To create the scaffolds, you use the `script/generate` script, like this:

```
jruby script/generate scaffold Product
```

As usual when generating something, you get some output that tells you exactly which files have been created or modified. Now start up the web server, and visit the address `http://localhost:3000/products`. If everything has gone right, you'll see an empty listing of products and a link to add a new one. Go ahead and explore the interface and see what you can do. You probably won't be able to add a new product yet, because there's no way to choose among the product types available yet. So, your first step is to change the addition of products so you can get data in there.

A Rails scaffold is a controller (that can be found in `app/controllers/products_controller.rb`) and a set of views, which almost always are RHTML files. To make it possible to work with product types within the `Product` scaffold, you first need to open up `app/controllers/products_controller.rb`. Find the method called `new`. It looks like this:

```
def new
  @product = Product.new
end
```

You simply need to provide the `ProductTypes` available here. You'll later need to add `ProductCategories` too, so just chuck that in while you're at it. The method should look like this when you're finished:

```
def new
  @product = Product.new
  @product_types = ProductType.find(:all)
  @product_categories = ProductCategory.find(:all)
end
```

That is all that's needed to provide the necessary information to the view. The scaffolds are smart, though; Rails uses the same code that views the RHTML for adding a new product to edit an existing product, so you'll want to make the same change to the edit method, which should look like this now:

```
def edit
  @product = Product.find(params[:id])
  @product_types = ProductType.find(:all)
  @product_categories = ProductCategory.find(:all)
end
```

The next step is to alter the file called app/views/products/_form.rhtml. The underscore means it's a partial, and it is used from the views edit and new. You want to change this file a little bit, so just go ahead and change the contents into this:

```
<%= error_messages_for 'product' %>


<!--[form:product]-->
<p><label for="product_name">Name</label><br/>
<%= text_field 'product', 'name'  %></p>


<p><label for="product_description">Description</label><br/>
<%= text_area 'product', 'description'  %></p>


<p><label for="product_product_type">Product Type</label><br/>
<%= select 'product', 'product_type_id', @product_types.collect {|p|
    [ p.name, p.id ] },{}%></p>


<p><label for="product_price">Price</label><br/>
$<%= text_field_tag 'product[price]', price(@product)[1..-1]  %></p>
<!--[eoform:product]-->
```

You've changed just the entries for ProductType and Price, but those are important changes. First, the ProductType change means you can switch among the available product types, and choose the one you want. The select helper method makes a select box with all types in it. The price is a little trickier, though. Remember that you represent it as cents? Well, it should be formatted in the regular format when viewed by the end user. So, you'll add a helper method that accomplishes this for you. The place to add this helper is in the file app/helpers/application_helper.rb because you want all of your application to have access to this helper. You just add these two methods to the module within:

```
def price(product)
  money product.price
end


def money(pr)
  pr ? "$%d.%02d" % pr.divmod(100) : "$0.00"
end
```

Because you most often want to display the price with a dollar sign in front, you have to strip out that sign when displaying the price in the box. The next step is making sure that saving these objects works too. To do this, you need to change the `create` and `update` methods. First of all, though, you need a small helper method in the controller that allows you to handle price more easily. So, in the end of the class, add this method declaration:

```
private
def intern_price
  if params[:product] && params[:product][:price]
    v = params[:product][:price].split('.').map(&:to_i)
    params[:product][:price] = v[0]*100 + v[1]
  end
end
```

This helper would reformat the price into cents if a `price` parameter was submitted. The `private` in the beginning says that this method should not be available as an action on the controller.

Next you need to change the `create` method to handle the new price:

```
def create
  intern_price
  @product = Product.new(params[:product])
  if @product.save
    flash[:notice] = 'Product was successfully created.'
    redirect_to :action => 'list'
  else
    @product_types = ProductType.find(:all)
    @product_categories = ProductCategory.find(:all)
    render :action => 'new'
  end
end
```

The other thing you added was `@product_types` and `@product_categories`, in case something goes wrong. This lets you see the original page again, with error messages attached. You need to do the same thing with the `update` method:

```
def update
  @product = Product.find(params[:id])
  intern_price
  if @product.update_attributes(params[:product])
    flash[:notice] = 'Product was successfully updated.'
    redirect_to :action => 'show', :id => @product
  else
    @product_types = ProductType.find(:all)
    @product_categories = ProductCategory.find(:all)
    render :action => 'edit'
  end
end
```

Now you can go ahead and create a product or two. You don't need to restart the web server either. If everything works correctly, you should also be able to see your new products in the list. You can edit and destroy products without trouble, too. You might note that the listing of products isn't that good right now. It shows a lengthy description, but not product type. That should probably be changed, so we'll take a look at that next. Now, you don't need to change anything in the controller to change those parts of the listing, because you have all the data you need already. You can find the listing at app/views/products/list.rhtml, and it contains a generic mechanism that walks you through the available attributes and shows these. We'll change it a bit:

```
<h1>Products</h1>

<table width="400">
  <tr>
    <th align="left">Name</th>
    <th>Type</th>
    <th>Price</th>
    <th> </th>
    <th> </th>
  </tr>
  <% for product in @products %>
    <tr>
      <td align="left" valign="top"><%= link_to h(product.name),
          {:action => 'show', :id => product},
                    :class=>'productLink' %></td>
      <td align="right" valign="top"><%=h product.product_type.name%></td>
      <td align="right" valign="top"><%=price product %></td>
      <td> </td>
      <td><%= link_to 'Remove', {:action => 'destroy', :id => product},
                          :confirm => 'Are you sure?', :post => true %></td>
    </tr>
  <% end %>
</table>

<%= link_to 'Previous page',
    { :page => @product_pages.current.previous } if
                  @product_pages.current.previous %>
<%= link_to 'Next page',
    { :page => @product_pages.current.next } if
                  @product_pages.current.next %>

<br />
<%= link_to 'New product', :action => 'new' %>
```

As you can see, you hard code the columns, and you only display the name, type, and price. By using the link_to helper, you make it possible to show a Product by clicking the product name. In that way you can remove the separate edit and show links. The h helper takes a string and returns a string where all HTML-specific characters have been encoded;

it's a good habit to always use this when displaying data. Also note that you use the price helper here again, and that you've added a CSS class called productLink to the name display. This makes it easy to add some good looks later on. While we're working on the layout of displaying products, let's also fix the show page. You can find it in app/views/products/ show.rhtml, and you should turn it into something like this:

```
<p><b>Name:</b> <%= @product.name %></p>
<p><b>Description:</b><br/>
  <%= @product.description %>
</p>
<p><b>Price:</b> <%= price(@product) %></p>
<p>
  <b>Product Type:</b> <%=h @product.product_type.name %>
</p>

<%= link_to 'Edit', :action => 'edit', :id => @product %> |
<%= link_to 'Back', :action => 'list' %>
```

Once again, there's nothing unexpected. You just use the price helper and show the name of the product type.

Ajax

Our administrative user interface for products is starting to look good. Except for some CSS styling, only one thing is missing: the product categories. These are slightly more tricky. You want it to be possible to choose zero or more products while editing or adding a product, but the only choices available should be the ones that match the currently selected product type. That means you'd need to reload the page each time the product type changed. However, there's a better way. Ajax is the new hype word in web development. I won't talk too much about it here, but suffice it to say, it's a perfect technology for the current problem. With Ajax you can create a listener that updates just part of the page when product types have been changed. This is ideal right now. So, how do you go about it? Well, the first step is to create a partial. This partial will be used both by the forms on the full request, and by the Ajax call that will update the page later on. First, create a file called app/views/products/_categories.rhtml with this content:

```
<%= select_tag 'product_categories[]',
      options_for_select(@product_categories.select {|p|
            p.product_type.id ==  ((@product &&
         @product.product_type) || @product_types.first).id
        }.collect {|p| [ p.name, p.id ] },
   (@product && @product.product_categories.collect(&:id)) || nil),
   :multiple=>true, :size=>5 %>
```

It isn't much code, but it's slightly messy. What you do is, based on the current @product, walk through all product categories in the system, only using those that match the product's product type. Add these to the select box. The next step is to collect all categories that should be selected, which is the next parameter to the select_tag call. The next step is to use this partial from within the forms. So, open up app/views/products/_form.rhtml again and add this code after the part that displays the product type:

```
<p><label for="product_categories[]">Product Categories
<span id="waitOut"></span></label><br/>
<div id="categoriesSelector">
<%= render :partial => 'categories' %></div></p>
```

Notice that you've added a span that is empty, and a div tag that contains the output generated from the partial. You'll need these two elements later on for the Ajax-y parts of the system. But right now, you need to alter the products_controller.rb again, to make sure everything will be saved when you save a product. This is a little bit outside the box, because Rails doesn't handle these multiple selections out of the box. In the create method, you need to add this code directly after the call to Product.new:

```
if params[:product_categories]
  @product.product_categories <<
          ProductCategory.find(
        params[:product_categories].collect(&:to_i))
end
```

This code adds all product_categories to the product, if there are any. You need to change the update method a little bit more, because you now have to make sure validation takes place. The new update method should look like this:

```
def update
  @product = Product.find(params[:id])
  intern_price
  if @product.update_attributes(params[:product])
    if params[:product_categories]
      @product.product_categories = ProductCategory.find(
          params[:product_categories].collect(&:to_i))
    end
    if @product.save
      flash[:notice] = 'Product was successfully updated.'
      redirect_to :action => 'show', :id => @product
    end
  end
  if !@product.valid?
    @product_types = ProductType.find(:all)
    @product_categories = ProductCategory.find(:all)
    render :action => 'edit'
  end
end
```

The big difference here is that you check if the product is valid explicitly, because it can become invalid in two different places (in update_attributes, or save). You could do this in other ways, but that would mean you'd have to duplicate code in the method.

While you're still in the controller, you'll add another action that the Ajax call is supposed to use to update the partial. The method is called `categories_partial` and looks like this:

```
def categories_partial
  @product = Product.find_by_id(params[:id]) || Product.new
  @product.product_type = ProductType.find(params[:tp])
  @product_types = ProductType.find(:all)
  @product_categories = ProductCategory.find(:all)
  render :partial => 'categories'
end
```

You need to create a dummy product for the partial to work and set the `product_type` correctly. After you've done that, you fetch the needed product types and categories, and render the partial. Nothing strange here, really. However, now you're slowly moving in to the part that makes Ajax so practical. Ajax uses JavaScript to asynchronously update parts of the view. So, what you have to do is provide a listener on the product type select box that updates the `categories` partial. Once again, open up app/views/products/_form.rhtml and change the product type parts to look like this:

```
<p><label for="product_product_type">Product Type</label><br/>
<%= select 'product', 'product_type_id',
          @product_types.collect {|p| [ p.name, p.id ] },{},
            :onChange => "\$(waitOut).innerHTML=
            '<i>(Updating categories, please wait...)</i>';
          new Ajax.Updater('categoriesSelector','#{url_for(
  :controller=>'products',:action=>'categories_partial',
  :id=>@product)}?tp=' + this[this.selectedIndex].value,
            {onComplete:function(){\$(waitOut).innerHTML='';
          new Effect.Highlight('categoriesSelector');},
 asynchronous:true});"%></p>
```

What you do here is a little involved. The first two rows are exactly the same. On the fourth row, you add an `onChange` handler that first sets the `innerHTML` attribute of the span with the ID `waitOut` to a text that lets the user know something is happening. The code then creates a new `Ajax.Updater` that asynchronously does an HTTP request to the `categories_partial` action. When completed it replaces the content of the `div` with the ID `categoriesSelector` with what it got from the HTTP request. It also removes the "please wait" text and highlights the new contents when they arrive.

To get all this working, you need to make a slight detour to layouts. If you remember from Chapter 3, you can define a layout that defines the look for many pages. Because the Ajax parts need some JavaScript included, you need to create a layout that manages this for you. So, open the file called app/views/layouts/products.rhtml and change it to look like this:

```
<html>
<head>
  <title>Products: <%= controller.action_name %></title>
  <%= stylesheet_link_tag 'scaffold' %>
  <%= javascript_include_tag :defaults %>
</head>
```

```
<body>

<p style="color: green"><%= flash[:notice] %></p>

<%= yield  %>

</body>
</html>
```

The only thing you change right now is to make the view call `javascript_include_tag` with an argument of `:defaults`. This includes all the commonly used JavaScript files needed for Ajax to work. After you've made this change, go create a new product and you'll notice that the product categories now work. Try to change `ProductType`; you'll notice that you get a message to wait patiently, and then the product categories are updated.

This is just a small taste of what can be achieved with Ajax. We'll look more at Web 2.0 techniques in Chapter 8. For now, you also need to update the `show` view to display the product categories. This should be done in the file `app/views/products/show.rhtml` and is simple. You just add this after the entry for `ProductType`:

```
<p>
  <b>Product Categories:</b><br/>
  <% @product.product_categories.each do |cat| %>
  <%=h cat.name %><br/>
  <% end %>
</p>
```

Adding Some Good Looks

Finally, you need to make everything look slightly more presentable. The first step is to create a new layout called `admin.rhtml` that the entire administrative user interface will use. So, create the file `app/views/layouts/admin.rhtml` and fill it with this code:

```
<html>
<head>
  <title>Shoplet Online Store Administration:
          <%=controller.action_name%>
          <%=h params[:controller]%></title>
  <%= stylesheet_link_tag 'shoplet' %>
  <%= javascript_include_tag :defaults %>
</head>
<body>
  <table width="100%" height="100%">
    <tr>
      <td width="250" class="leftMenu" align="center" valign="top">
        <h2><%= link_to 'Shoplet', :controller => 'store',
                        :action=>'index'%></h2>
        <h3><%= link_to 'Online Shopping', :controller => 'store',
                        :action=>'index'%></h3>
```

```
        <h3><%= link_to 'Administration', :controller => 'store',
                          :action=>'index'%></h3>
        <br/>
        <ul style="text-align: left;">
          <li><%= link_to 'Administrate products', {:controller =>
                      'products'},:class => 'adminLink' %></li>
          <li><%= link_to 'Handle orders', {:controller =>
                      'orders'},:class => 'adminLink' %></li>
          <li><%= link_to 'Authenticated users', {:controller =>
                      'users'},:class => 'adminLink' %></li>
        </ul>
        <br/>
      </td>
      <td class="main" valign="top">
        <p style="color: green"><%= flash[:notice] %></p>
        <p style="color: red"><b><%= flash[:error] %></b></p>

        <%= yield  %>
      </td>
    </tr>
  </table>
</body>
</html>
```

Note that I've added some links here to controllers that you haven't created yet. That's where the rest of the administrative user interface will be found. After you've created this file, you need to edit products_controller.rb to use it, too. That's easy enough. Just add this method call on the second row:

```
layout "admin"
```

Before you try it out, you should add a new style sheet too. Create a file called public/stylesheets/shoplet.css and fill it with this code:

```
body {
  margin: 0px;
  padding: 0px;
}

h3 {
  font-size: 1em;
  font-weight: bold;
}

h2 a {
  text-decoration: none;
  color: black;
}
```

```
h3 a {
  text-decoration: none;
  color: black;
}

a {
  text-decoration: none;
  font-weight: bold;
}

thead td {
  font-weight: bold;
}

.productLink {
  color: black;
  font-weight: normal;
}

.adminLink {
  color: black;
  font-weight: normal;
}

.leftMenu {
  padding-top: 20px;
  border: 1px solid black;
  border-left: none;
  font-family: arial, sans-serif;
  background-color: #CCCCEE;
}

.main {
  padding: 30px;
  color: dark-grey;
}
```

If you now update the web browser, you'll note that everything looks many magnitudes better. If you open up the file test/functional/products_controller_test.rb, you'll also see that lots of test cases have already been created for you, entirely for free. You need to modify these slightly in some cases to accommodate the structure you've adopted, with price and categories handled specially. But I'll wait and show you how to do that when we talk about testing the login engine we'll write in the sections "Adding Some Authentication" and "Functional Tests," because that changes the functional tests a bit.

More Models

Because you have more or less finished the administration side of Products, it's time to think about the other parts the user interface should sport. If you remember the links we added to the layout in the end of the last section, the two parts needed will be one for order handling, and one for user administration. I've modeled the order system like this: An Order has zero or more OrderLines, and each Order is associated with a Customer. Regarding users, there will be a User model object. You'll begin by generating these models:

```
jruby script/generate model Customer
jruby script/generate model Order
jruby script/generate model OrderLine
jruby script/generate model User
```

After you've generated these models, you should open up the file db/migrate/004_cre-ate_customers.rb and change it to look like this:

```
class CreateCustomers < ActiveRecord::Migration
  def self.up
    create_table :customers do |t|
      t.column :given_name, :string
      t.column :sur_name, :string

      t.column :shipping_address_street, :string
      t.column :shipping_address_postal, :string
      t.column :shipping_address_zip, :string
      t.column :shipping_address_country, :string

      t.column :billing_address_street, :string
      t.column :billing_address_postal, :string
      t.column :billing_address_zip, :string
      t.column :billing_address_country, :string
    end
  end

  def self.down
    drop_table :customers
  end
end
```

This is arguably not such a good database design, but extending it more would take too much focus from the core you need for the current project. The Order model that you find in db/migrate/005_create_orders.rb should look like this:

```
class CreateOrders < ActiveRecord::Migration
  def self.up
    create_table :orders do |t|
      t.column :customer_id, :integer
      t.column :time, :timestamp
      t.column :status, :string
```

```
      end
    end

    def self.down
      drop_table :orders
    end
  end
```

This is all you need to specify an order. You want to know the customer information, the time the order happened, and if it has been handled or not. The file db/migrate/006_create_order_lines.rb contains the database definitions for OrderLine:

```
class CreateOrderLines < ActiveRecord::Migration
  def self.up
    create_table :order_lines do |t|
      t.column :order_id, :integer
      t.column :product_id, :integer
      t.column :amount, :integer
    end
  end

  def self.down
    drop_table :order_lines
  end
end
```

An OrderLine is associated with an Order and a Product, and can contain more than one of the same Product. Last, here's db/migrate/007_create_users.rb:

```
class CreateUsers < ActiveRecord::Migration
  class User < ActiveRecord::Base; end

  def self.up
    create_table :users do |t|
      t.column :username, :string
      t.column :password, :string
    end

    User.create :username => 'admin',
                :password => 'admin'
  end

  def self.down
    drop_table :users
  end
end
```

The only thing that's different about this model is that you need to create at least one user from scratch, which you can use to add further users. Before you go any further, it's important that you migrate the database, so all these new tables are available:

```
jruby -S rake db:migrate
jruby -S rake db:migrate RAILS_ENV=test
```

When this is done, you can edit the model files and add all relationships that until now you only had in the database. You begin with Customer, in the file app/models/customer.rb. It should look like this:

```
class Customer < ActiveRecord::Base
  has_many :orders

  def to_s
    "#{given_name} #{sur_name}"
  end
end
```

The only thing you would possibly want from a Customer is to know which orders he or she is associated with. In some circumstances printing a Customer is interesting, so you add a custom to_s method to cater for this. Next, open the file app/models/order.rb and change it into this:

```
class Order < ActiveRecord::Base
  has_many :order_lines
  belongs_to :customer
end
```

An Order has many OrderLines and has one Customer. You can find the definitions for OrderLine in app/models/order_line.rb and you should change them into this:

```
class OrderLine < ActiveRecord::Base
  belongs_to :product
  belongs_to :order
end
```

All this is obvious. Finally, the User model is good as it is.

User Administration

Now it's time to add a new controller. The purpose of this one is to allow us to add or remove users, because you'll need this as soon as you switch on the authentication system. You'll begin with a scaffold for this:

```
jruby script/generate scaffold User
```

Then you'll tear a whole lot of stuff out of it, because you just want to be able to do three things: list the users, add a user, and remove a user. (You can implement password changing if you want, but at this stage it doesn't matter if you change passwords or just re-create the user.) So, open up app/controllers/users_controller.rb and remove the show, edit, and update methods. Also remove the reference to `update` in the `verify` call at the top. Next, add a directive to use the `admin` layout on the second line:

```
layout "admin"
```

That's all that's needed for the controller. Next, on to the views. You can safely remove the files app/views/users/show.rhtml and app/views/users/edit.rhtml. Next, change the app/views/users/list.rhtml file to read like this:

```
<h1>Authenticated users</h1>

<table width="300">
  <tr>
    <th align="left">Username</th>
    <th align="right">Password</th>
  </tr>

<% for user in @users %>
  <tr>
    <td align="left"><%= h user.username %></td>
    <td align="right"><%= h user.password.gsub(/./,'*') %></td>
    <td> </td>
    <td><%= link_to 'Remove', { :action => 'destroy',
            :id => user }, :confirm => 'Are you sure?', :post => true %></td>
  </tr>
<% end %>
</table>

<%= link_to 'Previous page', { :page =>
            @user_pages.current.previous } if
        @user_pages.current.previous %>
<%= link_to 'Next page', { :page =>
            @user_pages.current.next } if
        @user_pages.current.next %>

<br />
<%= link_to 'New user', :action => 'new' %>
```

Try it out by going to http://localhost:3000/users. If all is well, you should see one entry for the "admin" user, and nothing else. This concludes the user administrative interface. Go ahead and add a user or two. Later on you'll protect these pages from entry if you don't have a valid username and password.

Order Handling

For order handling, the flow is that you get a list of unhandled orders. Then you choose one order, see all information about it, and from that step you can mark the order as handled, or remove the order completely. You'll once again begin with a scaffold to make your work easier:

```
jruby script/generate scaffold Order
```

Next, open up the controller just generated (app/controllers/orders_controller.rb) and remove the show, new, create, edit, update, and destroy methods. The new complete file should look like this:

```ruby
class OrdersController < ApplicationController
  layout "admin"

  def index
    list
    render :action => 'list'
  end

  # GETs should be safe
  # (see http://www.w3.org/2001/tag/doc/whenToUseGet.html)
  verify :method => :post, :only => [ :remove, :handled ],
         :redirect_to => { :action => :list }

  def list
    @orders = Order.find(:all,:conditions => "status = 'placed'")
  end

  def handle
    @order = Order.find(params[:id])
    @price = @order.order_lines.inject(0) do |sum,l|
      sum + l.amount * l.product.price
    end
  end

  def remove
    Order.find(params[:id]).destroy
    redirect_to :action => 'list'
  end

  def handled
    @order = Order.find(params[:id])
    @order.status = "handled"
    if @order.save
      flash[:notice] = 'Order has been handled.'
      redirect_to :action => 'list'
    else
      @price = @order.order_lines.inject(0) do |sum,l|
        sum + l.amount * l.product.price
      end
      render :action => 'handle'
    end
  end
end
```

There's lots of new information here. First of all, you've added the admin layout so you get a unified layout. Second, the parameters to the verify method have been changed, so the only parameter includes remove and handled. The list method has been changed, so it only shows orders where the status is 'placed'. This is so you can retain the orders in the database, but you don't have to see them when they've been handled.

There are also three new methods. Rails will call the handle method when a specific order should be shown and handled. It finds the order in question, and then sums the total price together.

The remove method removes the order in question from the database.

The handled method sets the status to "handled" on the order in question, and redirects to the listing. Open up the app/views/orders/list.rhtml file and change it so it looks like this:

```
<h1>Orders to handle</h1>

<table width="500">
  <tr>
    <th>Customer</th>
    <th>Time</th>
    <th>Amount</th>
    <th>Items</th>
  </tr>

<% for order in @orders %>
  <tr>
    <td><%= h order.customer %></td>
    <td><%= order.time.strftime("%F %H:%M") %></td>
    <td align="right"><%= money(order.order_lines.inject(0){
            |sum,ol| sum + ol.amount*ol.product.price}) %></td>
    <td align="right"><%= order.order_lines.inject(0){
            |sum,ol| sum + ol.amount} %></td>
    <td align="right" width="150"><%=
        link_to "Handle order", :action => 'handle', :id => order %></td>
  </tr>
<% end %>
</table>
```

This shows a pleasing list of orders, showing the time each order was placed, how much money it amounts to, and how many items there are. The next step is to create a new file called app/views/orders/handle.rhtml. This will be a big file, because it's the main place for watching data about an order. Here it is:

```
<h2>Handle order</h2>

<p><b>Customer:</b> <%= h @order.customer %></p>
<p><b>Shipping address:</b><br/>
<%= h @order.customer.shipping_address_street %><br/>
<%= h "#{@order.customer.shipping_address_postal}
      #{@order.customer.shipping_address_zip}"%><br/>
<%= h @order.customer.shipping_address_country %></p>
```

```
<p><b>Billing address:</b><br/>
<%= h @order.customer.billing_address_street %><br/>
<%= h "#{@order.customer.billing_address_postal}
        #{@order.customer.billing_address_zip}"%><br/>
<%= h @order.customer.billing_address_country %></p>

<br/>

<table width="480">
  <thead>
    <td width="300" align="left">Product Name</td>
    <td width="20" align="right">Quantity</td>
    <td width="80" align="right">Each</td>
    <td width="80" align="right">Price</td>
  </thead>

  <% @order.order_lines.each do |ol| %>
    <tr>
      <td width="300" align="left"><%= h ol.product.name %></td>
      <td width="20" align="right"><%= ol.amount %></td>
      <td width="80" align="right"><%= price ol.product %></td>
      <td width="80" align="right"><%= money(
            ol.amount * ol.product.price) %></td>
    </tr>
  <% end %>
  <tr height="60">
    <td colspan="4"> </td>
  </tr>
  <tr>
    <td colspan="3" align="right"><b>Total:</b></td>
    <td align="right"><%= money @price %></td>
  </tr>
</table>

<%= button_to 'Handled', :action=>'handled',:id=>@order %>
<%= button_to 'Remove', :action=>'remove',:id=>@order %>
```

As you can see, you first display the shipping address and billing address, then list all the items with quantity, price, and combined price. Finally, two buttons let the handler either remove or mark the order as handled.

Adding Some Authentication

You now have almost all functionality finished for the administration part of the Shoplet application. There's just a small piece missing. At the moment, anybody who knew the address could do anything they wanted with the shop, and because the addresses are easy to guess, this is no way to leave it. You've already prepared for adding authentication by creating the User model, and the scaffolds for handling these. Now you need to secure your actions. When you try to go to the admin parts of the application, you should be redirected to a login page, submit your username and password, and if it is correct you should be redirected back to the page you tried to access first. You'll accomplish this through controller filters.

Rails provides filters to let you perform some task before or after an action runs. This has profound implications and makes many tasks easy, not just authentication and security.

The first step you'll take is to create a new controller. This controller will be the base for all your protected controllers, and won't have any actions itself. Open up the file app/controllers/admin_controller.rb and write this into it:

```ruby
class AdminController < ApplicationController
  before_filter :authentication

  private
  def authentication
    unless session[:user_id] && User.find_by_id(session[:user_id])
      flash[:notice] = "Please log in"
      redirect_to(:controller => 'auth', :action =>
                        'login', :into => url_for(params))
    else
      @loggedin = true
    end
  end
end
```

You first declare that the method called authentication should be called as a before_filter, which means it should execute before an action. You then define the method itself, and mark it as private. You first check if the parameter called :user_id in the session object is set, and if it is you also make sure there is an existing user with that ID. Otherwise you place a message in the flash and redirect to the login action on the auth controller (which you'll create soon). If the person is logged in, you just set the instance variable @loggedin to true.

Next, create a new controller by using the generate script:

```
jruby script/generate controller auth login logout
```

This creates a new controller called AuthController, with two actions called login and logout available to it. In this way, you get some things for free, including tests and default views. Open up the file app/controllers/auth_controller.rb and change it so it looks like this:

```ruby
class AuthController < ApplicationController
  layout "admin"

  def login
    if request.post?
      if user = User.find_by_username_and_password(
                    params[:username],params[:password])
        session[:user_id] = user.id
```

```
          redirect_to params[:into] || {:controller => 'products'}
          return
        else
          flash[:error] = "Wrong username or password"
        end
      end
      @into = params[:into]
    end

    def logout
      session[:user_id] = nil
      redirect_to "/"
    end
  end
```

Several interesting things are going on here. First of all, you use the standard admin layout, but you'll modify it so it only shows the links on the left if someone is logged in. Next, the login method will do two different things depending on if it's called using an HTTP POST or not. In this way you can let the view post information back to itself, and the login method will handle it differently. So, if there was a POST, you check the username and password provided. If they match, you set the session information and redirect either to the into parameter, or if there is no such parameter you redirect to the products controller instead. If the username or password doesn't match, you fall through, setting a flash. Then you do the same thing as if it was a GET, which is that you set the @into instance variable and display the view.

The logout method just wipes the session and redirects to the starting URL.

Next, let's take a look at the login view that can be found in app/views/auth/login.rhtml. It should look like this:

```
<h2>Please login with your username and password</h2>

<%= start_form_tag %>
<%= hidden_field_tag 'into', @into %>
<table>
  <tr>
    <td>Username:</td><td><%= text_field_tag 'username' %></td>
  </tr>
  <tr>
    <td>Password:</td><td><%= password_field_tag 'password' %></td>
  </tr>
  <tr>
    <td colspan="2" align="right"><%= submit_tag 'Login' %></td>
  </tr>
</table>
<%= end_form_tag %>
```

Here you start a new form, but use all the default parameters, which means the browser will POST it back to the same address. You set a hidden field with the 'into' parameter and then ask for a username and password, display a login button, and end the form.

Now that you can make sure people can log in, you also need to modify all your controllers so they won't let anyone in if they haven't been authenticated. So, open up app/controllers/products_controller.rb, app/controllers/orders_controller.rb, and app/controllers/users_controller.rb, and change the first line by replacing the word ApplicationController with AdminController. The first line in the file for the ProductsController should look like this:

```
class ProductsController < AdminController
```

Because all three of our controllers inherit from the admin controller, the before_filter you applied earlier will act on all actions written in any of the controllers. The only thing left is to open the layout file called app/views/layouts/admin.rhtml and change it by replacing the part that looks like this:

```
<ul style="text-align: left;">
 <li><%= link_to 'Administrate products',
          {:controller => 'products'},:class => 'adminLink' %></li>
 <li><%= link_to 'Handle orders',
          {:controller => 'orders'},:class => 'adminLink' %></li>
 <li><%= link_to 'Authenticated users',
          {:controller => 'users'},:class => 'adminLink' %></li>
</ul>
```

Replace this part with an if statement that only shows this when the person is logged in:

```
<% if @loggedin %>
<ul style="text-align: left;">
 <li><%= link_to 'Administrate products',
          {:controller => 'products'},:class => 'adminLink' %></li>
 <li><%= link_to 'Handle orders',
          {:controller => 'orders'},:class => 'adminLink' %></li>
 <li><%= link_to 'Authenticated users',
          {:controller => 'users'},:class => 'adminLink' %></li>
</ul>
<br/>
<p><%= link_to 'Log out', :controller=>'auth',:action=>'logout'%></p>
<% end %>
```

You also add a small 'Log out' link here, if the person is logged in.

Now it's time to try it out. Remember that you added an "admin" user with password "admin" before? You should use this now, if you haven't already created an extra user. Try to visit http://localhost:3000/products and see what happens. Also try to log out and log in and add products. Everything should work fine as soon as you're logged in, but should stop working otherwise.

Functional Tests

Now the time has come to test a controller. You'll base the tests on the test code automatically generated for the products_controller, but it won't work in the current state, because you added authentication in the last section. So, first test that you can just run the tests and that they blow up in various interesting ways. However, before you do that, make sure the database migration is at the latest version. Do that by running this:

```
jruby -S rake db:migrate RAILS_ENV=test
```

Next, run the functional tests for products_controller by running this command:

```
jruby test/functional/products_controller_test.rb
```

Now, open up test/functional/products_controller_test.rb and begin the testing by adding two fixtures you're going to need. Add these lines:

```
fixtures :users
fixtures :product_types
```

Then open up the file test/fixtures/users.yml and change it so it looks like this:

```
admin:
  id: 1
  username: admin
  password: admin
other:
  id: 2
  username: other
  password: other
```

Next, change the test_index test case to make sure it redirects correctly to the auth controller, and also rename it to test_index_without_login. Do that by writing a method that looks like this:

```
def test_index_without_login
  get :index
  assert_redirected_to :controller=> 'auth', :action => 'login'
  assert_equal 'Please log in',flash[:notice]
end
```

As you can see, you first issue a get request for the index of the controller in question. You then make sure you've been redirected to the right place, and that the flash is also set.

To test a method that's protected by authentication, you'll use a trick. The get method in functional tests can take several optional parameters. One describes the parameters to set, and another describes what the session should look like. By adding this parameter, you can make it look like a user is logged in. Now create a new test_index method that looks like this:

```
def test_index
  get :index, {}, {:user_id => users(:admin).id}
  assert_response :success
  assert_template 'list'
end
```

The second parameter to get is the query string or post parameters, and because you don't want to add anything like these, you just provide an empty hash. The next parameter sets the variable :user_id in the session to a valid user ID, which means the action should succeed as expected.

You do the same transformation with test_list, test_show, and test_new, adding the empty hash if needed, and otherwise enclosing the parameters in an explicit hash.

Next you'll change the test_create method. Because a new product isn't valid without a few parameters, you'll change the line that posts information, and this results in a test_create method that looks like this:

```
def test_create
  num_products = Product.count

  post :create,{:product => {:product_type_id=>1,
        :name => 'abc', :price => '10.00'}},
      {:user_id => users(:admin).id}

  assert_response :redirect
  assert_redirected_to :action => 'list'

  assert_equal num_products + 1, Product.count
end
```

Here you have to provide a product_type_id, a name and a valid price, and the user_id for the session. You also make sure that the new product has been added by counting all available products before and after the action has been performed. You should also fix the tests test_edit, test_update, and test_destroy by adding the session parameter and enclosing the rest in an explicit hash. The end result of these methods should look like this:

```
def test_edit
  get :edit, {:id => 1}, {:user_id => users(:admin).id}

  assert_response :success
  assert_template 'edit'

  assert_not_nil assigns(:product)
  assert assigns(:product).valid?
end

def test_update
  post :update, {:id => 1}, {:user_id => users(:admin).id}
  assert_response :redirect
  assert_redirected_to :action => 'show', :id => 1
end

def test_destroy
  assert_not_nil Product.find(1)
```

```
  post :destroy, {:id => 1}, {:user_id => users(:admin).id}
  assert_response :redirect
  assert_redirected_to :action => 'list'

  assert_raise(ActiveRecord::RecordNotFound) {
    Product.find(1)
  }
end
```

Now you can run the test again, and ideally it will result in much better output. To be able to run all tests, you need to modify the `orders_controller_test.rb` and `users_controller_test.rb` too, so the test cases handle authentication, and also so that the methods you removed aren't used in the tests. However, I leave that as an exercise for you. When that is done, you can always run your tests by just invoking `rake` in the directory of your application:

```
jruby -S rake
```

Summary

We've walked through the administration parts of a completely new application that could well be the backbone for an online shop application. Of course, some things are missing, such as further validations and more testing, but the core is there. I hope this has also served as a fast, practical introduction to many of the day-to-day tasks in creating a Rails application. The next chapter will talk about how the user interacts with this application; we'll create the code for that, and then I'll take a few pages to talk about different databases for a JRuby on Rails application.

CHAPTER 5

■ ■ ■

A Database-Driven Shop

Walking through the last chapter, you'll have gotten a feel for how Rails development is done. You should also understand most of the basics about Rails.

In this chapter we'll expand on that knowledge. First, we'll continue with Shoplet, making it into a complete application that can be used as the base for many diverse purposes. We'll look at how to make the URLs as simple and pleasing as possible for a user by using routes. The chapter will also take a look at how a real payment system would work when using Rails. We'll finish the implementation of Shoplet by adding all the user interface parts. By the end, it will be possible to deploy the application with suitable data and let users browse around and order whatever they want.

This chapter will contain some test code for a subset of the functionality of the Shoplet application, but as mentioned before there isn't room enough to test to the degree that should be done in a real application.

The second part of this chapter will talk more in depth about the database capabilities offered by JRuby on Rails. Much of this information will differ from a regular Ruby on Rails installation. I'll also talk at some length about ActiveRecord-JDBC (AR-JDBC), which makes it possible to use JDBC drivers as a back end to Rails. I'll cover what databases are supported at the moment, and how you can add support to your own JDBC driver if that's needed.

By the time you're finished with this chapter you'll have a substantial grasp of the possibilities inherent in Rails. After this, the focus will be on how you can complement this with the resources in Java.

Browsing Products

The first step to the client side of your application is a new controller. You'll call this one `store`, just to make it easy. This controller shouldn't be a scaffolded controller, so you'll just generate it directly instead. You do know that you'll need at least an `index` action to show the front page, an action for showing products, and one for showing a single product, so take the opportunity to add these actions with the generator:

```
jruby script/generate controller store index products product
```

At the moment there isn't much that you can do with the controller, so instead you'll open up the index page and write some text into it. Go ahead with the newly generated file called `app/views/store/index.rhtml`, and change into some welcoming message, such as this:

```
<h2>Welcome</h2>
<p>Hi and welcome to the Shoplet Online Store</p>
```

```
<p>This store is built with JRuby on Rails and is the
first project application for the book Practical JRuby on Rails.</p>
<p>Here you can look at various products and order them at very fine prices.</p>
```

You can try this file by pointing your browser at http://localhost:3000/store. Now, because you need to be able to browse products, you'll need to change the products action in the store controller. Open app/controllers/store_controller.rb and change the empty products method into this code:

```
def products
  @products = Product.find(:all)
end
```

Now you also need to change the view to show the products, so once again go to the view directory and open app/views/store/products.rhtml:

```
<h2>Products</h2>
<table width="400">
  <% for product in @products %>
    <tr>
      <td align="left" valign="top"><%= link_to h(product.name),
                                        :action => 'product',
                                        :id => product %></td>
      <td align="right" valign="top"><%=price product %></td>
      <td align="right" valign="top"><%= button_to "Add to cart",
                                        :action => 'add_to_cart',
                                        :id => product%></td>
    </tr>
  <% end %>
</table>
```

You can try it out by visiting http://localhost:3000/store/products. You might notice that you create a button in this code that points to the action add_to_cart. That's something you haven't created yet, but you want that later on. Also notice that you use the h helper to avoid strange characters in the product name on the fifth line, and the price helper to format the product price correctly on the eighth line.

If you try to visit one of the products at the moment it will show a page with Rails' standard view message for views that you haven't changed yet. So, the next step is to open store_controller.rb once again and add a single line to the product method:

```
def product
  @product = Product.find(params[:id])
end
```

That takes care of finding the correct product. What's left is to display it in a pleasing way. This is accomplished in the file app/views/store/product.rhtml. It should look like this:

```
<h2><%= h @product.name %></h2>

<p><b>Description</b><br/>
<%= h @product.description %></p>
```

```
<br/>
<br/>
<p><b>Price</b>    
  <%=price @product%></p>
<p><%= button_to "Add to cart",
        :action => 'add_to_cart', :id => @product%></p>
```

Nothing fancy. You display the product name, description, and price, and follow that with a button that lets the customer add it to the nonexistent cart.

Right now there are some glaring deficiencies in the application. First, it doesn't look so usable. You need a menu or something. Second, when browsing products it would be helpful if you didn't get to see all of them at the same time. Maybe you should only display products within one product type at a time. Third, it looks abysmal at the moment. You'll solve these problems in one simple way: you'll add a new layout that gets used by the store controller. Create a new file called app/views/layouts/store.rhtml and edit it like this:

```
<html>
<head>
  <title>Shoplet Online Store<%= ": #@title" if @title %></title>
  <%= stylesheet_link_tag 'shoplet' %>
</head>
<body>
  <table width="100%" height="100%">
    <tr>
      <td width="250" class="leftMenu" align="center" valign="top">
        <h2><%= link_to 'Shoplet', :action=>'index'%></h2>
        <h3><%= link_to 'Online Shopping', :action=>'index'%></h3>
        <br/>
        <% for t in @types %>
          <p><%= link_to plural(t.name), :action=>'products',
                                         :id=>t %></p>
        <% end %>
        <br/>
      </td>
      <td class="main" valign="top">
        <p style="color: green"><%= flash[:notice] %></p>

        <%= yield  %>
      </td>
    </tr>
  </table>
</body>
</html>
```

There are a few interesting things to notice here. First, you display a title if the controller has set a title. This helps make the title bar more readable. Second, you use the same style sheet that you created for the administrative application. This lets you retain some of the looks you used in that part. Further down, you iterate over the types available, and link to them.

Here you also use a new helper called plural, which you'll define in a moment. First you need to make sure that the variable @types will be available at all points. So, open up store_controller.rb once again, and change it by adding a menu method that gets called from all the actions. The complete store controller should look like this:

```
class StoreController < ApplicationController
  def index
    menu
  end

  def products
    menu
    @type = ProductType.find(params[:id])
    @title = Inflector.pluralize(@type.name)
    @products = Product.find(:all,
                 :conditions => ['product_type_id=?', params[:id]],
                 :order => 'name ASC')
  end

  def product
    menu
    @product = Product.find(params[:id])
    @title = @product.name
  end

  private
  def menu
    @types = ProductType.find(:all, :order => 'name ASC')
  end
end
```

The menu method is simple; it just finds all product types and orders them by name. This method gets called from index, products, and product. You don't need to change anything more in the index method. The product method doesn't change much either; you just add a call to menu, and also set the @title variable to the current product name. However, in products, you need to do some extra things. First, you need to find the type of products that should be displayed. This is the id parameter to the products action. After you've done that, you need a title for the page. However, because your product types are singular, you need to make them plural instead. It doesn't make sense to have the title "Book" when you're showing several books. The Inflector class is a fancy part of Rails that's used in many places under the covers. Suffice it to say, it's capable of doing some easy transformations on the English language. Last, you find all products that match the SQL condition you provide. You also order the products by name.

At this point, you need to effect two small changes before it will work. First, you need Rails to know the plural of "music," which is "music." Rails contains knowledge about many special cases, but this isn't one of them. So, open up the file `config/environment.rb`, and at the end add this code:

```
Inflector.inflections do |inflect|
  inflect.uncountable %w(music)
end
```

This tells the `Inflector` class that the word "music" is uncountable. Right now you need to restart the web server, because changing `environment.rb` doesn't have any effect otherwise. However, before you do that, you should change another thing that needs a restart to get in effect. Wouldn't it be nice if people who are going to shop at your place didn't have to write `/store` after the URL? In fact, people should be able to go directly to `http://www.yourshop.com` and come to the right place. You achieve this in two ways. First, you have to change the port that the web server listens to into port 80 instead of 3000. We won't do that now, but instead we'll look at how to do it when we talk more about deploying an application. The second part is that a person who doesn't write any path after the URL should be redirected to the store. It's easy to make that happen. First, remove the file called `public/index.html` (it will get in the way otherwise). Then open up `config/routes.rb`. Right now it's lots of comments, and four lines of code. Without the comments, the new file should look like this:

```
ActionController::Routing::Routes.draw do |map|
  map.connect '', :controller => "store"
  map.connect ':controller/service.wsdl', :action => 'wsdl'
  map.connect ':controller/:action/:id'
end
```

What you say is just that an empty path should go to the `store` controller. So, go ahead and restart the web server right now! I'm waiting . . .

Good! One thing is left before you can browse around easily. You need that helper I mentioned before, called `plural`. Open `app/helpers/application_helper.rb` and add this code together with the rest:

```
def plural(name)
  h Inflector.pluralize(name)
end
```

As you see, you just use the `Inflector`. However, you hide it within a helper, because that's nice if you want to use it in other places.

It's now time for you to try out the application again. Just visit `http://localhost:3000`, and see the new menu that gives you access to fun product browsing. You're now about halfway finished. The next part is to add a shopping cart and allow the customer to check that out.

Adding a Shopping Cart

As mentioned before, the current application might be fun to play with, but there's still no way to buy anything, so the shop isn't likely to generate revenue. You'll help the situation by adding a cart. The first thing you have to do is decide how to implement this. I'll take a simple approach here. Because in your application the contents of the cart can be represented with a product ID and a number for quantity, you'll be able to save an array of these two numbers in the session and re-create the products and the price information from this array. So, the first thing you should do is add that add_to_cart method to the store controller. Open app/controllers/store_controller.rb and add this method:

```
def add_to_cart
  p = Product.find(params[:id])
  (session[:cart] ||= []) << p.id
  session[:price] ||= 0
  session[:price] += p.price
  flash[:notice] = "#{p.name} added to cart"
  redirect_to :action => :products, :id=> p.product_type.id
end
```

So, as you can see, the add_to_cart method first finds the Product specified, then creates a cart in the session unless it's already there. It then adds the product ID to this cart, and does the same thing with a running total for price. You add a message to the flash and then redirect to the products action, showing products for the same type as the product you just added, because that is a reasonable guess at where the customer originated.

At this point the earlier buttons you added make it possible to add contents to the cart, but there isn't any way to see what's in it, empty it, or see the running price. So you'll add that functionality to the menu. If you remember, you earlier created a menu method that gets called to provide the information the menu layout needs. You'll change this to incorporate some needed changes:

```
def menu
  @types = ProductType.find(:all, :order => 'name ASC')
  @cart = session[:cart]
  @price = session[:price] || 0
end
```

As you see, you only provide the cart and the price in instance variables. You'll also need a way to empty the cart, so add the action called empty_cart right now:

```
def empty_cart
  session[:cart] = []
  session[:price] = 0
  redirect_to params[:back_to]
end
```

Now you just need to provide these operations to the user. You'll do that by changing the layout slightly, by adding this to app/views/layouts/store.rhtml:

```
<% unless @cart.blank?%>
 <br/>
 <br/>
 <p>You have <%=pluralize @cart.length, 'item'%> in your
```

```
                cart for <%= money @price %>.</p>
  <p><%= link_to "Cart",:action=>'cart'%></p>
  <p><%= button_to 'Empty cart', :action=>'empty_cart',
                          :back_to=>url_for(params)%></p>
<% else %>
  <br/>
  <br/>
  <p>Your cart is empty</p>
<% end %>
```

Here you check if there is any cart, and if there is you pluralize the word item, based on the length of the cart, and also display the current price. You have a link to viewing the contents of the cart, where checkout will be possible. Last, you also have a button to empty the cart. Notice the way the url_for helper is used to create a complete URL for getting back to the current point after emptying the cart. If there's no content in the cart, you just write a small message about this.

Viewing the Cart

The first step toward being able to buy things is to see what you have in your cart. In the last section you added a link to an action called cart. This action doesn't exist yet, but you'll add it to app/controllers/store_controller.rb now:

```
def cart
  menu
  @pcart = canon_cart.map {|k,v| [Product.find(k),v] }
end
```

This method relies heavily on the canon_cart method, which you should add next:

```
def canon_cart
  rcart = Hash.new(0)
  c = session[:cart]
  unless c.blank?
    c.each do |v|
      rcart[v] += 1
    end
  end
  rcart
end
```

The method first creates a new hash, but it does this through the regular constructor. This is because you want the new hash to have a default value when looking up something that doesn't exist yet. The value nil (which is the original default) isn't that useful in this context, so you supply 0 instead. By doing this, you can count the quantities of all products in the cart, by adding one to the hash entry for the current product for each entry in the cart. What you get from this operation is a neat hash that maps from product ID to quantity. In the cart method, you use this to create a new array where each entry is an array of the product and the quantity.

After adding these methods you're ready to create the view that will display the cart. Create a file called app/views/store/cart.rhtml:

```
<h2>Your cart</h2>
<table width="480">
  <thead>
    <td width="300" align="left">Product Name</td>
    <td width="20" align="right">Quantity</td>
    <td width="80" align="right">Each</td>
    <td width="80" align="right">Price</td>
  </thead>
  <% for prod, qnty in @pcart %>
    <tr>
      <td width="300" align="left"><%= h prod.name %></td>
      <td width="20" align="right"><%= qnty %></td>
      <td width="80" align="right"><%= price prod %></td>
      <td width="80" align="right"><%=
                        money(qnty * prod.price) %></td>
    </tr>
  <% end %>
  <tr height="60">
    <td colspan="4"> </td>
  </tr>
  <tr>
    <td colspan="3" align="right"><b>Total:</b></td>
    <td align="right"><%= money @price %></td>
  </tr>
  <tr>
    <td colspan="4" align="right"><%= link_to "Checkout",
                        :action=>'checkout'%></td>
  </tr>
</table>
```

The code is easy. First you create a table with the correct headings, then iterate over the cart you prepared in the action, printing the product name, how many of that product, the price of a single product, and the combined price for that row. Last, you print a total price and a link to check out the products.

Checking Out

The last thing last. People would probably want to be able to order items, so you'll allow just that by adding two new actions to the store controller:

```
def checkout
  menu
  @customer = Customer.new
end

def order
```

```
  if params[:customer][:billing_address_zip].blank?
    ['street','postal','zip','country'].each do |v|
      params[:customer]["billing_address_#{v}"] =
              params[:customer]["shipping_address_#{v}"]
    end
  end
  cust = Customer.create(params[:customer])
  order = Order.create(:customer => cust,
               :time => Time.now, :status => 'placed')

  canon_cart.each do |k,v|
    order.order_lines.create(:product => Product.find(k), :amount => v)
  end

  session[:cart] = []
  session[:price] = 0
  flash[:notice] = "Order placed"
  redirect_to :action => :index
end
```

The checkout method is an exercise in simplicity. You call the menu method and create a new customer from scratch. (The new method on model objects doesn't add that model object to the database. That's the main difference between new and create for ActiveRecord models.)

The order method is a little more involved. The big complication is caused by something you'll add to the checkout.rhtml page soon. If the billing address should be the same as the shipping address, you shouldn't fill in the billing address at all. So, the order method checks if the ZIP code is blank, and if so copies the street, postal, zip, and country attributes from the shipping address to the billing address parameters. You then use create to make this customer exist in the database, then create a new Order, associate this with the customer, and set the time and status correctly. The next step is to create order lines for the order, and you use canon_cart for this step too. Last, the cart is blanked, because you usually don't want to retain the cart after checking out. As the final action, you redirect back to the index.

There's only one thing left to do with this application. You need to add that app/views/store/checkout.rhtml file:

```
<h2>Checkout</h2>

<% form_for :customer, @customer, :url => {:action => 'order'} do |f| %>
  <table>
    <tr>
      <td>Given Name:</td>
      <td><%= f.text_field :given_name %></td>
      <td>Sur Name:</td>
      <td><%= f.text_field :sur_name %></td>
    </tr>
    <tr><td colspan="4" align="left"><b>Shipping address</b></td></tr>
    <tr>
      <td>Street:</td>
```

```
        <td colspan="3"><%= f.text_field :shipping_address_street,
                                         :size=>60 %></td>
    </tr>
    <tr>
      <td>Postal address:</td>
      <td><%= f.text_field :shipping_address_postal %></td>
      <td>Zip code:</td>
      <td><%= f.text_field :shipping_address_zip, :size=>10 %></td>
    </tr>
    <tr>
      <td>Country:</td>
      <td colspan="3"><%= f.text_field :shipping_address_country %></td>
    </tr>
    <tr><td colspan="4" align="left"><b>Billing address</b>
                  <i>(leave blank if
              same as shipping address)</i></td></tr>
    <tr>
      <td>Street:</td>
      <td colspan="3"><%= f.text_field :billing_address_street,
                                       :size=>60 %></td>
    </tr>
    <tr>
      <td>Postal address:</td>
      <td><%= f.text_field :billing_address_postal %></td>
      <td>Zip code:</td>
      <td><%= f.text_field :billing_address_zip, :size=>10 %></td>
    </tr>
    <tr>
      <td>Country:</td>
      <td colspan="3"><%= f.text_field :billing_address_country %></td>
    </tr>
    <tr>
      <td colspan="4" align="right"><%= submit_tag "Place order" %></td>
    </tr>
  </table>
<% end %>
```

This is a long file, but simple. Most of the contents are just supposed to make the HTML look good. First, you use the form_for helper to create a new form that updates attributes on the customer model object. This process makes it simpler to add error processing if something like that is wanted.

The application is mostly finished now. You can add many innovations, but the only additional things I'll show here are some more unit and functional tests, to make sure that the store application's behavior matches what you expect from it.

Validation and Testing

The first step in testing what you've done so far is to add a few more checks to the `Customer` model. As it stands at the moment, you can supply whatever information you want, or abstain from providing necessary information. That's clearly not a good way to have it. So, add some validations for presence at least to the file app/models/customer.rb:

```
validates_presence_of :sur_name, :shipping_address_postal,
                      :shipping_address_zip, :shipping_address_country,
                      :billing_address_postal, :billing_address_zip,
                      :billing_address_country
```

If you know the rules for ZIP codes in various countries, it would probably be a good idea to add some recognition, so that someone in the United States won't try to submit an illegal United States ZIP. We won't do that now, though.

The next step to allow some testing is to add a fixture or two, so you have something to work with. Go ahead and open the file test/fixtures/customers.yml, remove what's in it, and replace it with something like this:

```
cust1:
  id: 1
  sur_name: Gaiman
  shipping_address_postal: San Francisco, CA
  shipping_address_zip: 94111
  shipping_address_country: USA
  billing_address_postal: San Francisco, CA
  billing_address_zip: 94111
  billing_address_country: USA
cust2:
  id: 2
  given_name: Alan
  sur_name: Moore
  shipping_address_street: Stora Kvinns vag 74
  shipping_address_postal: ALVSJO
  shipping_address_zip: 12559
  shipping_address_country: Sweden
  billing_address_street: 2 E 2nd Street
  billing_address_postal: NEW YORK, NY
  billing_address_zip: 10003
  billing_address_country: USA
```

The first customer should not have a given name, so you just don't provide that information in the file.

Now you have some test data. First you need to make sure that the customer object created by these fixtures will validate, so you begin by opening test/unit/customer_test.rb, remove the test_truth method, and add a test_valid one that just takes these two fixtures and ensures that they are valid:

```
def test_valid
```

```
  assert customers('cust1').valid?
  assert customers('cust2').valid?
end
```

Go ahead and run the test case now, to see whether it runs:

```
jruby test/unit/customer_test.rb
```

In this case there's no need to use Rake for testing. You can just run the file you want to specifically, so you won't have to wait for all the other tests to run too. The next point is to make sure that all those validates_presence_of work as they're expected to. So, you create a new test that sets the sur_name to an empty string, and then to nil, to make sure the preceding code catches both these cases:

```
def test_no_sur_name
  p = customers('cust1')
  p.sur_name = ''
  assert !p.valid?
  assert p.errors.invalid?(:sur_name)
  p.sur_name = nil
  assert !p.valid?
  assert p.errors.invalid?(:sur_name)
end
```

Now you could go ahead and write methods like this for the other six required attributes. But really, isn't that overkill? Shouldn't there be a better way to achieve this, because the methods will look exactly like the preceding one? Duplication is always evil, and you should practice DRY even while writing tests. The dynamic nature of Ruby makes it easy to define these methods through metaprogramming. So, scratch the test_no_sur_name method and replace it with this code:

```
%w(sur_name shipping_address_postal shipping_address_zip
   shipping_address_country billing_address_postal
   billing_address_zip billing_address_country).each do |name|
  define_method(:"test_no_#{name}") do
    p = customers('cust1')
    p.send :"#{name}=",''
    assert !p.valid?
    assert p.errors.invalid?(:"#{name}")
    p.send :"#{name}=",nil
    assert !p.valid?
    assert p.errors.invalid?(:"#{name}")
  end
end
```

Appendix A explains most of the tricks used in this snippet, but simply put, you create a list of all attributes you want to test the presence of, then iterate over this list, defining a new method for each attribute. The method name is test_no_ with the name appended. Then you define the method body. The big difference here is that you use send to set the attribute, instead of doing it directly. You also check for the name in the invalid? specification. Presto, you have seven tests instead of one. Always make sure to use the flexible nature of Ruby in these ways when possible.

At this point it would be prudent to add more unit tests for the models we haven't covered yet.

You should also add some basic functional tests to make sure the controller works as you expect it to do. Open test/functional/store_controller_test.rb and begin by removing the test_truth method. The next step is to add references to two fixtures you'll need, namely product_types and products:

```
fixtures :products
fixtures :product_types
```

You know that almost all actions in this controller will return menu information, and if you wanted to test that for all actions, you would need to duplicate that code many times. Fortunately you can extract that test case in another method in the test. You begin by adding this method:

```
def _test_menu
  assert_not_nil assigns(:types)
  assert_not_nil assigns(:price)
end
```

Notice that the name begins with an underscore. In this case, the underscore makes sure that Test::Unit won't think this is a separate test. You could have used whichever name didn't start with test_ for this method, but I like the symmetry in _test for these helper methods. Next, you should make sure that the index action works, and that it handles the menu correctly:

```
def test_index
  get :index
  assert_response :success
  assert_template 'index'
  _test_menu
end
```

Make sure that a regular get of the index page works as expected. Also, check that the return code is successful (HTTP 200), and that the template used is the one called 'index'. Last, call the _test_menu method to test the menu code.

Second, test the products action:

```
def test_products
  get :products, :id => product_types('book').id
  assert_response :success
  assert_template 'products'
  assert_equal product_types('book'), assigns(:type)
  assert_equal 'Books', assigns(:title)
```

```
  assert_not_nil assigns(:products)
  _test_menu
end
```

Once again you do a get, but because this action needs a parameter to work, you supply the one for the book product type. You make sure that the type created as an instance variable is the one you specified, that the title generation worked correctly, and that the products instance variable isn't nil. Then you test the menu.

You can test a few more of the actions like this:

```
def test_product
  get :product, :id => products('first').id
  assert_response :success
  assert_template 'product'
  assert_equal products('first'), assigns(:product)
  assert_equal 'Abc', assigns(:title)
  _test_menu
end

def test_cart
  get :cart
  assert_response :success
  assert_template 'cart'
  assert_not_nil assigns(:pcart)
  _test_menu

  get :cart,{},{:cart => [products('first').id,products('first').id,
                          products('another').id]}
  assert_not_nil assigns(:pcart)
  _test_menu
end

def test_checkout
  get :checkout
  assert_response :success
  assert_template 'checkout'
  assert_not_nil assigns(:customer)
  assert !assigns(:customer).valid?
  _test_menu
end
```

As you see, most of these tests are simple and don't do anything special. The only interesting part is the test_cart method, where at the first call there is no cart information in the session, but in the second request you make sure there is a cart with some information in it. You could also have made sure that the information in this cart got back correctly, but that is a task for another day.

You can run just these tests by calling the file directly:

```
jruby test/functional/store_controller_test.rb
```

REAL PAYMENT SYSTEMS

When writing a real online store application you would probably like to be able to handle payments with credit cards, or even through PayPal or any of the other online payment processors. Because this would introduce needless complications in the example code, I don't show the code for how to do this. In any case, all stores have their own needs for this functionality, so you'll have to let your own demands decide which system to choose.

In a regular Rails application, you'd probably use one of the several libraries for handling payments that exist for Ruby. One of the best is called Active Merchant, which according to its web site supports many gateways for payment systems of all different kinds. Work is also going on to tie it into various shipping gateways, such as FedEx, USPS, UPS, and Canada Post. By using something like this, you can offer much of the functionality needed for a shop, without needing to implement much of the structures behind.

Of course, because we're talking about JRuby on Rails, all the APIs that are published for handling payments through Java will work fine for such a solution. In fact, you can probably count on the provider of the service to already have a way of handling requests from Java clients. In this case, you're home free. Integrating the Java library through JRuby is almost always easy. You can also wrap the code in a Ruby class that makes the API less cumbersome. This is often interesting, because most payment APIs in Java use XML at one point or another.

A new Java Specification Request (JSR) is underway as I write this. It's JSR 182, and it's called JPay. Its purpose is to allow open source implementations of payment gateways to provide the resources underneath while still going through an open and standardized API.

As said before, which way you choose to go entirely depends on your current resources and requirements on the end process. However, using JRuby on Rails gives you more options than either Ruby or Java separately.

This book won't be able to give more than a cursory glimpse of how to do online systems that can handle payments. If that subject interests you, *Beginning Ruby on Rails E-Commerce* by Christian Hellsten and Jarkko Laine (Apress, 2006) is the way to go. The information in that book is only about the Ruby way of doing things, but the concepts should be easy to combine with JRuby.

ActiveRecord and JDBC

As mentioned in Chapter 2, which described what software you would need to install to follow along in this book, the component that makes it possible to use Java JDBC drivers within Rails is called ActiveRecord-JDBC, or AR-JDBC for short. In regular Rails applications, there's the concept of an adapter. In Rails, each adapter is specific for one database, so there's a MySQL adapter, an Oracle adapter, and so on. At the moment, there are few adapters that ship with ActiveRecord. This is also one of the major selling points for JRuby on Rails. Because AR-JDBC is implemented as an adapter, and that adapter can use any JDBC driver you'd like, it means that many more databases will be available for use with Rails.

All is not that easy, though. The JDBC adapter in AR-JDBC is written to be as generic as possible, but there are still problems with how Rails connects to the database that make it necessary to tweak the adapter in different ways, depending on which database will be used. One of the more common problems is differences in SQL quoting, which differ between database vendors. So, there still has to be some support code for each database, but the difference compared to regular Rails is that this code won't be so big, and it is easy to add this code to the system.

Further, not only can you use regular JDBC drivers to connect to databases; you can also use other deployment patterns for database access that make more sense in a Java enterprise environment. This support is continually evolving, but at the moment you can use simple JDBC drivers of all kinds, and you can also fetch a `DataSource` from Java Naming and Directory Interface (JNDI). Making it possible to use data sources opens up a few different possibilities. First of all, you can deploy database handles in an application server and the Rails application can fetch connections from that point. By splitting the configuration like this, it becomes easy to change the back-end database, make configuration changes, and even enable failover on the database, totally transparently from the Rails application. Another important possibility is the usage of database pooling. In regular Rails, some of the database adapters support pooling, but this is implemented inside the database-specific database driver. With Java, it's easy to use one of the many open source database pooling tools that exist; for example, Jakarta Commons DBCP is good enough for most purposes.

A single adapter for ActiveRecord makes all this possible. Some other ideas are floating around about how to extend Rails in other Java-specific ways. Some of the more interesting proposals concern making a Hibernate back end for Rails. If someone would do this, it would open up the Rails world to a completely new type of application, which until now has been difficult or impossible to accomplish due to Rails' opinionated way of doing things.

It's also possible to use AR-JDBC outside of Rails. For testing purposes, where it is interesting to talk directly to a database and watch what happens, a deployment with only ActiveRecord and AR-JDBC makes sense, especially because in many cases it's much easier to get a strange database working with JDBC than with C drivers.

Supported Databases

As mentioned before, AR-JDBC supports many databases out of the box. This section will walk through each of them, giving a little information about what's needed to get the database configuration set up in a way that will work with that database. The sections won't show how to set up the databases themselves, just how to configure Rails for them. The example configuration will be the development section of `config/database.yml`, and in most cases will use the `localhost`, with a database name of `ar_test`, a username of "ar_user," and a password of "ar_pass." Any deviations from this will be noted at the point they happen.

MySQL

The MySQL support in AR-JDBC is one of the more stable parts. Most of the strange parts in how Rails uses ActiveRecord are things that work well with MySQL. So, for many applications MySQL should be an easy choice. The configuration of a MySQL database in Rails is also straightforward. (You've already done it once for the Shoplet application.) A sample configuration should look like this:

```
development:
  adapter: jdbc
  driver: com.mysql.jdbc.Driver
```

```
url: jdbc:mysql://localhost:3306/ar_test
username: ar_user
password: ar_pass
```

All information will be familiar here if you've used JDBC before. The only strange part is the adapter, and that will be the same for all configurations of AR-JDBC. In fact, that definition tells ActiveRecord to use AR-JDBC instead of something else.

The `driver` parameter points to the regular JDBC driver class name. It's important that this class can be found on JRuby's `CLASSPATH`; otherwise it won't be found and Rails won't work.

The `url` parameter works in exactly the same way as with regular JDBC. The big difference is that you need separate username and password parameters for AR-JDBC. Because that URL is what gets sent to the JDBC driver, you can also include configuration settings in it, if you need the connection to MySQL handled in a different way from the defaults.

Oracle SQL

Next to MySQL and PostgreSQL, Oracle database support is the one that works best in AR-JDBC. The configuration is more or less exactly the same as the one for MySQL:

```
development:
  adapter: jdbc
  driver: oracle.jdbc.driver.OracleDriver
  url: jdbc:oracle:thin:@localhost:1521:ORCL
  username: ar_user
  password: ar_pass
```

The main difference with regard to other databases is that you won't specify an explicit database. Instead, your username defines which schema you're part of. Also, the JDBC URL looks slightly different, because you need to point out which System Identifier (SID) the Oracle driver should use. However, as is the case with MySQL, you can append any configuration options that are valid for a regular JDBC Oracle connection here. Using a full Oracle Call Interface (OCI) JDBC adapter instead of the thin driver also works, if that is more fitting for the application in question.

PostgreSQL

As mentioned earlier, PostgreSQL also works well with Rails. For almost all interesting purposes, it works exactly like the MySQL driver, and the configuration is similar:

```
development:
  adapter: jdbc
  driver: org.postgresql.Driver
  url: jdbc:postgresql://localhost/ar_test
  username: ar_user
  password: ar_pass
```

Microsoft SQL Server

The SQL Server driver is slightly more involved. In fact, it allows the use of two different JDBC drivers. I'll show here the driver configuration for the JDBC driver that Microsoft ships for SQL Server, but AR-JDBC works just as well with the TDS driver that can be found on the Internet.

```
development:
  adapter: jdbc
  driver: com.microsoft.sqlserver.jdbc.SQLServerDriver
  url: jdbc:sqlserver://localhost;databaseName=ar_test
  username: ar_user
  password: ar_pass
```

Once again, the JDBC configurations follow the same pattern.

IBM DB2

The database drivers from IBM for DB2 are in good working order, and the configuration looks almost exactly like the rest of the JDBC adapters:

```
development:
  adapter: jdbc
  driver: com.ibm.db2.jcc.DB2Driver
  url: jdbc:db2://localhost:50000/ar_test
  username: ar_user
  password: ar_pass
```

Firebird

What makes Firebird a little strange to work with is how it names the databases. In most cases, Firebird wants your database to reside as a regular file, and the database name is the path to that file. Except for that, Firebird is nice enough to work with:

```
development:
  adapter: jdbc
  driver: org.firebirdsql.jdbc.FBDriver
  url: jdbc:firebirdsql://localhost:3050//home/ola/ar_test.gdb
  username: ar_user
  password: ar_pass
```

Derby

Derby is a nice database that also ships with recent versions of Java. There are two different ways to set Derby up, and I'll show the configuration for each here. The first—and easiest— way is to have Derby automatically create an in memory database when it gets used. To achieve that, configure AR-JDBC like this:

```
development:
  adapter: jdbc
  driver: org.apache.derby.jdbc.EmbeddedDriver
  url: jdbc:derby:ar_test;create=true
```

As you can see, in this case neither username nor password is necessary. What happens is that the first time the database is requested, it's created, but only in memory. That means the content of the database won't persist. It's a good way to run test cases, though.

The other way to use Derby is through the more usual server setup:

```
development:
  adapter: jdbc
  driver: org.apache.derby.jdbc.ClientDriver
  url: jdbc:derby://localhost:1527/ar_test
  username: ar_user
  password: ar_pass
```

When used in this way, you see that the configuration looks exactly like the other databases.

HSQLDB

HSQLDB is another in memory database that makes it easy to test things. The difference from Derby in embedded mode is that HSQLDB saves the results from the database to a file between processes:

```
development:
  adapter: jdbc
  driver: org.hsqldb.jdbcDriver
  url: jdbc:hsqldb:mem:ar_test
  username: sa
  password:
```

As you see, you define a URL that specifies the name of the database. HSQLDB requires you to use the "sa" user if you want to create tables and such, so in this case you connect with "sa," without any password, because you want complete rights.

Mimer SQL

Mimer SQL is a small, relatively unknown database from Sweden. It's fast and extremely SQL compliant. The support for Mimer is also the most recent to get added to AR-JDBC. However, as such, it works well indeed, and you won't notice much difference in configuration compared with the other JDBC drivers:

```
development:
  adapter: jdbc
  driver: com.mimer.jdbc.Driver
  url: jdbc:mimer://localhost/ar_test
  username: ar_user
  password: ar_pass
```

How to Support a New Database

This is all well and good. But say you want to support a database that AR-JDBC doesn't support yet. There are many databases in the world, and if your database has a functional JDBC driver, it potentially could work with Rails. Adding this support is easy indeed. First of all, you should try and see if your database works with AR-JDBC without changing anything. Say you want support for FooDB, which has a JDBC driver called org.foo.db.Driver. Just write the configuration for it and try it with Rails. If you're lucky, it will just work:

```
development:
  adapter: jdbc
  driver: org.foo.db.Driver
  url: jdbc:foodb://localhost/?db=ar_test
  username: ar_user
  password: ar_pass
```

If you're not lucky, you'll need to add some parts to AR-JDBC. You won't have to modify the source code for AR-JDBC to effect changes in it, though. However, to be able to make good changes, it will help you to see how the other databases have been implemented, so go to http://rubyforge.org/projects/jruby-extras and from there on find your way to the most recent AR-JDBC source code. If you want some more information on this, take a look in Chapter 15 where I describe some more about what's needed to support new databases to AR-JDBC. You can find the support for the different databases in lib/jdbc_adapter/. The added support is divided into two different parts: Column and Adapter. Possibly, you won't have to add code for both, but we'll just assume that for now. If your code works well, you'll probably want to publish it somewhere, but for now you'll develop the code in the lib directory of a Rails application. Say your file is called lib/foo_adapter.rb. In that case you should add a require for that file in config/environment.rb after the require for jdbc_adapter:

```
require 'jdbc_adapter'
require 'foo_adapter'
```

Further, the usual organization of the adapters for AR-JDBC means you should have a skeleton in your foo_adapter.rb code that looks like this:

```
module JdbcSpec
  module Foo
    module Column
      #Column specific code
    end
    #Code for the rest of the adapter
  end
end
```

The naming is arbitrary, but it's the way AR-JDBC does it. After you've defined these modules, you should hook them into AR-JDBC so they'll be used. You achieve that by changing two hashes in the internals of the JDBC adapter:

```
ActiveRecord::ConnectionAdapters::
  JdbcColumn::COLUMN_TYPES[/foo\.db/i] =
        lambda {|cfg,col| col.extend JdbcSpec::Foo::Column }
```

```
ActiveRecord::ConnectionAdapters::
  JdbcAdapter::Adapter_TYPES[/foo\.db/i] =
          lambda {|cfg,ad| ad.extend JdbcSpec::Foo }
```

In this way, when a JDBC configuration with a driver that matches the regular expression used is initialized, the code in `JdbcSpec::Foo::Column` and `JdbcSpec::Foo` will be mixed into their respective classes and the functionality in them will be added. Exactly what those two modules should contain, though, is something that depends very much on what kind of database `FooDB` is. One thing that usually needs to change, though, is the migration code. In the adapter you should make sure that `create_table`, `rename_table`, `drop_table`, and corresponding methods for columns do what you expect them to, though, in your database. Another thing that usually differs between different database vendors is how quoting of strings and other database types is handled. This typically needs to be changed in both the `Column` and the `Adapter`, but once again the existing adapters display many ways of doing this.

Of course, the current set of databases is just what is known at the time of writing. It's possible that the amount of databases supported has been extended at the time you're reading this. The only way to make sure is to check the documentation for AR-JDBC.

Summary

We've walked through the rest of the Shoplet application, and you've seen how to simplify browsing for the user, while still not having to duplicate code to manage a menu. We've also looked more at how to test models and functionality with Rails' built-in testing support. I couldn't show all testing that should have been done, but I hope what was covered was enough to whet your appetite enough to research more testing by yourself.

The second half of the chapter looked at AR-JDBC a little more closely. It delved into the different databases supported, how you should configure them, and also what you can do if you need to use a database that isn't supported by AR-JDBC yet.

The purpose of the preceding chapters has been mainly to introduce you to how Rails works, and to some of the quirks that come up in conjunction with JRuby. You should know now how to handle the day-to-day tasks of building a simple application in JRuby on Rails.

From the next chapter on, we'll work with much more Java code, and there will also be a high amount of JRuby-specific code. The next chapter will describe JRuby in more detail, describing how to accomplish all the usual tasks you'll need when integrating Java with Ruby. We'll also start on a completely new project that makes much more use of this integration. That means there won't be much place for things you've learned in the last few chapters, so some of the code will be omitted, and some just described in prose instead of code. The full code is available online, though, in the Source Code/Download area of the Apress web site (`http://www.apress.com`).

PROJECT 2

A Content Management System (CoMpoSe)

CHAPTER 6

■■■

Java Integration

The last few chapters mainly served to introduce Ruby and Rails, and only incidentally used JRuby to achieve this. From now on much more Java will be involved. That doesn't necessarily mean that you need to write and build Java classes, but you'll interact with the Java ecosystem in different ways that aren't possible with regular Ruby.

To make this transition easier on you, this chapter will be a detour into these issues. It will be a focused chapter; I won't talk about the next project application at all. This is the crash course about the areas where JRuby differs from Ruby.

I'll begin by describing how you can reference Java classes, Java primitives, and Java arrays, and what you can do with them from JRuby. The primitives and arrays especially are handled in a way that isn't natural for a Java programmer, so it's important to get these facts down.

One of the nicer things you can do when interfacing Java and Ruby is to implement Java interfaces, extend Java classes from Ruby, and then send that code back to Java. For example, you could implement an OutputStream in a few lines of Ruby code, send it right back into some FilterOutputStream or whatnot, and it will just work.

JRuby also adds several handy new ways of working with Java collections and Java arrays by adding many new methods to them. Because of this, some of the more useful things you can do are to call map on a SortedMap, for example. The possibilities are endless, and useful.

There's also another side to the Java integration in JRuby. Sometimes you want to use Ruby from Java. I'll describe three different techniques for how to do this: two that are recommended, and one that is not so recommended. That part of the chapter will be of most interest to you if you want to create a Java application that uses Ruby as an extension language, or to provide macro/plug-in capabilities. It could also be interesting if you want to use Ruby as a scripting language for web pages instead of Java Server Pages (JSP) or Velocity.

The final part will discuss some gotchas. Because the Java integration in JRuby is on the boundary between two different kinds of systems, it also contains most of the things that can go wrong if you don't know all the tricks and interesting things that can happen. I'll describe in some detail how the Java integration works, so that you understand the capabilities and limitations inherent in it.

But enough talking about what we're going to talk about. Let's get started.

Using Java Resources

The major selling point for using JRuby instead of regular Ruby is that all the Java code in the world is available to your Ruby program, and it's as easy to use as Ruby libraries. JRuby aims to be compatible with Ruby. Because of that, you first need to say you want to use the Java features in your Ruby program. There are two ways of doing this: the first explicit, the second implicit. The explicit way looks like this:

```
require 'java'
```

That's all there is to it. The implicit way of getting at the Java goodness is to reference the Java module in your code. Say you'd like to use the Java class se.ologix.HelloWorld. In that case you could just do it like this:

```
k = Java::se.ologix.HelloWorld
```

Because you referenced the Java module, you don't have to require java; it's done beneath the covers. That's it when it comes to getting hold of the Java information. One thing can be good to know, though. If you want to write code that runs on both ordinary Ruby and JRuby, and you'd like to see if you are using JRuby or not, there is one cumbersome way:

```
jruby = false
begin
 require 'java'
 jruby = true
rescue
end
```

As you can see, if there isn't any java to require, a LoadError will be raised and the variable jruby won't be set to true. However, this can fail for several reasons. One of the big ones is that maybe there is a library on the load path called java. A better way to see if you're on JRuby or not is to check the RUBY_PLATFORM constant. If RUBY_PLATFORM =~ /java/, then you know you're running JRuby:

```
jruby = RUBY_PLATFORM =~ /java/
```

Currently, the best solution to finding out this information is to check for the JRUBY_VERSION:

```
jruby = defined?(JRUBY_VERSION)
```

Next we'll look at how to use the things you can find in the Java module. Every Java library you want to use must be on the CLASSPATH prior to running JRuby. There are two ways of circumventing this restriction, though, but they don't work for all Java classes. The last part of Appendix B has more information about this caveat. However, in most cases both ways work, so try and see. The first is by using require on a JAR file:

```
require 'commons-discovery.jar'
```

This adds commons-discovery.jar to the CLASSPATH JRuby uses to find classes. The second way is more explicit. It demands that you execute require 'java' before doing it:

```
$CLASSPATH << 'commons-discovery.jar'
```

Classes

In many cases, it's incredibly easy to use Java classes. There are several ways to get hold of references to Java classes, though, and different solutions fit different use cases. All the examples from here on depend on the Java integration libraries being loaded, as described earlier.

The first way to get hold of classes is the oldest, and is still the only way in JRuby to reference classes without a package. This version uses a method called `include_class`:

```
include_class "java.util.HashMap"

x = HashMap.new
x.put("foo","bar")
```

After executing `include_class` with a string describing the class to load, a local constant with the same name as the class will be made available to your code. In some cases this isn't so good. For example, you might want to change the name of the included class, so it doesn't clash with existing Ruby classes. Then you can send a block to `include_class`, and that block is used to decide the name for the resulting constant:

```
include_class("java.lang.String") {|pkg,name| "JString"}

JString.new "Hello, world"
```

The `include_class` method can take an array of class names, and in that case the block version is especially convenient:

```
include_class(["java.lang.String",
               "java.lang.Runtime",
               "java.util.Map"]) {|pkg, name| "J#{name}"}

JString.new "Hello, world"
```

Usually, though, it's easier just to refer to the classes directly. If the top package is `java`, `javax`, `org`, or `com`, you can use the direct way of referring to Java classes. The easiest way is to use this in conjunction with setting local constants. You can also use import on a single class name, if you miss Java:

```
JString = java.lang.String

import org.jruby.Main

org.jruby.util.ByteList.new
```

As you can see, you don't even need to set a local constant. It's easy enough just to call the method you're after directly. So, what do you do when the package you want to reference isn't one of the four shortcut packages? Well, you could use `include_class`, but you can also find all these reference methods in the `Java` module. You can find the Java `String` there, but also all other packages that can exist:

```
JString = Java::java.lang.String

HelloWorld = Java::se.ologix.HelloWorld
```

This can often make it much more obvious what's happening, even if it's slightly more verbose.

So, when you have a class reference, what can you do with it? Well, you can do most of the things with it from Java code. JRuby also tries to be smart about things, doing implicit conversions of different kinds. Say that you want to call `System.out.println` from Ruby. You do it mostly the same way:

```
java.lang.System.out.println("Hello, world")
```

It's important to notice that the `"Hello, world"` string is a Ruby `String`, not a Java `String`. These are different types, but a Ruby `String` is converted beneath the covers for all obvious cases. For example, a Ruby `Fixnum` matches against all the integer types in Java, and also the primitive wrapper types. The goal with all this integration is that you won't have to care what type objects are. For almost all cases, things will just work.

To create a new instance of a Java class, just call the `new` method on it:

```
m = java.util.HashMap.new

m.put "hello", "world"
m.put "goodbye", "life"

puts m.get("hello")

iter = m.keySet.iterator
while iter.hasNext
  key = iter.next
  puts "#{key}=#{m.get(key)}"
end
```

As you can see, all these things work more or less exactly as they would in Java. The big difference is that you don't have to write parentheses in most cases, and you don't have to care about the types of variables. Ruby takes care of that. Obviously, this is not the best way to work with Java collections from Ruby. We'll take a look at the Ruby way later in this chapter.

There's one thing to be careful about when creating a new instance of a class and things aren't working as expected. What's wrong with this example?

```
m = java.util.SortedMap.new

m.put "Hello", "World"
```

Yes, `SortedMap` isn't a class; it's an interface. In Java that code wouldn't even compile. However, due to Ruby's dynamic nature, this is allowed. JRuby also allows it, but it probably won't do what you expect. This code creates an anonymous implementation of `SortedMap` that raises an error any time you try to call a method on it. This is the main way you can implement interfaces from Ruby, as you'll see later, so the behavior is expected.

JRuby tries to make method names and variables work as expected from the Ruby perspective. One of the ways it does this is by adding aliases for most methods. Because Ruby usually uses method names `do_foo_to_bar`, where the Java equivalent would be `doFooToBar`, JRuby makes aliases available in the underscore style for all methods. That means the `HashMap` example from earlier could've been written like this:

```
m = java.util.HashMap.new

m.put "hello", "world"
m.put "goodbye", "life"

puts m.get("hello")

iter = m.key_set.iterator
while iter.has_next
  key = iter.next
  puts "#{key}=#{m.get(key)}"
end
```

It's maybe not a big difference, but it does make your Ruby code more consistent. The second thing to note is that common getters and setters in Java are also aliased to make things more obvious from a Java perspective. Say you have a Java class called com.example.FooBar, which has three methods called getName, setName, and getValue. These methods are also available in the Ruby attribute accessor form, so this code does what's expected:

```
foo = com.example.FooBar.new

foo.name = foo.name + foo.value
```

What happens is that all instances of getFoo are available as foo. All instances of setFoo are available as foo=. I encourage you to use these shortcuts because, as I said before, it makes your code more Ruby-like, even if it's calling Java code.

A thing to notice is the interface java.lang.Runnable. Say you have Java code implementing this interface, and you want to call run in a block, say something like this:

```
t = java.lang.Thread.new

foo { t.run }
```

You could instead use a shortcut:

```
t = java.lang.Thread.new

foo &t
```

The t variable is automatically turned into a block by the to_proc method that java.lang.Runnable has.

Primitives

Working with primitives from JRuby isn't recommended. Of course, sometimes you need to do so. However, in most cases you can just count on the automatic conversions to handle things correctly. You need to be able to do a few things, though. First of all, you need to get at the primitive classes. There are two ways to do this, the easy and the hard, where hardness is mostly about typing more:

```
b1 = Java::byte
b2 = java.lang.Byte::TYPE
```

If you remember your Java, the TYPE static variable is available on all the primitive wrappers, giving you easy access to that class instance. You cannot do much with this class, though; not in itself. The only thing it's good for is when you need to provide a Class instance and to handle primitive arrays, which the next section will cover.

If you want to create primitive versions of objects directly, use the wrapper classes instead. These will be automatically coerced into the real primitive types when needed:

```
a = java.lang.StringBuffer.new
```

```
a.append java.lang.Character.new(13244)
```

This call uses the method java.lang.StringBuffer.append(char).

Arrays

Usually you only need to use arrays in the sense of creating them so you can send them in to Java code. Arrays returned from Java code are mostly indistinguishable from the Ruby class Array. In the cases where you need a real Ruby Array, you can call to_a on the Java array.

So, in many cases, it suffices to be able to create a Java array from a Ruby Array. In these cases, the to_java method does what you want it to. The thing making it annoying is that you must specify what type of array it should be. If you don't, the to_java method will create a basic Object[]. So, you can create Java arrays from Ruby Arrays like this:

```
[1,2,3].to_java        # new Object[] {new Integer(1),
                       #               new Integer(2), new Integer(3)}
[1,2,3].to_java :byte  # new byte[] {1,2,3}
[1,2,3].to_java :char  # new char[] {1,2,3}
[1,2,3].to_java :float # new float[] {1,2,3}
# etc
["str", "str2"].to_java java.lang.String   # new String[]{"str","str2"}
```

As you can see, you can provide either a symbol representing the primitive type, or a class instance. The primitive types you can use are :boolean, :byte, :char, :double, :float, :int, :long, and :short. There are also shortcuts for java.lang.Object, java.lang.String, java.math.BigDecimal, and java.math.BigInteger, as well as for by :object, :string, :big_decimal or :decimal, and :big_integer or :big_int.

In most cases, this is all you need. However, sometimes you might need to create an empty array, or an array of more than one dimension. In these cases there are [] helpers on all Java classes in the system. So, for example, you could create an empty String[] with length 3 like this:

```
java.lang.String[].new 3
```

Or you could create it like this:

```
java.lang.String[3].new
```

If you need a two dimensional array, you can just add a new parameter to the call. For example, you do this to create something akin to new String[3][3]:

```
java.lang.String[].new [3,3]
```

or

```
java.lang.String[3][3].new
```

or

```
java.lang.String[3,3].new
```

To work with such an array, just do it the normal way:

```
d = java.lang.String[3,3].new
d[0][0] = "Hello"
d[0][1] = "World"
```

Working with arrays in this way works fine with the primitive types too:

```
Java::byte[256].new
```

If you need to reference the Java classes for arrays, you use the same form:

```
java.lang.String[][][]
```

The preceding code returns the class represented by `[[[Ljava.lang.String;`. In the same manner, this code returns the class `[[Z`:

```
Java::boolean[][]
```

There are some more caveats and things to know about handling Java code, but we'll look at those as we go along.

Extending Java

Being able to use Java code from Ruby is useful, and in many situations that's all you need. On the other hand, sometimes you want to send code back into Java, in the form of callbacks or handlers. The two major ways you can do this from JRuby are by implementing interfaces or by extending existing classes. JRuby has extensive support for both these situations.

Interfaces

In many cases, it's enough to implement an interface in Ruby and send that back to Java. It's simple to achieve this. Remember that you could call new on an interface class from Java? Well, to implement an interface in Ruby, you just import it as if the interface was a Ruby module. All methods you don't implement will call method_missing, in the manner of regular Ruby code:

```
class RaiseErrors
  import org.xml.sax.ErrorHandler
  def error exception
    raise "ValidationError", exception.to_s
  end
  def fatalError exception
    raise "ValidationError", exception.to_s
  end
  def warning exception
```

```
    end
end
```

```
builder.set_error_handler RaiseErrors.new
```

As you can see, there's nothing strange with implementing interfaces this way, and it works as you expect.

■Caution You should be careful to name methods with the exact same name as their Java counterparts. The aliasing used when calling methods isn't available when implementing them. That's why you have to write `fatalError`, and not `fatal_error`.

■Caution If the method you're implementing should return a Java value, make sure the value you return from the method can be coerced into Java without problems.

You can also implement more than one interface, in mostly the same way:

```
class RunCompare
  import java java.lang.Runnable
  import java.lang.Comparable

  def compareTo o
    this <=> o
  end

  def run
    puts "running..."
  end
end
```

```
java.lang.Thread.new(RunCompare.new)
java.util.TreeSet.new(RunCompare.new)
```

Notice that you can only do this the first time you open up a class. Because Java integration needs to generate a proxy class beneath the covers, this can only be done once. As you can see from the example, you can send instances of this class into everything that can take either a `Runnable` or a `Comparable`. One thing to note about implementing interfaces is that up until now you've had to create a new class explicitly. This can pollute the namespace, and isn't always necessary. Many times you just want something like an anonymous implementation of the interface. You can also have that with the `impl` method:

```
button.set_action_listener java.awt.event.ActionListener.impl { |_,e|
  e.source.text = "Hello World"
}
```

impl is a method that exists on all interfaces. It takes a block in some form that should be executed when any of the methods in the interface is called. The block should take the same arguments as the method or methods in question, and a last argument that is a string that names the method called. If the interface methods take different lengths of arguments, you can use *args instead. For an explicit example, you could create an implementation of KeyListener like this:

```
java.awt.event.KeyListener.impl do |method, e|
 case method
  when "keyPressed": puts "A key was pressed"
  when "keyReleased": puts "A key was released"
  when "keyTyped": puts "A key was typed"
 end
end
```

Of course, in many cases you don't care what method was called, and in those cases you can just name the method argument to an underscore or something else. If you don't need any arguments to the method, such as Runnable, you can just omit the arguments:

```
java.lang.Runnable.impl do
  puts "Running"
end
```

Note that the impl method creates a new anonymous class beneath the covers that calls the block. There's nothing strange going on; the Java integration layer just hides those parts. At the moment, most of the Java integration layer is totally written in pure Ruby, and the parts involved in the impl method don't use any Java at all.

You can use the initialize method in the same way as you do from Ruby. In earlier versions of JRuby this didn't work as expected, and you had to call super explicitly to avoid strange errors. This is no longer true; both initialize and super calls in initialize work as you would like them to:

```
class Abc
  import java.lang.Runnable
  def initialize(pu)
    puts "init #{pu}"
  end

  def run
    puts "running"
  end
end

java.lang.Thread.new(Abc.new("foo")).start
```

Of course, interfaces only get you so far. Sometimes you need to be able to work with Java classes too.

Classes

Until recently, there was no way to extend Java classes and have those extensions be visible to Java code. You could inherit from any Java class, and the Ruby code would see all the changes. But that has changed; now you can extend any Java class, create instances of that extended class, and the changes will be visible to Java code too. Here's a simple example:

```
class FooStream < java.io.OutputStream
  def write(p)
    puts p
  end
end

s = java.io.BufferedOutputStream.new(FooStream.new)
s.write([1,2,3].to_java(:byte), 0, 3)
s.flush
```

As you see here, the write method gets implemented in Ruby, and you use the array form of write to see that the BufferOutputStream calls the Ruby-implemented write method. It is important to get the number of arguments correct when overriding Java methods. Also note that if you override a method with just one argument, and there are several versions of that method with different argument types, the Ruby overloading will have to take care of them all. For example, say you did something like this:

```
class MyStringBuffer < java.lang.StringBuffer
  def append(v)
  end
end
```

This would end up overriding *all* the append methods with one argument in StringBuffer. That isn't a good thing, but because Ruby doesn't have static type information to help out, it's the only possible route at the moment. All these instructions about arguments work the same for constructors. Calling super in an initialize method ends up calling the constructor that matches the arguments most correctly.

You can implement interfaces and extend a Java class at the same time, using import to implement interfaces the same way you would do when not inheriting from a Java class:

```
class MyStringBuffer < java.lang.StringBuffer
  import java.lang.Runnable
end
```

Java Collections

One of the things I love most about JRuby's Java integration is its support for working with Java collections in much the same way as you would a Ruby collection. You can easily express many productive things in Ruby that are cumbersome in regular Java. For example, say that you want to sort a collection of FooObjects by an attribute called name. In Java this could look something like this:

```
Collections.sort(foos, new Comparator() {
  public int compare(Object o1, Object o2) {
    return ((FooObject)o1).getName().compareTo(((FooObject)o2).getName());
  }
});
```

That's pretty much the best case scenario, provided the objects don't implement Comparable. How would you do the preceding with JRuby?

```
foos.sort_by {|o| o.name}
```

Of course, if you have Facets or Rails loaded you can do it like this:

```
foos.sort_by &:name
```

Some difference, huh? So, Java collections get almost all the regular Ruby collection
methods for free. In plain English, these are the current extensions to Java collections:
java.util.Map has an each method, a [] method, and a []= method. Map mixes in Enumerable
and gets all the methods there for free. The interface java.lang.Comparable has the <=>
method, and mixes in the Ruby module Comparable. All classes descended from
java.util.Collection have each, <<, +, -, length, and mix in Enumerable. In this way, Java lists
are almost indistinguishable from Ruby collections. Further, java.util.List has [] and []=,
and also implements fast versions of sort and sort! that use java.util.Collections.sort
beneath the covers.

You can create Java collections in much the same way as other Ruby collections. A Ruby
Hash implements java.util.Map, and a Ruby Array implements java.util.List. This means
you can create a new LinkedList like this:

```
java.util.LinkedList.new [1,2,3]
```

One thing to note about all these methods is that for Lists, the [] and []= don't implement slicing or ranges at the moment. They are just wrappers for get and set. If you want
slicing, you can use the to_a method:

```
a = java.util.ArrayList.new [1,2,3,4,5,6]
a.to_a[2..4]
```

Note that to_a returns a new array, and changes to that array won't reflect on the original
Java collection. As you might remember, to_a exists in Enumerable, so you can call to_a on Maps
too:

```
h = java.util.HashMap.new
h['a'] = 'b'
h['c'] = 'd'

p h.to_a        #=> [['c','d'],['a','b']]
```

The more useful parts of Enumerable all work as you would expect. I find myself using collect, select, and sort_by most, because it takes so much code to do the equivalent in Java.
inject, grep, reject, partition, and all the others work well too.

It's important to remember that if you find something that would be useful to add to all the Java collection classes, you can do so easily. You shouldn't use the regular Ruby class syntax for this, though, because there's a fair amount of magic involved. However, say you'd like all Java collections to have an implementation of each_cons. (each_cons returns each pair of values consecutively available in the collection). You could add the each_cons method with a little help from extend_proxy like this:

```
JavaUtilities.extend_proxy('java.util.Collection') {
  def each_cons(&block)
    iter = iterator
    if iter.hasNext
      first = iter.next
      while iter.hasNext
        val = first, iter.next
        first = val[1]
        block.call *val
      end
    end
    nil
  end
}
```

As you can see, the method definition works as usual, but you have to execute it within a block sent to JavaUtilities.extend_proxy. Say you have this defined and execute this code:

```
a = java.util.LinkedList.new [1,2,3,4,5]
a.each_cons do |v|
  p v
end
```

You'd see this:

```
[1,2]
[2,3]
[3,4]
[4,5]
```

The method would be available to all code implementing java.util.Collection, even new classes loaded after the fact.

Gotchas

As noted in the introduction to this chapter, several things can go wrong when interacting between Ruby and Java code. Most of these are caused by Ruby being much more dynamic than Java, which means it's hard for JRuby to know whether what you did was a mistake, or meant to be that way. So, when doing things that would have generated warnings or compile errors in Java, JRuby happily lets you go ahead with it, because it can't know if you intended to do what you did.

The failures when dealing with Java integration can also be cryptic. Sometimes everything looks as if it's working fine, but beneath the covers, something has gone wrong. In other situations, interpretation can shut down without any message at all. However, usually you get something to work with, at least. When researching the reason for a Java integration failure, it helps to check out the JRuby Wiki and JRuby FAQ. You're probably not alone in experiencing the problem in question. You can find links to these resources in Appendix C.

So, where should you look first when trying to find the cause of a strange error? First of all, check if the method you're calling takes the same amount of arguments that you've provided to it. Java programmers are used to the compiler finding this type of problem, but that isn't possible with JRuby, so the wrong number of arguments is the number one cause of Java integration problems. Another common cause of problems is that JRuby cannot find a method with matching argument types. These are a little harder to see, but in many cases it's caused by you sending in another value than you intended to.

When creating implementations of interfaces and extending classes, make sure that the argument arity (number of arguments) matches. If it doesn't, JRuby will happily continue running, and you won't notice anything wrong until the method you thought you overrode is called, but the wrong operation is executed. Also remember the earlier caution about overriding overloaded methods with the same argument arity. If you don't handle all cases, things invariably won't work.

All these problems can be easily remedied and combated by having extensive test suites covering both your Ruby and Java code. Because it's easy to write tests in Ruby that test Java code, there isn't any good reason not to do it. If you test all your code, these dynamic failures will be found before you try to execute the code in production. RSpec is an especially good framework for testing, particularly when programming with Test-Driven Development. Otherwise, the `Test::Unit` framework that comes with Ruby's standard library works well too. Just remember to test the Java integration code closely, because it's easier to get errors in those areas of your code.

Using Ruby from Java

As I mentioned in the beginning of this chapter, it can sometimes be useful to be able to call out to Ruby from Java. You could accomplish many things with this; some interesting examples would be to use Ruby as an extension language for writing macros and plug-ins to an application. You could also easily write a Java application that's configured by a custom configuration DSL, executed by JRuby. Of course, you can do many other things too.

What I'll show you here is three different ways to call out to custom Ruby code from Java. I'll show a complete Java program for each approach, but they are about as minimal as they can get. The approaches are ordered by level of recommendation. That is, you should probably use JSR223 if you can; if not, use Bean Scripting Framework (BSF), and if that also fails, use the JRuby runtime directly.

The JRuby Runtime

Let me begin this section by saying this once again: you probably shouldn't call out to the JRuby runtime directly. There is almost certainly a better solution. The reason it's better to use one of the standardized frameworks is that the runtime demands that you wrap and unwrap values manually. There are many more things to keep in mind, and you can't be certain that it will just work, as BSF and JSR223 pretty much guarantee.

So, on to the example program. You want to get some data in there too, so the example program will print out the result from adding 13 to a value you send in from Java. Here's the code to achieve this (and this is pretty much the most minimal Ruby runtime code there can be). It will be more complex for more complicated tasks.

```
package c6;

import org.jruby.Ruby;
import org.jruby.javasupport.JavaEmbedUtils;

public class JRubyRuntime {
    public static void main(String[] args) {
        Ruby runtime = Ruby.getDefaultInstance();
        runtime.getGlobalVariables().set("$label",
                         JavaEmbedUtils.javaToRuby(runtime, 27));
        runtime.evalScriptlet("puts 13 + $label");
    }
}
```

At the moment, you need just two classes. First, the Ruby class is the central runtime. The JavaEmbedUtils class provides some utilities that can be useful for working with Ruby code.

So, what's happening here? Well, you define a new Java class and its main method. The easiest way to get hold of a Ruby runtime is to call the getDefaultInstance method. It almost always gives you what you want, if you don't want to redirect the engine's input and output, or something fancy like that. That runtime is something you'll have to use extensively when interacting with Ruby code.

The next line gets the GlobalVariables object, and sets the label global. The javaToRuby method on JavaEmbedUtils is handy, because it's often a nasty procedure to convert a Java object or primitive into its Ruby counterpart.

After you've set the global, you call the method evalScriptlet. This is one of about a dozen ways you can evaluate Ruby code with a runtime. Other versions include preparsing the code and sending the parsed abstract syntax tree (AST) to the evaluator. There are other possibilities, too.

To compile and run this code, place it in a file called c6/JRubyRuntime.java and execute these commands:

```
javac -cp $JRUBY_HOME/lib/jruby.jar c6/JRubyRuntime.java
java -cp $JRUBY_HOME/lib/jruby.jar:. c6.JRubyRuntime
```

If you're lucky, you'll see the result of adding 13 to 27. Amazing!

To give you a glimpse of how you can call methods on objects you get back and things like this, this snippet shows how to get hold of a JRuby object for a number, and calling a Ruby method on that object called "succ", which returns the next value for the integer:

```
IRubyObject num  = JavaEmbedUtils.javaToRuby(runtime, 27);
IRubyObject num2 = num.callMethod(runtime.getCurrentContext(), "succ");
```

When this code is executed in a relevant context, num2 will contain a Ruby Fixnum with the value 28. You probably understand why I don't recommend working directly with this interface. It works well for implementing libraries around the engine, but it's not that useful for application development.

Bean Scripting Framework

Bean Scripting Framework, or BSF for short, is an open source project hosted by Apache Jakarta. It was originally developed by IBM and later open sourced. The purpose is to make different so-called scripting engines available to a Java program with a language-agnostic interface. That means the code looks almost exactly the same, whether you are working with JavaScript, TCL, Python, Ruby, or any other language with BSF bindings. You need to have BSF and Commons Logging on your CLASSPATH for this example to work.

```
package c6;

import org.apache.bsf.BSFManager;

public class JRubyBSF {
    public static void main(String[] args) throws Exception {
        BSFManager.registerScriptingEngine("ruby",
                                "org.jruby.javasupport.bsf.JRubyEngine",
                                new String[] { "rb" });

        BSFManager manager = new BSFManager();
        manager.declareBean("label", "hello world", String.class);
        manager.exec("ruby", "(java)", 1, 1, "puts $label");
    }
}
```

First of all, you only need to import the BSFManager. This is the central point for all evaluations with BSF, and should be the only thing needed. You first need to register Ruby as a script engine, so that BSF can recognize which evaluator to use. The String array passed to registerScriptEngine details which file endings this script engine should evaluate. After you've registered Ruby, you create a new manager, and then declare a bean on that manager. As you can see, there's no mention of wrapping or converting the object. BSF does this completely beneath the covers. The exec method takes several parameters that you can use for detailed error reporting. The first string is which language you're evaluating. The next is the file name this code belongs to. The numbers are line and column indexes where this code comes from.

To compile and run this code, place it in c6/JRubyBSF.java and execute these commands:

```
javac c6/JRubyBSF.java
javac -cp ${CLASSPATH}:. c6.JRubyBSF
```

If everything works as expected, you should see hello world printed on your console.

Of course, this approach is more verbose than using the JRuby engine directly. That is mainly caused by the initial setup and the need to provide some extra information to the evaluation process. You'll find that this code is much easier to maintain, though, and when the JRuby engine changes its interface (which it will do, over and over again), you won't have to change your own code to accommodate. BSF takes care of that. Also, if you would like to add another script engine for some reason, it will be easy to include it in the current setup, because BSF handles one language much like the other.

JSR223—Java Scripting

The superior way of running JRuby from your own application is through the Java Scripting API, also known as JSR223. It became a standard part in Java with the Java 6 SE release. The goals of JSR223 are pretty much the same as those of BSF. Simply enough, you should be able to use a scripting language with a standard Java installation, without any extra libraries except those for the engine of the language you're interested in. Java bundles a JavaScript engine, and will probably bundle more languages in the future.

The usage of Java Scripting is similar to BSF. You need to have Java 6 installed, and you need to download the JSR223 Engines package from its home page (http://scripting.dev.java.net). After you've done that, you should unpack it, and add the file jruby/lib/jruby-engine.jar to your CLASSPATH. With all that done, you should be set to go.

```
package c6;

import javax.script.ScriptEngine;
import javax.script.ScriptEngineManager;

public class JRubyJSR223 {
    public static void main(String[] args) throws Exception {
        ScriptEngineManager m = new ScriptEngineManager();
        ScriptEngine rubyEngine = m.getEngineByName("jruby");
        rubyEngine.getContext().setAttribute("label", new Integer(4),
                                ScriptContext.ENGINE_SCOPE);
        rubyEngine.eval("puts 2 + $label");
    }
}
```

As you can see, the concepts are mostly the same. You create a new ScriptEngineManager, and fetch an engine for JRuby from that. You then set an attribute named label on the context of the engine. The value should be 4 and the scope should be ENGINE_SCOPE, which is mostly the same as global scope. You then evaluate the same code as before. If everything is done correctly, you should see a 6 appear when this code runs.

In all these examples, you mostly do the same thing: get hold of an engine, set some value for a name, and then evaluate some code. The big positive about using Java Scripting is that it's available everywhere. You need the JRuby engine JAR, and then it will work. You don't have to handle BSF and Commons Logging, and you get all interaction with the script engine done in such a way that you'll never have to work with the engine's internal objects. Because those internal objects can be quite cumbersome in JRuby, that's a good thing.

Summary

As you've seen in this chapter, the Java integration issues can be complicated, but in most cases things work as you should expect them to. JRuby tries hard to get out of your way and do things in the most reasonable way possible. That doesn't mean there aren't corner cases where it's hard to do right without hints from the programmer, but JRuby also provides ways for you to help it.

Because the Java integration is one of the most important parts of JRuby, this chapter detailed quite a bit of information about this subject. You can turn back to this text when something is unclear in the example code in the rest of the book. This chapter didn't cover all there is to know about Java integration, but it did cover much of it. You can find more updated information on the Internet.

Now it's time to get started with the next project application, called CoMpoSe.

CHAPTER 7

■■■

A Rails CMS

In the last chapter we explored the mechanics involved in crossing the border between Java and Ruby. As you no doubt have learned, there are several tricky things to keep in mind. In this chapter we'll start looking at the first application in the book that uses Java libraries actively, instead of just relying on JDBC and otherwise doing things the Ruby way.

We'll take a look at the basic parts of a content management system, called CoMpoSe. This system isn't a full-fledged Content Management System (CMS). First of all, most help texts are missing. A few other areas also should be improved before deploying it in production. However, CoMpoSe will still serve to illustrate how a Rails application that uses Java can work. Further, it could absolutely form the skeleton for a real CMS application.

The project is divided into two different areas. The one we'll mostly explore in this chapter is the administrative part, where a user can edit the content and metacontent of the system. The other part is the rendering engines that will show the content to end users, which Chapter 8 will mostly cover.

I've decided to divide the content management tasks into several different parts, and these parts will mesh nicely with the different models in the system. The tasks will be divided into administrating the styles of the system, where styles can be Extensible Stylesheet Language Transformations (XSLT) style sheets that transform XML, or Cascading Style Sheets (CSS) styles that will change the user interface for the end user. The next tasks are administrating layouts (where a layout is an ordered collection of styles), administrating paths (a path is a subdomain within the system), and writing articles. Further, there will be a separate part for handling users authenticated to the system.

CoMpoSe won't have any authorization; every administrator can do anything in the system. Authorization would be easy to add, though, and should be implemented in a real application. Although we won't have authorization, we'll add a simple authentication system, much like in the last project, so that the administration parts of CoMpoSe aren't open to the whole world.

CoMpoSe will render content in different stages, where the text of an article can be styled with either Textile (through RedCloth), Markdown (through BlueCloth), or just as plain text. The end result of rendering the article will then be processed with the layout associated with the article, or with the path this article is part of. Each style will be used to process the current content sequentially, until no more tasks remain. At this point, the content is finished, and can be returned to the user's browser. The point of having all these steps and different rendering engines is that you should be able to switch in other rendering engines easily, or even switch layouts or styles based on which kind of request you get. So, for example, in an extension to CoMpoSe it would be possible to associate styles or layouts with conditions, and that style or layout would only be executed if the condition was true. In that way, it's possible to build extremely powerful systems.

So, let's get started with the base of the application.

The Database

First of all, you need to create a new application and configure the database for it. I'll call the application "compose," but feel free to name it whatever you'd like. So, generate it with the rails program, add a require for jdbc_adapter to the config/environment.rb file, and then edit the config/database.yml file to suit your needs. After that's done, you need to create the migrations that you'll use for this project. As I mentioned before, we're interested in creating five models. You'll also add a sixth migration that adds the article name, so you can see how that's done.

Go ahead and create the models:

```
jruby script/generate model User
jruby script/generate model Path
jruby script/generate model Style
jruby script/generate model Layout
jruby script/generate model Article
```

After all the required files have been created, you should also add the sixth migration:

```
jruby script/generate migration AddArticleName
```

After everything has been generated, it's time to define the tables. You begin with users, which is basically a list of usernames and passwords, just like in the Shoplet application (see Listing 7-1).

Listing 7-1. *db/migrate/001_create_users.rb*

```
class CreateUsers < ActiveRecord::Migration
  class User < ActiveRecord::Base; end

  def self.up
    create_table :users do |t|
      t.column :username, :string
      t.column :password, :string
    end

    User.create :username => 'admin',
                :password => 'admin'
  end

  def self.down
    drop_table :users
  end
end
```

You need to create an initial user, with a known username and password, so you can bootstrap the system. This migration is basically the same as the corresponding one in Shoplet (see Listing 7-2).

Listing 7-2. *db/migrate/002_create_paths.rb*

```ruby
class CreatePaths < ActiveRecord::Migration
  def self.up
    create_table :paths do |t|
      t.column :path, :string
      t.column :layout_id, :integer
      t.column :name, :string
    end
  end

  def self.down
    drop_table :paths
  end
end
```

A path should have a name, a path that is the primary mapping string, and an associated layout (see Listing 7-3).

Listing 7-3. *db/migrate/003_create_styles.rb*

```ruby
class CreateStyles < ActiveRecord::Migration
  class StyleType < ActiveRecord::Base; end

  def self.up
    create_table :style_types do |t|
      t.column :name, :string
    end

    StyleType.create :name => 'CSS'
    StyleType.create :name => 'XSLT'

    create_table :styles do |t|
      t.column :name, :string
      t.column :style_type_id, :integer
      t.column :data, :text
    end
  end

  def self.down
    drop_table :styles
    drop_table :style_types
  end
end
```

The migration for styles is a bit more complex, because you first need to create a table for style types, and populate it with the values CSS and XSLT. You could have saved this information in a string field in the style table, but it's good database design to externalize this information. That way, you don't have to change things in many different places should you decide to add a new style type.

A style is just a load of data that has a name and a type.

As you can see in Listing 7-4, a Layout is a collection of styles in a specified sorting order. You save this information in a separate table called stylings. You could have used a join table for this purpose, but when adding an attribute such as sort, it makes sense to have the styling connection as a fully featured model object. You'll see how this makes sense later on, when looking at the model classes.

Listing 7-4. *db/migrate/004_create_layouts.rb*

```
class CreateLayouts < ActiveRecord::Migration
  def self.up
    create_table :layouts do |t|
      t.column :name, :string
    end

    create_table :stylings  do |t|
      t.column :layout_id, :integer
      t.column :style_id, :integer
      t.column :sort, :integer
    end
  end

  def self.down
    drop_table :layouts
    drop_table :stylings
  end
end
```

Listing 7-5 defines the migration for articles. An article should have a content type, so you create a table for that first, and add three values for now.

Listing 7-5. *db/migrate/005_create_articles.rb*

```
class CreateArticles < ActiveRecord::Migration
  class ContentType < ActiveRecord::Base; end

  def self.up
    create_table :content_types do |t|
      t.column :name, :string
    end

    ContentType.create :name => 'RedCloth'
    ContentType.create :name => 'BlueCloth'
    ContentType.create :name => 'text'
```

```
    create_table :articles do |t|
      t.column :path_id, :integer
      t.column :subject, :string
      t.column :content, :text
      t.column :content_type_id, :integer
      t.column :user_id, :integer
      t.column :layout_id, :integer
    end
  end

  def self.down
    drop_table :articles
    drop_table :content_types
  end
end
```

We'll take a look at the meaning of RedCloth and BlueCloth later on. However, as you can see, an article is associated with a path; it has a subject, content, and a content type. It's also associated with the user who created it, and an optional layout. However, something is missing. You know that paths had a path attribute that could help you select them, but how can a controller know, from a request, which article to render for that path? Clearly, a field for article name is missing. So, the last command you executed, to create a migration called AddArticleName, should do that (see Listing 7-6).

Listing 7-6. *db/migrate/006_add_article_name.rb*

```
class AddArticleName < ActiveRecord::Migration
  def self.up
    add_column :articles, :name, :string
  end

  def self.down
    remove_column :articles, :name
  end
end
```

Here, you just add a new column to the articles table, called name, which contains the pattern to match against when trying to find the correct article.

Wow. That was many database definitions quickly. Now, let's migrate this and take a look at the corresponding models:

```
jruby -S rake db:migrate
```

The Model

After creating the database, it's time to get the model in shape. You aren't adding validations or testing at the moment, just so you can get something working fast. You'll go through the models one at a time in the same order as you created them in the database. There's almost nothing new here, so I'll present the model files straight up. Let's begin with the User model:

```
class User < ActiveRecord::Base
  has_many :articles
end
```

Next up, create the Path model:

```
class Path < ActiveRecord::Base
  belongs_to :layout
  has_many :articles
end
```

Now, styles are a little bit more complicated. One reason for this is that you need to create a new file for the model called app/models/style_type.rb:

```
class StyleType < ActiveRecord::Base
  has_many :styles
end
```

Next, create the Style model:

```
class Style < ActiveRecord::Base
  belongs_to :style_type
  has_many :stylings, :order => 'stylings.sort'
  has_many :layouts, :through => :stylings, :order => 'stylings.sort'
end
```

As you can see here, you have a few new things. First of all, you use the Style model, and order it. You might remember that you created a table for stylings in the migration for layouts. The model association between Style and Layout is mediated through stylings. This works mostly the same way as a join table, but it lets us add attributes to the association in a way that's much easier than has_and_belongs_to_many. You can still work with these associations in the regular has_many ways.

The next model you should look at is the one for Layout:

```
class Layout < ActiveRecord::Base
  has_many :stylings, :order => 'stylings.sort'
  has_many :styles, :through => :stylings, :order => 'stylings.sort'
  has_many :articles
  has_many :paths
end
```

Here you see the inverse of the relationship, sorted the same way. You need to create the styling model by hand, so add a new file called app/models/styling.rb:

```
class Styling < ActiveRecord::Base
  belongs_to :style
  belongs_to :layout
end
```

Finally, you need a new file called app/models/content_type.rb so you can add the Article model, too. You should define ContentType like this:

```
class ContentType < ActiveRecord::Base
  has_many :articles
end
```

Add Article like this:

```
class Article < ActiveRecord::Base
  belongs_to :user
  belongs_to :content_type
  belongs_to :path
  belongs_to :layout

  def matcher
    Regexp.new('^'+self.name+'$')
  end
end
```

Notice that you use the name attribute to create a new regular expression that's anchored at both ends. That means the matching should only be done on a complete string. You'll see later how you use this part of the model. This is all there is to our model at the moment. It will be more complicated later, though.

Some Layout

Well, you have the model in place—at least partly. It's time to add some looks, and then to start work on the administrative user interface. It makes sense to get the basic style sheet in place before you start work. A layout will also be handy, because you have to think about how the overall navigation should work to get the layout in place.

First of all, you need to add a style sheet. Add a file called public/stylesheets/compose.css to your project, and add these definitions:

```
body {
  margin: 0px;
  padding: 0px;
}

h3 {
  font-size: 1em;
  font-weight: bold;
}

h2 a {
  text-decoration: none;
  color: black;
}
```

```
h3 a {
  text-decoration: none;
  color: black;
}

a {
  text-decoration: none;
  font-weight: bold;
}

thead td {
  font-weight: bold;
}

.topMenu {
  padding-top: 20px;
  border: 1px solid black;
  border-top: none;
  font-family: arial, sans-serif;
  background-color: #CCCCEE;
}

table {
  text-align: center;
}

.centered {
  display: block;
  margin-left: auto;
  margin-right: auto;
}

.main {
  padding: 30px;
  color: dark-grey;
  text-align: center;
}
```

The only interesting part of the CSS file is the centered class. There are reasons that this is hard to do consistently in HTML, so using a CSS class such as this for centering is quite useful.

You're going to change the route definition for your application before doing anything else. Open up config/routes.rb, comment out all lines beginning with map.connect, and add this line instead:

```
map.admin 'admin/:controller/:action/:id', :controller => 'styles'
```

This makes the administration parts easily recognized by the system, and defaults to the styles controller, which you'll create soon. In the next chapter, you'll add some more definitions to this routing, but for now it's fine to leave it like this.

The final part of the layout for the administrative parts is a layout file. Open a new file called app/views/layouts/admin.rhtml and add HTML that looks like this:

```
<html>
<head>
  <title>CoMpoSe: <%=controller.action_name%> <%=h params[:controller]%></title>
  <%= stylesheet_link_tag 'compose' %>
  <%= javascript_include_tag :defaults %>
</head>
<body>
  <table width="100%" height="100%">
    <tr>
      <td class="topMenu" align="center" valign="top" height="100">
        <h2>CoMpoSe</h2>
        <h3>Administration</h3>
        <p align="center">
          <%= link_to 'Users', :controller => 'users' %> -
          <%= link_to 'Styles', :controller => 'styles' %> -
          <%= link_to 'Layouts', :controller => 'layouts' %> -
          <%= link_to 'Paths', :controller => 'paths' %> -
          <%= link_to 'Articles', :controller => 'articles' %>
        </p>
        <% if @loggedin %>
        <p align="right"><%= link_to 'Log out', :controller=>'auth',
                                     :action=>'logout'%></p>
        <% end %>
      </td>
    </tr>
    <tr>
      <td class="main" valign="top" align="center">
        <p style="color: green"><%= flash[:notice] %></p>
        <p style="color: red"><b><%= flash[:error] %></b></p>

        <%= yield %>
      </td>
    </tr>
  </table>
</body>
</html>
```

You're using several things from the Shoplet application here, especially checking for the @loggedin instance variable, and providing a logout action on the auth controller. You can also see that you have five parts of the system, one for each model you'd like to be able to administrate. With this file added, you're ready to get started on the user interface.

Administration Interface

You'll create the administrative user interface one controller at a time, beginning with the easiest. I'll try to keep the descriptions short, but still include the information you need to follow along. This interface will also have a few more bits of Ajax functionality, mostly in the administration of Layouts.

Users

The User controller is very much based on the scaffolding, so go ahead and generate a scaffold for User. Then open up the generated controller and remove the show, new, edit, and update methods. Also go ahead and remove the files app/views/users/show.rhtml, app/views/users/new.rhtml, and app/views/users/edit.rhtml, because those aren't needed anymore. Next, edit the list method to look like this:

```
def list
  @user_pages, @users = paginate :users, :per_page => 10
  @user = User.new
end
```

Because you don't have a separate new action anymore, you need to add a form to the list page that creates a new user. That is much simplified by putting a blank user model in an instance variable too. At this point you should also make sure that the controller uses the admin layout by adding this directive beneath the row that starts the class:

```
layout "admin"
```

You need to change the create method too, because it will redirect to the new action if something goes wrong. That will fail because there is no new action anymore. So, change it into this:

```
def create
  @user = User.new(params[:user])
  if @user.save
    flash[:notice] = 'User was successfully created.'
    redirect_to :action => 'list'
  else
    @user_pages, @users = paginate :users, :per_page => 10
    render :action => 'list'
  end
end
```

The only change here is that you provide the pagination parts for the list action, and render list instead of new. The destroy method is good as it is, so now it's time to edit the view files. The _form view is good as it is too, so the only thing you need to change is the file app/views/users/list.rhtml:

```
<h1>Authenticated users</h1>

<table width="400" class="centered">
  <tr>
```

```
    <th align="left" width="100">Username</th>
    <th align="right" width="100">Password</th>
    <th align="right" width="50"></th>
    <th align="right" width="150"></th>
  </tr>

<% for user in @users %>
  <tr>
    <td align="left"><%= h user.username %></td>
    <td align="right"><%= h user.password.gsub(/./,'*') %></td>
    <td> </td>
    <td><%= link_to 'Remove', { :action => 'destroy', :id => user },
                    :confirm => 'Are you sure?', :post => true %></td>
  </tr>
<% end %>
</table>

<%= link_to 'Previous page', { :page =>
        @user_pages.current.previous } if @user_pages.current.previous %>
<%= link_to 'Next page', { :page =>
        @user_pages.current.next } if @user_pages.current.next %>

<br />

<h1>New user</h1>

<%= start_form_tag :action => 'create' %>
  <%= render :partial => 'form' %>
  <%= submit_tag "Create" %>
<%= end_form_tag %>
```

This view looks very much like the one for Shoplet users, actually. Note that you have a partial at the bottom where you can create new users. The table that lists users is centered through the CSS class called centered.

You can now start up the web server and try this controller out. This will allow you the chance to look at the new layout too. So, start it up and visit http://localhost:3000/admin/users.

Paths

The Path model is easy to administrate. We're interested in working on just three attributes: name, path, and default layout. Because this is the case, beginning with a basic scaffold seems like a good idea:

```
jruby script/generate scaffold Path
```

You can begin by removing the file app/views/paths/show.rhtml, because that isn't necessary. Next, let's start editing the controller, making it do what you want it to. First of all, you need to make sure the admin layout is used. You should also remove the show action. It's mostly good enough now, except for one detail. You want the administrator to be able to choose a default layout from among the available ones. Edit the new method so that information is provided too:

```
def new
  @path = Path.new
  @layouts = Layout.find :all, :order => 'name'
end
```

Also, you need to change the create, edit, and update actions in a similar manner:

```
def create
  @path = Path.new(params[:path])
  if @path.save
    flash[:notice] = 'Path was successfully created.'
    redirect_to :action => 'list'
  else
    @layouts = Layout.find :all, :order => 'name'
    render :action => 'new'
  end
end

def edit
  @path = Path.find(params[:id])
  @layouts = Layout.find :all, :order => 'name'
end

def update
  @path = Path.find(params[:id])
  if @path.update_attributes(params[:path])
    flash[:notice] = 'Path was successfully updated.'
    redirect_to :action => 'show', :id => @path
  else
    @layouts = Layout.find :all, :order => 'name'
    render :action => 'edit'
  end
end
```

This is all you need to do to get the Path controller working as you want it to. The next step is to change the views, and as it happens, they don't need much editing either. First of all, the list view needs to be changed a little bit:

```
<h1>Listing paths</h1>

<table width="400" class="centered">
  <tr>
```

```
      <th width="150" align="left">Name</th>
      <th width="150" align="right">Path</th>
      <th width="50"></th>
      <th width="50"></th>
    </tr>

<% for path in @paths %>
    <tr>
      <th width="150" align="left"><%= link_to h(path.name),
                        { :action => 'edit', :id => path }%></th>
      <th width="150" align="right"><%= h path.path%></th>
      <th width="50"></th>
      <td><%= link_to 'Destroy', { :action => 'destroy', :id => path },
                        :confirm => 'Are you sure?', :post => true %></td>
    </tr>
<% end %>
</table>

<%= link_to 'Previous page', { :page =>
            @path_pages.current.previous } if @path_pages.current.previous %>
<%= link_to 'Next page', { :page =>
            @path_pages.current.next } if @path_pages.current.next %>

<br />

<%= link_to 'New path', :action => 'new' %>
```

Second, the form for new and edit also needs to be changed. Most of what is there is good enough, but you need to add a field for the layout selection:

```
<%= error_messages_for 'path' %>

<!--[form:path]-->
<p><label for="path_name">Name</label><br/>
<%= text_field 'path', 'name'  %></p>

<p><label for="path_path">Path</label><br/>
<%= text_field 'path', 'path'  %></p>

<p><label for="path_layout_id">Layout</label><br/>
<%= select 'path', 'layout_id', @layouts.collect {|l| [l.name, l.id]} %></p>
<!--[eoform:path]-->
```

As you can see, you use the select helper. It takes care of everything for you; you just need to provide an array of arrays, where the first entry is what should be displayed as the option caption, and the second entry is the value that should be sent to the server. Rails automatically makes select the correct option when editing an existing value. Now everything is finished enough so that you can test it. Visit http://localhost:3000/admin/paths and see how it looks.

Styles

The basis of Style administration should also be built on scaffolding, so go ahead and create it. Also remove the new.rhtml and show.rhtml files, because those won't be needed. As with all other parts of this user interface, you should make the controller use the admin layout. You should also remove the show action and the create action from the controller. You should change the new action into this:

```
def new
  @style = Style.create :name => 'NEW STYLE',
              :style_type => StyleType.find_by_name('CSS'), :data => ''
  goto_list
end
```

You create a new style by adding default values and then redirecting to the list action. You should add the helper method goto_list at the bottom of the class:

```
private
def goto_list
  redirect_to admin_url(:controller => 'styles', :action => 'list')
end
```

Here's something new: usually, when using redirect_to you can just provide the parameters to construct the URL directly to it. But in this case, you want the generated URL to begin with "/admin." Therefore, you use an automatically generated method, which is based on the route you created earlier. If you create a named route, you'll be able to create URLs from that route by taking the name and appending "_url" to it to get the method name to use.

You need to have all available style types on hand when editing a Style, so the edit action should look like this:

```
def edit
  @style = Style.find(params[:id])
  @style_types = StyleType.find :all
end
```

You need to update the update action in the same manner; it should also use goto_list:

```
def update
  @style = Style.find(params[:id])
  if @style.update_attributes(params[:style])
    flash[:notice] = 'Style was successfully updated.'
    goto_list
  else
    @style_types = StyleType.find :all
    render :action => 'edit'
  end
end
```

Finally, the destroy method should use the goto_list helper:

```
def destroy
  Style.find(params[:id]).destroy
  goto_list
end
```

As you might have noticed at this point, the controllers for these applications you're creating aren't complicated at all. In fact, if your controllers become complicated, that is a sure sign that you should refactor them, and put more code in external libraries instead.

Once again, the controller is finished, and you should go ahead and work on the views. First of all, open up the list.rhtml file and edit it to look something like this:

```
<h1>Listing styles</h1>

<table width="500" class="centered">
  <tr>
    <th width="200" align="left">Name</th>
    <th width="150" align="right">Type</th>
    <th width="150" align="right"></th>
  </tr>

<% for style in @styles %>
  <tr>
    <td align="left"><%=link_to h(style.name), admin_url(
        :controller => params[:controller],:action => 'edit',
        :id => style)%></td>
    <td align="right"><%=h style.style_type.name %></td>
    <td align="right"><%= link_to 'Destroy', admin_url(
        :controller => params[:controller], :action => 'destroy',
        :id => style), :confirm => 'Are you sure?',
        :post => true if style.stylings.empty?%></td>
  </tr>
<% end %>
</table>

<%= link_to 'Previous page', { :page =>
       @style_pages.current.previous } if @style_pages.current.previous %>
<%= link_to 'Next page', { :page =>
       @style_pages.current.next } if @style_pages.current.next %>

<br />

<%= link_to 'Create new style', admin_url(:controller =>
                    params[:controller],:action => 'new') %>
```

As you can see, you've used the admin_url helper again here. Also notice that you only show the destroy link if the style has no associated stylings. That means you can only remove a style that isn't used by anyone.

The _form.rhtml file doesn't need to change so much:

```
<%= error_messages_for 'style' %>

<!--[form:style]-->
<p><label for="style_name">Name</label><br/>
<%= text_field 'style', 'name' %></p>
```

```
<p><label for="style_data">Content</label><br/>
<%= text_area 'style', 'data'  %></p>

<p><label for="style_style_type">Style Type</label><br/>
<%= select 'style', 'style_type_id',
            @style_types.collect {|p| [ p.name, p.id ] },{}%></p>
<!--[eoform:style]-->
```

You just add a select box over all style types in the same way you did with the paths. That's all there is to the administration of styles. Try it out now!

Layouts

Editing layouts is much more interesting than the other parts we've been discussing up until now. Because a layout is basically an ordered list of styles, you need to have a good way to order something. Ajax and the Prototype library will provide exactly what you need to accomplish this. But first, begin as always by generating a scaffold.

Also as before, start by removing the show.rhtml and new.rhtml views. As usual, you'll begin by adding the admin layout to the layouts controller. Also, remove the show action and the new action. You won't do everything in the controller in one go, because the Ajax implementation needs a few helpers. It makes more sense to look at those methods later. But first, change the list action:

```
def list
  @layout_pages, @layouts = paginate :layouts, :per_page => 10
  @layout = Layout.new
end
```

Also, change the create action:

```
def create
  @layout = Layout.new(:name => 'New layout')
  if @layout.save
    flash[:notice] = 'Layout was successfully created.'
    redirect_to :action => 'list'
  else
    @layout_pages, @layouts = paginate :layouts, :per_page => 10
    render :action => 'list'
  end
end
```

The edit action needs to know which styles are available:

```
def edit
  @layout = Layout.find(params[:id])
  @styles = Style.find :all, :order => 'name'
end
```

Finally, update the update action by removing the reference to the show action, and change that to edit instead. That's about it for now. Open up list.rhtml and change it into this:

```
<h1>Listing layouts</h1>

<table width="500" class="centered">
  <tr>
    <th width="350" align="left">Name</th>
    <th width="150" align="right"></th>
  </tr>
<% for layout in @layouts %>
  <tr>
    <td align="left"><%= link_to h(layout.name),
              :action => 'edit', :id => layout %></td>
    <td align="right"><%= link_to 'Destroy',
            { :action => 'destroy', :id => layout },
              :confirm => 'Are you sure?', :post => true %></td>
  </tr>
<% end %>
</table>

<%= link_to 'Previous page', { :page =>
        @layout_pages.current.previous } if @layout_pages.current.previous %>
<%= link_to 'Next page', { :page =>
        @layout_pages.current.next } if @layout_pages.current.next %>

<br />
<%= link_to 'Create new layout', {:action => 'create'}, :post => true %>
```

There's nothing new here. You just change the code to match the other views. The _form.rhtml file needs some more changes, though. This is where the Ajax magic happens, so I'm going to go through it thoroughly:

```
<%= error_messages_for 'layout' %>

<!--[form:layout]-->
<p><label for="layout_name">Name</label><br/>
<%= text_field 'layout', 'name'  %></p>

<div id="styles">
<%= render :partial => 'style_list' %>
</div>
<p>
<%= select_tag 'layout_add_style',@styles.inject("") {|sum, s|
            sum << "<option value=\"#{s.id}\">
                            #{s.name} (#{s.style_type.name})
                      </option>" } %>
<%= link_to_remote 'Add style', :update => 'styles',
```

```
                    :url=>"'+theUrl+'", :before => "theUrl = '#{url_for(
                :action => 'add_style', :id => @layout)
                }?style='+$(layout_add_style).value" %>
</p>
<!--[eoform:layout]-->
```

There are two important parts in this file, both new. First, the partial called `style_list` is wrapped inside a `div` element. This allows you to switch the content of that element when you need it later. Before we look at that partial, let's unravel the `select` tag at the next line. You cannot use the `select` helper in this situation, because you don't want the value to be set when submitting the form. Instead, you use this `select` tag to add styles dynamically to the preceding style list. You do this with `link_to_remote`.

`link_to_remote` does the same thing as the `link_to` helper, with the exception that `link_to_remote` uses Ajax to make the call, without submitting the complete web page. The `update` parameter causes the `div` with id `"styles"` to be updated with the return value from the call. You need to do some hacking with the URL for the link, so that the currently chosen style is part of the submit to the server. The other part of adding styles is the `add_style` action in `layouts_controller`:

```
def add_style
  @layout = Layout.find(params[:id])
  @style = Style.find(params[:style])
  newSort = 1
  newSort = @layout.stylings.max {|a,b| a.sort <=>
                       b.sort }.sort+1 unless @layout.stylings.empty?
  @layout.stylings.create :layout => @layout,
                                    :style => @style,
                                    :sort => newSort

  render :partial => 'style_list'
end
```

As you can see, you add the new style to the layout in question, and then you find a new sort value that places the new style at the last point in the list. After that, you render the partial `style_list` and return it.

The `style_list` partial should look like this:

```
<ol id="styles-list">
  <% for styling in @layout.stylings %>
  <li id="item_<%=styling.id%>" style="cursor:move;">
    <%=styling.style.name%> (
          <%=styling.style.style_type.name%>)
        <%= link_to_remote 'Remove', :update => 'styles',
              :url=>{:action => 'remove_style', :id => @layout,
                         :styling => styling} %>
  </li>
  <% end %>
</ol>
```

```
<%= sortable_element 'styles-list',
    :url => {:action => 'sort', :id => @layout},
    :complete => visual_effect(:highlight, 'styles-list') %>
```

This is also a bit complicated. First of all, this style list is an ordered list. You need to provide an id to the ol element, so the sorting can happen later. Walk through each styling and
create an li tag for it, with ids that begin with item_ and the ID of the styling. There's also a
link to remove_style for each entry. That is a link_to_remote element too, and it updates the
styles element in the same way as add_style. We'll look at remove_style soon. First though,
look at the sortable_element part in the preceding code. That helper makes the magic Ajax
tricks available so your list can be sorted by drag and drop. At the first row, you name the element to sort. The second line provides the url, which is the action sort. Third, you provide an
optional complete action that is a visual_effect called highlight. There are many ways of
providing visual effects for the user with Ajax, and it's usually a good idea to provide a cue that
an update has happened.

So, the remove_style action is easy. You just remove the styling provided from the layout,
and then render the style_list partial again:

```
def remove_style
  @layout = Layout.find(params[:id])
  @layout.stylings.delete Styling.find(params[:styling])

  render :partial => 'style_list'
end
```

The sort action isn't that complicated either:

```
def sort
  @layout = Layout.find(params[:id])
  @layout.stylings.each do |styling|
    styling.sort = params['styles-list'].index(styling.id.to_s) + 1
    styling.save
  end
  render :nothing => true
end
```

First you fetch the layout to sort, then you change the sort value for each styling based on
the parameters for the styles list element. Finally, nothing should be rendered, because the
sort action doesn't update anything on the page.

Well, go ahead and try it out. The sort action is slick and useful. If you look back at the
code for the style_list partial, you can see that you use CSS to provide a hand as a cue that
you can drag and drop the elements in the list. This technique is incredibly useful when handling ordered data that it should be possible to update in some way. There are also many
variations on the looks of the sorted list. You can use the different HTML tags available to provide lists without numbers, or through CSS you can have lists with Roman numerals instead.
You'll also notice that the numbers follow along when you're dragging an element. In
Figure 7-1 you can see how editing of Layouts should look.

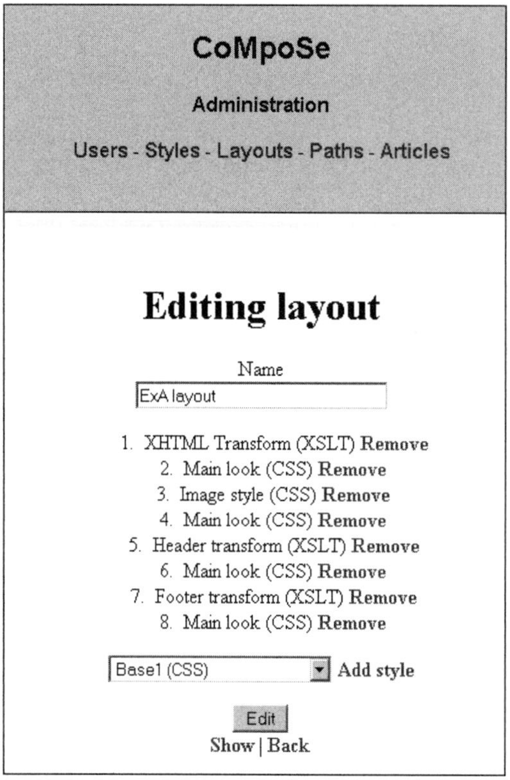

CoMpoSe

Administration

Users - Styles - Layouts - Paths - Articles

Editing layout

Name

ExA layout

1. XHTML Transform (XSLT) **Remove**
2. Main look (CSS) **Remove**
3. Image style (CSS) **Remove**
4. Main look (CSS) **Remove**
5. Header transform (XSLT) **Remove**
6. Main look (CSS) **Remove**
7. Footer transform (XSLT) **Remove**
8. Main look (CSS) **Remove**

Base1 (CSS) ▼ Add style

Edit

Show | Back

Figure 7-1. *Editing a layout*

Articles

Finally, it's time to edit articles. I know you've been waiting for it. Articles are quite simple. You only need a big text box and some smaller ones. The only thing complicating matters is the need for a way to preview articles. You won't add that at this point, but defer that action until the next chapter. You will add the button to request a preview, though.

Begin by—as always—creating a scaffolding. Then remove the show view and the corresponding show action in the controller. You'll begin with the controller again. The articles controller should use the admin layout; the list action can remain as is. However, the new action needs to include a call to the form method:

```
def new
  @article = Article.new
  form
end
```

The form helper method provides a few things you'll need in several actions. It looks like this:

```
private
def form
  @content_types = ContentType.find :all, :order => 'name'
  @layouts = Layout.find :all, :order => 'name'
  @paths = Path.find :all, :order => 'name'
end
```

It doesn't do anything complicated at all; rather, it just provides all the model objects you need to render most of the article pages. In the same manner, the create method needs to call form before rendering the new view:

```
def create
  @article = Article.new(params[:article])
  if @article.save
    flash[:notice] = 'Article was successfully created.'
    redirect_to :action => 'list'
  else
    form
    render :action => 'new'
  end
end
```

edit works the same way too:

```
def edit
  @article = Article.find(params[:id])
  form
end
```

Finally, edit the update method, which will change some when you add the ability to preview an article. However, right now it should look like this:

```
def update
  @article = Article.find(params[:id])
  if @article.update_attributes(params[:article])
    flash[:notice] = 'Article was successfully updated.'
    redirect_to :action => 'list'
  else
    form
    render :action => 'edit'
  end
end
```

Once again, adding the invocation of the form method is the only thing that has changed. Ideally, your controller should now be in good shape for working with articles, but you still need to edit the views. The `list` view is close to the original, except that you only display select elements. For example, it isn't a good idea to display the article content in the list:

```
<h1>Listing articles</h1>

<table width="800" class="centered">
  <tr>
    <th width="50" align="left">ID</th>
    <th width="200" align="left">Subject</th>
    <th width="150" align="left">Name</th>
    <th width="100" align="right">Content Type</th>
    <th width="100" align="right">Layout</th>
    <th width="100" align="right">Path</th>
    <th width="50" align="right"></th>
    <th width="50" align="right"></th>
  </tr>

<% for article in @articles %>
  <tr>
    <td width="50" align="left"><%=h article.id %></td>
    <td width="200" align="left"><%= link_to h(article.subject),
              :action => 'edit', :id => article %></td>
    <td width="150" align="left"><%= h article.name %></td>
    <td width="100" align="right"><%= h(article.content_type.name) %>
            </td>
    <td width="100" align="right">
          <%= h(article.layout.name) if article.layout %></td>
    <td width="100" align="right"><%= h(article.path.name) %></td>
    <td width="50" align="right"> </td>
    <td width="50" align="right"><%= link_to 'Destroy',
                  { :action => 'destroy', :id => article },
                  :confirm => 'Are you sure?', :post => true %></td>
  </tr>
<% end %>
</table>

<%= link_to 'Previous page', { :page =>
        @article_pages.current.previous } if @article_pages.current.previous %>
<%= link_to 'Next page', { :page =>
        @article_pages.current.next } if @article_pages.current.next %>

<br />

<%= link_to 'Create new article', :action => 'new' %>
```

Instead, you need to manually list those attributes that you're interested in displaying. In this case, there are quite a few, including the article ID. At the moment, both the new.rhtml and edit.rhtml files are fine. You'll change them when it gets time to add preview, though.

Finally, change the _form.rhtml file. It should look something like this:

```
<%= error_messages_for 'article' %>

<!--[form:article]-->
<p><label for="article_subject">Subject</label><br/>
<%= text_field 'article', 'subject' %></p>

<p><label for="article_name">Name (will be used
            in the URL to identify article, can have regexp parts)</label><br/>
<%= text_field 'article', 'name' %></p>

<p><label for="article_content">Content</label><br/>
<%= text_area 'article', 'content' %></p>

<p><label for="article_content_type_id">Content Type</label><br/>
<%= select 'article', 'content_type_id',
            @content_types.collect {|c| [c.name, c.id]} %></p>

<p><label for="article_layout_id">Layout</label><br/>
<%= select 'article', 'layout_id',
            @layouts.collect {|l| [l.name, l.id]}, :include_blank => true %></p>

<p><label for="article_path_id">Path</label><br/>
<%= select 'article', 'path_id',
            @paths.collect {|p| [p.name, p.id]} %></p>
<!--[eoform:article]-->
```

There's nothing strange here. You just add the associated values, with select boxes for them. You also make sure that the captions for all fields are correct and descriptive.

This is all there is to articles. Go ahead and create some now! In the next chapter we'll take a look at how to go about rendering the content created in this interface. First you have a more pressing concern: security, or the lack thereof.

Some Security

We've neglected that this should be an administrative user interface, which means it should be protected. Of course, there is a model for users, and you've added support for updating that, but there is no real protection yet. However, as you might remember, it's simple to fix that. So, create a new controller named AdminController. It should look like this:

```
class AdminController < ApplicationController
  before_filter :authentication

  private
  def authentication
    unless session[:user_id] && User.find_by_id(session[:user_id])
      flash[:notice] = "Please log in"
```

```
      redirect_to(:controller => 'auth', :action => 'login',
                  :into => url_for(params))
    else
      @loggedin = true
    end
  end
end
```

As you can see, the code is more or less the same as the authentication parts for the Shoplet. It tries to find a user in the session, and if it's not there sends the request on to the auth controller:

```
class AuthController < ApplicationController
  layout "admin"

  def login
    if request.post?
      if user = User.find_by_username_and_password(
                params[:username], params[:password])
        session[:user_id] = user.id
        redirect_to params[:into] || admin_url(:controller => 'products')
        return
      else
        flash[:error] = "Wrong username or password"
      end
    end
    @into = params[:into]
  end

  def logout
    session[:user_id] = nil
    redirect_to url_for(:action => 'login')
  end
end
```

You also need to add a login view for the auth controller:

```
<h2>Please login with your username and password</h2>

<%= start_form_tag %>
<%= hidden_field_tag 'into', @into %>
<table width="400" class="centered">
  <tr>
    <td>Username:</td><td><%= text_field_tag 'username' %></td>
  </tr>
  <tr>
    <td>Password:</td><td><%= password_field_tag 'password' %></td>
  </tr>
```

```
<tr>
  <td colspan="2" align="right"><%= submit_tag 'Login' %></td>
</tr>
</table>
<%= end_form_tag %>
```

That's about it. You now need to make sure all the other controllers you've created inherit from the `AdminController`, and then you can try the application out. Ideally, the security should work as expected.

Summary

We've seen the first part of the CMS application. We've looked at all the parts that don't have anything to do with actual content rendering. We've seen that in most cases Rails controllers will be simple and readable. We've also taken a look at an advanced Ajax feature: using remote Ajax links to invoke code on the server asynchronously, and also how to create a list that can be sorted through dragging and dropping.

In the next chapter it's finally time to look at how to get all this working together with Java libraries. We'll look at different approaches to XML rendering and also how to use other Ruby libraries, such as BlueCloth and REXML, from your JRuby code.

■ ■ ■

## CHAPTER 8

Content Rendering

Chapter 6 explained in some detail how to use JRuby to get access to Java resources, and Chapter 7 described the implementation of most of the administrative user interface for the CoMpoSe application. This chapter is split in two parts. First of all, we're going to take a thorough look at different ways of doing content rendering. The examples here will be small standalone programs that can be executed outside Rails. In this way we can see many different ways of handling XML content, and also some other interesting approaches.

In the second part of the chapter we use what we learned from Chapters 6 and 7, and from the first part of this one, to finally create the rendering engine for CoMpoSe. The final system will be layered and use all the information available about an article, including its own data, the path it resolved through, and all layouts and styles associated with these. The final system will have some flexibility and will also be something you can extend and make powerful with little effort.

Rendering content that should be consumed by human readers is a complex task, and it can never be totally automated. A real CMS system must provide an intuitive user interface where authors can write without being troubled by layout questions, and designers can create and change looks without having impact on the articles. CoMpoSe won't be all that right now, but with some work it could be an interesting possibility. Also, it's the first application in this book to use the strengths of both Ruby (through Rails) and Java (through its XML APIs).

Let's get cracking!

Content Rendering with XML

Whether you like it or not, XML is the most common way of storing data nowadays. There are also many standards that define how content can be marked with rendering data in XML. Extensible HyperText Markup Language (XHTML) is probably the most well known of these, but there are many others. Also, it's common to define your own XML schema for content when you know the domain well.

You can do the actual handling and transformation of XML data in several different ways, and with JRuby you have even more choices in the matter. I'll talk about one approach from the Ruby world first, and then several variations using Java XML APIs.

The examples shown here won't use schema or Document Type Definitions (DTDs); that would only make the examples hard to read. But we'll make both schema validation and transformation possible in the final content rendering approach for CoMpoSe.

Most of the example programs are written to be run against the XML file called projects.xml:

```xml
<?xml version="1.0" encoding="utf-8"?>

<company>
  <projects>
    <project id="shoplet">
      <title>
        The Store: Shoplet
      </title>
      <description>
        The Shoplet application is supposed to
        teach the reader about basic Rails functionality.
      </description>
      <manager ref="hmank"/>
    </project>
    <project id="compose">
      <title>
        CoMpoSe: Content made easy
      </title>
      <description>
        CoMpoSe is a content management system,
        based on high tech buzzwords like XML, RedCloth and Rails.
      </description>
      <manager ref="slars"/>
      <manager ref="adahl"/>
    </project>
    <project id="bigbrother">
      <title>
        Big Brother, administration in a nutshell
      </title>
      <description>
        Big Brother is the swiss army knife of administration tools
      </description>
      <manager ref="adahl"/>
    </project>
  </projects>
  <managers>
    <manager id="adahl">Arne Dahl</manager>
    <manager id="hmank">Henning Mankell</manager>
    <manager id="slars">Stieg Larsson</manager>
  </managers>
</company>
```

Ruby XML

In Ruby, there are three ways to work with XML data. The fastest way for small XML documents is to parse them using regular expressions. Because Ruby's text processing support is fairly good, this approach scales better than you would expect, but it's not good enough for a real application. The second approach is the Ruby `libxml2` bindings. These are fast, due to being written in C, but the API isn't really Ruby-like. Further, it doesn't work in JRuby, so I won't cover it at all in this book. The third approach—which this section is about—is called REXML, and it's part of the Ruby standard distribution. It conforms to XML 1.0, but it doesn't do validation.

A simple test program will show you how to walk all the nodes in the file and print their names and attributes (see Listing 8-1).

Listing 8-1. *rexml_print.rb*

```ruby
require 'rexml/document'
include REXML

input = File.new(ARGV[0])
doc = Document.new input


def print_element(el, indent=0)
  print " "*indent
  print el.name
  if el.attributes.size > 0
    print ": #{el.attributes.map{|k,v| "#{k}=>#{v}"}}"
  end
  if el.text && el.text.strip.size > 0
    print ": #{el.text.strip}"
  end
  puts
  el.elements.each { |e|
    print_element(e,indent+2)
  }
end


doc.elements.each { |e|
  print_element e
}
```

You can run the file like this:

```
jruby rexml_print.rb projects.xml
```

This would generate output that looks like this:

```
company
  projects
    project: id=>shoplet
```

```
        title: The Store: Shoplet
        description: The Shoplet application is supposed to
          teach the reader about basic Rails functionality.
        manager: ref=>hmank
    project: id=>compose
      title: CoMpoSe: Content made easy
      description: CoMpoSe is a content management system,
        based on high tech buzzwords like XML, RedCloth and Rails.
      manager: ref=>slars
      manager: ref=>adahl
    project: id=>bigbrother
      title: Big Brother, administration in a nutshell
      description: Big Brother is the swiss army knife of administration tools
      manager: ref=>adahl
  managers
    manager: id=>adahl: Arne Dahl
    manager: id=>hmank: Henning Mankell
    manager: id=>slars: Stieg Larsson
```

I'll briefly walk you through what's happening here: you walk the XML Document Object Model (DOM), printing text if there is any, attributes if any, and all sub-elements. There are other ways to walk data with REXML if you don't like the DOM flavor. You can include a `StreamListener` that you can send into a Simple API for XML (SAX) parser, which will let you do mostly the same operations. REXML also supports XPath in several nice ways. For example, you can send an XPath string to the `elements.each` method call, like this, and it would yield all manager elements in the document:

```
doc.elements.each("//manager")
```

There are a few problems with REXML, though. First of all, it's slow. It's also cumbersome to use in some places. Further, there is no support for validation with DTDs or schemas. The parsing of XML is also done in a way that introduces subtle bugs that can be hard to find. For simple XML parsing in Ruby or JRuby, REXML is still your best choice. However, for other applications you need some or all of the missing features. In those cases, it makes sense to turn to the Java XML APIs, which are generally fast, support everything you'd ever need, and aren't so hard to work with either.

Java DOM Parsing

The DOM implementation for Java has been in Java SE for a long time. It's not the easiest way to work with XML, but it works fine for most cases. We'll get right at it, and implement the same XML dumper as we did with REXML.

```
require 'java'

xparsers = javax.xml.parsers

factory = xparsers.DocumentBuilderFactory.new_instance
d = factory.new_document_builder.parse(ARGV[0])
e = d.get_document_element
```

```
def print_attributes(attrs)
  print ": "
  for i in 0...(attrs.get_length)
    print attrs.item(i)
  end
end

def print_element(el, indent=0)
  print " "*indent
  print el.get_node_name
  if el.has_attributes
    print_attributes(el.get_attributes)
  end

  els = el.get_child_nodes
  str = ""
  for i in 0...(els.get_length)
    if els.item(i).get_node_type == 3
      str << els.item(i).get_node_value
    end
  end

  if str.strip.size > 0
    print ": #{str.strip}"
  end
  puts

  for i in 0...(els.get_length)
    if els.item(i).get_node_type == 1
      print_element els.item(i), indent+2
    end
  end
end
print_element e
```

Invoke this in the exact same way as the last example, and you should see almost the same output, except that the attributes are printed in a different way. As you can see, this implementation is longer, and harder to use. On the other hand, you have full control over what happens, and the DOM model is closer to W3C's specification. What makes things hard is that you can't get the text content of an element explicitly. Instead you have to iterate over the child nodes and look for text nodes (which have the type 3), and concatenate these. It's all closer to how XML works, and you can process any XML node you want, including comments and processing instructions.

Based on just these two examples, REXML obviously seems much better. But you have to remember all the extra features you get from DOM. For example, namespaces would just work. And if you wanted validations, you could set an attribute on the DocumentBuilderFactory, and XML schema or DTD validations would just work. That isn't possible with REXML.

Java SAX Parsing

The SAX API is much more useful in situations where you have a large input to handle, and don't need to keep it all in memory. For example, say you're collecting specific parts of data but don't care about the whole thing. SAX is a stream-based API, which means the different parts of the XML document are made available to you sequentially.

In Java, the easiest way to handle SAX events is by creating a subclass of DefaultHandler, and overriding the methods that provide interesting information. This means it won't be easy to make it have exactly the same output as the other examples, but we'll try to get it as close as possible. The large difference will be text handling, because there's no way to get the text inside an element until after it has been parsed.

```ruby
require 'java'

class PrintHandler < org.xml.sax.helpers.DefaultHandler
  def initialize
    @indent = 0
    @text = ""
  end

  def characters(ch, start, length)
    @text << java.lang.String.new(ch,start,length).to_s
  end

  def startElement(uri,name,qname,attrs)
    print " "*@indent
    print name
    if attrs.getLength > 0
      print ":"
      for i in 0...(attrs.getLength)
        print " #{attrs.getLocalName(i)}=>#{attrs.getValue(i)}"
      end
    end
    puts
    @indent+=2
  end

  def endElement(uri,name,qname)
    if @text.strip.length > 0
      print " "*@indent
      puts "::#{@text.strip}"
      @text = ''
    end
    @indent-=2
  end
end

xr = org.xml.sax.helpers.XMLReaderFactory.createXMLReader
```

```
handler = PrintHandler.new
xr.setContentHandler handler
xr.setErrorHandler handler

xr.parse org.xml.sax.InputSource.new(java.io.FileReader.new(ARGV[0]))
```

A quick walkthrough: `DefaultHandler` implements the `ContentHandler` and `ErrorHandler` interfaces with `null` operations. So, your `PrintHandler` overrides the `characters`, `startElement`, and `endElement` methods to provide the things you need. What happens is that `startElement` is called each time an element starts, and so on. Because you know your elements cannot contain both text and elements, you can just collect all the text in an instance variable, and then print it afterwards. As you can see, you get hold of all the necessary namespace information here, and you can also tell the `XMLReaderFactory` that you want it to validate the content. If the content is malformed, you'll get an exception.

All this is pretty straightforward. The only cumbersome part is that you have to create a new Java string from the characters sent to the `characters` method. You also need to explicitly turn it into a Ruby `String`.

A SAX-based API can be useful, because the overhead is small for most applications. It's fast and you don't need to write much code to get it working. On the other hand, sometimes you need more code to do something that doesn't come naturally to SAX APIs. In those cases you'll have to write more than the equivalent DOM solution.

Java DOM and XSLT

In my opinion, when you need to do content management of some sort, the best solution is to use XSLT to transform the XML directly into what you want it to be. When you're doing content rendering, it's great not to have to manually walk the tree or take care of the nodes. Instead, define an XSLT style sheet that defines how the output should look. In the case of printing data, it's easy, so you'll begin with the XSLT for printing the same output as the previous examples.

```
<?xml version="1.0" encoding="utf-8"?>

<xsl:stylesheet version="1.0" xmlns:xsl="http://www.w3.org/1999/XSL/Transform">
  <xsl:output method="text"/>
  <xsl:template match="*">
    <xsl:value-of select="name()"/>
    <xsl:if test="@*">: <xsl:value-of select="@*"/>
    </xsl:if>
    <xsl:text> </xsl:text>
    <xsl:value-of select="normalize-space(text())"/>
    <xsl:text>
    </xsl:text>
    <xsl:apply-templates select="*"/>
  </xsl:template>
</xsl:stylesheet>
```

Now, this XSLT document doesn't provide all the features from before. This is mostly caused by you not wanting to emit XML or HTML. You don't have any control over indent in this example, and the attribute names don't get printed either. But when you're using XSLT to generate XML or XHTML, the situation is much different. You can do some interesting things with it at that point.

The code for processing this XSLT document against an XML document could look like this:

```
require 'java'
require 'stringio'

TransformerFactory = javax.xml.transform.TransformerFactory
StreamSource = javax.xml.transform.stream.StreamSource
StreamResult = javax.xml.transform.stream.StreamResult

f = TransformerFactory.new_instance
t = f.new_transformer StreamSource.new(java.io.FileReader.new(ARGV[1]))
s = StringIO.new
t.transform StreamSource.new(java.io.FileReader.new(ARGV[0])),
            StreamResult.new(org.jruby.util.IOOutputStream.new(s))
puts s.string
```

The major problem here is that you have to create readers for the command line arguments explicitly. You use a StringIO object to capture the output, and that's about it. You use a TransformerFactory to create a new transformer from an XSLT source, and you can use the resulting transformer to transform XML documents.

The output from this example looks like this:

```
company
    projects
    project: shoplet
    title The Store: Shoplet
    description The Shoplet application is supposed
       to teach the reader about basic Rails functionality.
    manager: hmank
    project: compose
    title CoMpoSe: Content made easy
    description CoMpoSe is a content management system,
       based on high tech buzzwords like XML, RedCloth and Rails.
    manager: slars
    manager: adahl
    project: bigbrother
    title Big Brother, administration in a nutshell
    description Big Brother is the swiss army knife
       of administration tools
    manager: adahl
    managers
    manager: adahl Arne Dahl
    manager: hmank Henning Mankell
    manager: slars Stieg Larsson
```

As you can see, there are a few differences. The indent is one; the attribute keys are another. However, this approach still gives you more flexibility than the other approaches, so this is what you'll use in CoMpoSe. Because the administrator can change the XSLT too, this offers more power, allowing the user and designer to create more flexible content and design.

Other Java APIs

I haven't covered nearly all the approaches available to process XML data in Java. If you're looking around for something interesting, both XOM and JDOM are libraries that look useful, depending on what your domain is. There's also dom4j and Electric XML, which have some neat points. In fact, REXML takes much inspiration from Electric XML, so if you find yourself liking the REXML APIs, but need something faster and more validating, Electric XML could well be it.

There are also some other ways to handle content rendering. Next we'll take a look at how you can solve this problem with other technologies.

Other Ways to Render Content

XML isn't the end of content rendering. There are many alternative techniques to generate content, and especially so when you want the result to become XHTML or HTML. This section will present a few of these, in the context of Ruby, because most of the solutions are much easier to use that way. Most of them do have implementations in Java too, if speed becomes an issue.

RedCloth (Textile)

Textile is a lightweight markup language designed to be easy to read, and easy to transform to XHTML at the same time. It handles many of the worst parts about writing content in HTML, and lets you concentrate on writing, instead of writing angle brackets. RedCloth is the premier implementation of Textile in Ruby, and it's nice to work with generally. A new, faster version, called SuperRedCloth, is in development, and can also be used with JRuby. The API works almost exactly the same way, so we'll just be using regular RedCloth here. For example, say you have this text:

```
h1. Welcome to CoMpoSe

This is a small example of what you can do with something like
*Textile*. Most of what you'd like to do just works, so write everything
like you're used to, and it will be fine.

For example, a list of things could look like this:

* A thing
* Another thing
** Some subthings
** More subthings
* A final thing
```

You can also create tables and other formatting tools with Textile, but all that information is available in the documentation, which can be easily found with Google.

You can render this with a Ruby program that looks like this:

```
require 'rubygems'
require 'redcloth'

puts RedCloth.new(File.read(ARGV[0])).to_html
```

That would generate this HTML:

```
<h1>Welcome to CoMpoSe</h1>
 <p>This is a small example of what you can do with something like
 <strong>Textile</strong>.
Most of what you&#8217;d like to do just works,
so write everything like you&#8217;re used to,
and it will be fine.</p>
 <p>For example, a list of things could look like this:</p>
 <ul>
  <li>A thing</li>
  <li>Another thing
  <ul>
   <li>Some subthings</li>
   <li>More subthings</li>
  </ul>
  </li>
  <li>A final thing</li>
 </ul>
 <p>You can also create tables and other formatting tools with Textile,
but all that information is available in the documentation, which
can be easily found with Google.</p>
```

As you can see, Textile handles all strange characters automatically, by turning them into the corresponding XHTML entity.

BlueCloth (Markdown)

Markdown is close to Textile. They have the same aim: to be a small markup language that gets out of your way when trying to write content, and also to be able to generate valid XHTML from almost anything, which ends up looking more or less like you expect it to. The official aims for Markdown are to maximize readability and "publishability" of both its input and output forms.

You can take the last example and convert it into Markdown:

```
# Welcome to CoMpoSe

This is a small example of what you can do with something like
**Markdown**. Most of what you'd like to do just works, so
```

write everything like you're used to, and it will be fine.

For example, a list of things could look like this:

```
* A thing
* Another thing
* A final thing
```

You can also create tables and other formatting tools with Markdown, but all that information is available in the documentation, which can be easily found with Google.

Note that having sublists within lists doesn't work that well. You can render the preceding file with BlueCloth, like this:

```
require 'rubygems'
require 'bluecloth'

puts BlueCloth.new(File.read(ARGV[0])).to_html
```

Now you can see that the API for the basic rendering is exactly the same as RedCloth, so the learning curve isn't that big. The output will also look much like the RedCloth one:

```
<h1>Welcome to CoMpoSe</h1>

<p>This is a small example of what you can do with something like
<strong>Markdown</strong>. Most of what you'd like to do just works, so
write everything like you're used to, and it will be fine.</p>

<p>For example, a list of things could look like this:</p>

<ul>
<li>A thing</li>
<li>Another thing</li>
<li>A final thing</li>
</ul>

<p>You can also create tables and other formatting tools with Markdown,
but all that information is available in the documentation, which
can be easily found with Google.</p>
```

ERb

If you need to handle somewhat more dynamic data, then maybe ERb is for you. ERb is closer to technologies such as JSP and Active Server Pages (ASP) than BlueCloth and RedCloth. What happens is that you write data exactly like you want it to be displayed, but also input dynamic parts where you can execute any Ruby you want. You could even execute code that outputs data from other rendering engines. Here's a simple example:

```
<h1>Hello</h1>

A random number: <%= rand(100) %>
```

You enclose the Ruby code inside special tags. Everything inside these tags is executed, and the return value is turned into a string and input in the text document. To evaluate an ERb file, you can execute like this:

```
require 'erb'

puts ERB.new(File.read(ARGV[0])).result(binding)
```

Because the parsing of an ERb file is separated from the actual evaluation, first you have to create a new instance of the ERb object, and then ask it for the result. The `result` method takes a binding, which is where all the evaluations in the ERb file will be evaluated under. The result from the preceding would be this, where 16 could be any number between 0 and 99:

```
<h1>Hello</h1>

A random number: 16
```

YAML

Sometimes you don't want to specify the formatting in the content at all. You just want the content to contain structured, hierarchical data, and then format it as you see fit. In some cases XML is good for this, but if you want a more readable data format I recommend YAML:

```
Welcome to CoMpoSe:
- This is a small example of what you can do with something like
  YAML. Most of what you'd like to do just works, so write everything
  like you're used to, and it will be fine.
- "For example, a list of things could look like this:"
- - A thing
  - Another thing
  - - Some subthing
    - More subthings
  - A final thing
- You can also create tables and other formatting tools with Textile,
  but all that information is available in the documentation, which
  can be easily found with Google.
```

You still have some structure here, but almost all presentation information is gone. To render this, you need to get more low level, though. First of all, you need to load the YAML file, and then walk the tree generated and execute operations depending on where you are. Here's the program:

```ruby
require 'yaml'

content = YAML.load_file ARGV[0]

def print_para para
  case para
    when String: puts "<p>#{para}</p>"
    when Array:
      puts "<ul>"
      para.each do |el|
        print "<li>"
        print_para el
        puts "</li>"
      end
      puts "</ul>"
  end
end

content.each do |heading, c|
  puts "<h1>#{heading}</h1>"
  c.each do |e|
    print_para e
  end
end
```

The program generates output like this, when applied to the preceding YAML document:

```html
<h1>Welcome to CoMpoSe</h1>
<p>This is a small example of what you can do with something like Textile.
Most of what you'd like to do just works, so write everything
like you're used to, and it will be fine.</p>
<p>For example, a list of things could look like this:</p>
<ul>
<li><p>A thing</p>
</li>
<li><p>Another thing</p>
</li>
<li><ul>
<li><p>Some subthing</p>
</li>
<li><p>More subthings</p>
</li>
</ul>
</li>
<li><p>A final thing</p>
</li>
</ul>
<p>You can also create tables and other formatting tools with Textile,
but all that information is available in the documentation,
which can be easily found with Google.</p>
```

This approach is more verbose, but if you have specialized needs, it's good to have something like this to fall back on. When you need data-driven rendering, YAML is almost always a good choice, because it gets turned into regular Ruby data objects when parsed.

Other Solutions

There are lots of other solutions to content rendering. You could let the user input information in HTML directly. You could use RDoc (which is the format Ruby uses internally to format documentation, and incidentally the format in which I wrote the first draft of this book). An entirely different solution would be one of the Java template engines, such as JSP or Velocity. All these work fine, but you should make sure to use what's best suited for your current needs. Using a too-powerful rendering solution is likely to make things harder on your users and designers.

Finishing CoMpoSe

After a detour through content handling, it's finally time to finish the CoMpoSe application. The solution to how the application will handle content rendering will use many of the techniques already seen. There will also be support for generating intermediate content in another format, through several runs of the XSLT style sheet transformer. In that way, you can define much of the content in the same way, and then you could add provisions for outputting other data as the outermost layer.

We'll begin by taking a look at the helper classes that will handle rendering. These classes will live in the lib directory, and it's important to remember that they won't be reloaded when modified, so you should always restart the web server when changing any of these files.

Rendering Engine

The main system that collects all the different methods is found in the file lib/render_engine.rb and should look like this:

```
require 'xslt_transformer'

class RenderEngine
  include Singleton

  def render article, controller = nil
    layout = article.layout || article.path.layout
    options = { :title => article.subject }
    current = self.send :"render_content_#{article.content_type.
                name.downcase}", article.content, options, controller
    if layout
      for style in layout.styles
        current = self.send :"render_style_#{style.style_type.
                name.downcase}", style, current, options, controller
      end
    end
```

```ruby
    current
  end

  private
  def render_style_xslt style, content, options, controller
    options[:document] ||= XML::JDocument.new(content)
    opts = options.dup
    opts.delete :document
    options[:document].transform_with! style.data, opts
    options[:document].content
  end

  def render_style_css style, content, options, controller
    (options[:headlinks] ||= []) << {:href => "/style/#{style.id}",
                  :media => 'screen', :rel => 'Stylesheet', :type => 'text/css'}
    content
  end
end

require 'render_engine/redcloth'
require 'render_engine/bluecloth'
require 'render_engine/text'
```

This class is more complicated than what you've seen until now. First of all, you'll keep the XSLT transformer in another file; you require that first. The RenderEngine itself is a class that uses the Singleton module. It defines three methods: one (render) is the main entrance to rendering functionality; the other two are private helper methods. The render method first takes the layout to use, and then sends a dynamic render message based on the content type of the article. In this case, it could be bluecloth, redcloth, or text. You'll define the actual render_content_* methods later. After you've rendered the base content in this way, you iterate over the styles available in the layout and call each style with its specific method—either render_style_xslt or render_style_css. The render_style_css method is interesting, because it doesn't do anything. It just adds a new parameter to the options, so it's up to the other renderings to use this.

The XSLT renderer creates an XML::JDocument and transforms that with the data provided. You define all these operations in the XSLT transformer.

Finally, you require all available render engines for content. These are all simple (see Listings 8-2, 8-3, and 8-4).

Listing 8-2. *lib/render_engine/redcloth.rb*

```ruby
require 'redcloth'

module RenderEngine
  def render_content_redcloth content, options, controller
    RedCloth.new(content).to_html
  end
end
```

Listing 8-3. *lib/render_engine/bluecloth.rb*

```
require 'bluecloth'

module RenderEngine
  def render_content_bluecloth content, options, controller
    BlueCloth::new(content).to_html
  end
end
```

Listing 8-4. *lib/render_engine/text.rb*

```
module RenderEngine
  def render_content_text content, options, controller
    content
  end
end
```

All these just do what we saw before when talking about RedCloth and BlueCloth. In the case of text rendering, you return exactly the same content that you got.

The final part of rendering is the XSLT transformer. Because that one is a little bit more complicated I'll show it to you in pieces, explaining the different things to do.

Everything should be in a file called `lib/xslt_transformer.rb` and contained in the module XML:

```
require 'java'
require 'stringio'

module XML
  # content here
end
```

You need StringIO, because like before you're going to capture the output of the transformation into a `String`. Before that you need to define some classes, and also include some Java code:

```
class XMLError < StandardError;end
class ValidationError < XMLError;end

class RaisingErrorHandler
  include org.xml.sax.ErrorHandler
  def error exception
    raise ValidationError, exception.to_s
  end
  def fatalError exception
    raise ValidationError, exception.to_s
  end
  def warning exception
  end
end
```

```
InputSource = org.xml.sax.InputSource
StringReader = java.io.StringReader
DocumentBuilderFactory = javax.xml.parsers.DocumentBuilderFactory
TransformerFactory = javax.xml.transform.TransformerFactory
StreamSource = javax.xml.transform.stream.StreamSource
StreamResult = javax.xml.transform.stream.StreamResult
IOInputStream = org.jruby.util.IOInputStream
IOOutputStream = org.jruby.util.IOOutputStream
```

This is all standard. You just create the new Exceptions you need, and define a new implementation of ErrorHandler that raises the correct Ruby exceptions. Finally, you pull in all the Java classes you need.

The meat of the transformation is the class JDocument, which also holds state about the current content:

```
class JDocument
  attr_reader :content

  def initialize content
    @content = content
    @factory = DocumentBuilderFactory.newInstance
    @document = @factory.new_document_builder.parse input_source_for(content)
  end
end
```

The initialization creates a new DocumentBuilderFactory and parses the content with that. The next step is validation, which you won't use from the RenderEngine. However, it's still good to be able to add this later on (see Listing 8-5).

Listing 8-5. *In the JDocument Class Definition*

```
def validate_with schema
  schema = schema.content if JDocument === schema
  @factory.set_namespace_aware true
  @factory.set_validating true
  @factory.set_attribute "http://java.sun.com/xml/jaxp/properties/schemaLanguage",
  "http://www.w3.org/2001/XMLSchema"
  @factory.set_attribute "http://java.sun.com/xml/jaxp/properties/schemaSource",
  input_source_for(schema)
  builder = @factory.new_document_builder
  builder.set_error_handler RaisingErrorHandler.new
  builder.parse input_source_for(content)
end
```

You need to set a few options on the factory, and then create an InputSource for the schema provided. I'll show the input_source_for method later; it creates an InputSource in different ways depending on the type of schema. After you've set the validation options, you can just parse the content again with a RaisingErrorHandler:

```
def transform_with! style, options = {}
  style = style.content if JDocument === style
  f = TransformerFactory.new_instance
  t = f.new_transformer source_for(render_options(style,options))
  s = StringIO.new
  t.transform source_for(@content), StreamResult.new(IOOutputStream.new(s))
  @content = s.string
end
```

This transformation code does almost exactly the same thing as our previous XSLT translation example. The only new parts are the source_for and render_options methods. These are all helpers to make the code easier to read:

```
private
def render_options content, options
  options.each do |k,v|
    val = v.map{|ll| '<link ' + ll.map{|lk,lv|"#{lk}=\"#{lv}\""}.join(' ') +
                      '/>' }.join("\n")
    content.gsub! "<!--$$#{k}$$-->",val
  end
  content
end
def source_for io
  case io
    when IO: StreamSource.new(IOInputStream.new(io))
    when String: StreamSource.new(StringReader.new(io))
    else raise ArgumentError, "couldn't handle argument of type #{io.class}"
  end
end
def input_source_for io
  case io
    when IO: InputSource.new(IOInputStream.new(io))
    when String: InputSource.new(StringReader.new(io))
    else raise ArgumentError, "couldn't handle argument of type #{io.class}"
  end
end
```

The only strange part of these helpers is render_options, which allows you to add something like <!--$$headlinks$$--> to your XSLT output, which is replaced with the corresponding data generated with the link strings. This isn't dynamic enough, but you see how it would be possible to add any kind of content here. The options hash could contain blocks that generate the correct strings when called, or something similar to that.

This is all there is to the rendering of content in CoMpoSe. As said before, you can do almost anything with this code and add whatever kinds of features you'd like, but this is the basis for content rendering.

Content

You need a controller that's responsible for generating the content. It shouldn't be secured, and you don't need any views for it either:

```
jruby script/generate controller compose default_render style
rm -rf app/views/compose
```

You need two different actions for this: one for regular rendering, and one for serving style sheets. Both of these are simple. The full ComposeController should look like this:

```
require 'render_engine'

class ComposeController < ApplicationController
  def default_render
    current_path = "/#{params[:anything]}"
    paths = Path.find :all
    path = paths.detect { |p| current_path[0...p.path.length] == p.path }

    unless path
      no_such_page
      return
    end

    artid = current_path.dup
    artid[path.path] = ''

    article = path.articles.detect {|a| a.matcher =~ artid }

    unless article
      no_such_page
      return
    end

    render :text => RenderEngine.instance.render(article,self)
  end

  def style
    v = Style.find(params[:anything].to_s.to_i)
    unless v
      no_such_page
      return
    end

    render :text => v.data, :content_type => 'text/css'
  end

  private
  def no_such_page
    render :text => 'no such page', :status => 404
  end
end
```

The no_such_page helper just renders the text "no such page" with a status of 404. The style action isn't that complicated either. You try to use the anything parameter in the params hash to find a Style. If there is one, you render it with the correct content type; otherwise, you call the no_such_page action and are done with it.

Finally, the default_render action first tries to find all Paths that begin with the same string as the current request. If there is such a path, you try to find an article whose matcher matches the rest of the path, and if you find such an article you just render the text that RenderEngine generates for you.

For this to work, the routing needs to change somewhat. The new config/routes.rb should look like this:

```
ActionController::Routing::Routes.draw do |map|
  map.admin 'admin/:controller/:action/:id', :controller => 'styles'

  map.connect 'style/*anything', :controller => 'compose', :action => 'style'
  map.connect '*anything', :controller => 'compose', :action => 'default_render'
end
```

You need three different routes: one for administration, one that matches everything that begins with style, and a last one that matches anything. The special parameter *anything in routes matches absolutely anything, and makes that available in the params hash with the key :anything. In that way you can take routing in your own hands and do dynamic applications.

Previews

At this point you're almost finished, and all things needed to render content for a user work. However, as you might remember in the last chapter, I said there would be a way to add previews to article editing with small changes in the current code. Now is the time to add this support. There isn't much to it, actually. You just need to make the RenderEngine available from the articles_controller. So, open up the articles_controller.rb file and replace the update method with this:

```
def update
  if params[:preview]
    preview
  else
    commit
  end
end
```

Here you use two private helper methods, depending on if the preview parameter is provided or not. The commit helper is basically the old update method:

```
def commit
  @article = Article.find(params[:id])
  if @article.update_attributes(params[:article])
    flash[:notice] = 'Article was successfully updated.'
    redirect_to :action => 'list'
  else
    form
```

```
    render :action => 'edit'
  end
end
```

The `preview` helper should look like this:

```
def preview
  article = Article.new params[:article]
  render :text => RenderEngine.instance.render(article,self)
end
```

It's exceedingly simple to preview an article, because you don't need to find all paths and articles matching the route string. You just render the text for the `Article`. The final part you need to change is the `edit` view for articles so you can do a preview. Open `app/views/articles/edit.rhtml` and change it into this:

```
<h1>Editing article</h1>

<%= start_form_tag({:action => 'update', :id => @article},
                                    {:name => 'main_form'}) %>
  <%= render :partial => 'form' %>
  <%= submit_tag 'Edit' %>
  <%= submit_tag 'Preview', :name => 'preview',
    :onClick => "$(main_form).target='_new';return true;" %>
<%= end_form_tag %>

<%= link_to 'Show', :action => 'show', :id => @article %> |
<%= link_to 'Back', :action => 'list' %>
```

This is almost the same as before, but you added a new `submit_tag` that also needs to execute some JavaScript so the preview will open in a new window. You could also do the same thing with the `new` view, but then you'd have to replace the `create` action to check for a preview too. I leave this as an exercise.

Right now, you should start up Mongrel and try the application out. See what kinds of things you would have to add to make into a real product!

Summary

In the last three chapters we've seen how the judicious use of Java libraries can make a Rails application much better. By using native Java XML APIs that support lots of things Ruby doesn't have yet, we made an application that combines the best of both worlds.

You've also learned the mechanics of how to use JRuby's Java integration support. This will be even more important in the project we'll create next, which will use much more Java technology. We'll look at how to shift the responsibility for application and business logic to the place where it should be, and we'll also discuss the different deployment options available for an application written in JRuby on Rails.

An Administration System (Big Brother)

CHAPTER 9

■■■

A JRuby Enterprise Bean

After the last chapter's focus on XML and content rendering, we'll spend a few pages talking about a service application. For a few years, one of the most important cornerstones of Java enterprise applications has been Enterprise JavaBeans (EJBs). At the moment, EJBs are seeing a bit of a resurgence with the new EJB 3.0 standard. In this chapter, we'll focus on combining EJB3 with JRuby.

The next three chapters will describe a service application and a web interface that uses this service. We'll create that service in this chapter. It will have no user interface at all; the only way to access it will be through an EJB. The purpose of doing it this way is twofold. First, I'll show you how to wrap a JRuby engine within an EJB, and expose some operations from Ruby to EJB consumers. Second, in the next chapter, we'll be able to look at how to make JRuby on Rails use an EJB. In most situations, you'd probably have either a Java consumer that uses a Ruby EJB, or a Rails application that uses a regular EJB.

The application you create will be small, because it will be used first and foremost to show the infrastructure necessary. The service you'll expose allows a user to get named sequence values. You'll add authorization to the service, and also timestamps and the possibility to reset sequences or create them.

To make the application as easy as possible to write, you'll make use of ActiveRecord in the service engine implemented in Ruby. Further, you'll also use the JRuby classes directly, because you need to have some functionality that can't be done through BSF or JSR223.

You won't use migrations, instead resorting to regular SQL, because we don't have the framework necessary to make migrations easy to use . When it gets time to deploy the enterprise bean, you'll do that in the excellent GlassFish container. This chapter will require you to use at least Java 5, because the EJB3 standard is too tempting to resist for an application like this.

When you're through, you should have many new ideas and approaches to handle your enterprise problems. What's interesting about the EJB approach is that you deploy a regular enterprise bean, but you still get all the benefits from using Ruby. You don't even need to develop the Ruby code within the EJB framework at all; just make sure it runs correctly on its own, and then wrap the code in the EJB. In this way, you get the power of Ruby, accessible through all the major application servers in the world.

ENTERPRISE JAVABEANS

EJB is a Java API for creating managed, server-side components that provide modular construction of enterprise systems. In practice, that means EJBs define how you should write JavaBeans in a way that allows them to be deployed in an application server. The application server more or less transparently gives the bean access to enterprise capabilities such as transactions, security, modularity, declarative configuration, persistence, and management.

The first version of the specification was released in 1998 and was later enhanced under the Java Community Process. The first few versions were close to unusable, but 2.0 and 2.1 provided several important improvements. It did help that best practices had been developed at that point, and that tools and application servers were more mature. Until 2006, when EJB3 was released, the usage of EJBs declined, because most developers felt that they created more problems than they solved. Some of these problems were caused by too much XML configuration and requirements to create many classes with repetitive code.

EJB3 changed all that by making heavy use of Java 5 annotations and also providing a new version of Entity Beans based on the Java Persistence APIs (JPA). The new version doesn't require nearly as much code, and it's intuitive because you add annotations with required information directly in the business code. It also means that in the best case you don't need any configuration at all. Some people do believe that the time for EJBs is over and that more lightweight alternatives should reign. However, even if that's the case, there are many enterprise beans in the world, and it's a good bet that you'll need to work with them at some point.

There are three different types of enterprise beans, and they are different enough that it's good to talk about them separately.

Entity Beans

Entity Beans are distributed, persisted objects. You use them to talk to the database with Java Enterprise Edition. The state of the bean can be handled by the bean itself or by the container. Entity Beans are the main reason EJBs have such a bad reputation. In most circumstances, you're better off just writing your own Data Access Objects (DAOs) and using Hibernate or something similar. But once again, JPA and EJB3 have changed things. Today Entity Beans are lightweight and much closer to Hibernate and Java Data Objects (JDO) than before.

Session Beans

There are two types of session beans: stateless and stateful. Both are distributed objects, but stateful session beans retain client-specific information between calls to the same bean instance. This means you don't need to provide all information in one call, but can use more fine-grained methods. Stateless beans, on the one hand, require you to provide all information at each call, but on the other hand are lightweight for the container to maintain. Because no state needs to be preserved, any stateless session bean can handle any request.

Message-Driven Beans

Message-driven beans (MDBs) are the only bean type that cannot be invoked directly. Instead, they subscribe to JMS topics or queues, and are invoked in response to messages showing up there. This means they're substantially easier than the other varieties, because there's no need for all the handling of remote conversations. MDBs always act locally, don't have state, and it's up to the container to take care of the message handling for them.

The Sequence Database

The first thing you need to do is to create a database for the EJB service to use. Because this won't happen within the framework of Rails, I'll instead show simple SQL scripts for this, in Listing 9-1 and Listing 9-2 . You should run both of these against the MySQL database with root privileges.

Listing 9-1. *auth.sql*

```
CREATE DATABASE seq;
GRANT ALL ON seq.* TO 'seq'@'%' IDENTIFIED BY 'Sekventially';
FLUSH PRIVILEGES;

USE seq;

CREATE TABLE authorized_users (
        id int(11) DEFAULT NULL auto_increment PRIMARY KEY,
        uid varchar(255) NOT NULL,
        password varchar(50) NOT NULL
);

CREATE TABLE authorizations (
        id int(11) DEFAULT NULL auto_increment PRIMARY KEY,
        authorized_user int(11) NOT NULL,
        operation varchar(255) NOT NULL
);

INSERT INTO authorized_users(uid,password) VALUES('admin','admin');
INSERT INTO authorizations(authorized_user,operation) VALUES(1,'next');
INSERT INTO authorizations(authorized_user,operation) VALUES(1,'last_updated');
INSERT INTO authorizations(authorized_user,operation) VALUES(1,'last_updated_by');
INSERT INTO authorizations(authorized_user,operation) VALUES(1,'reset');
INSERT INTO authorizations(authorized_user,operation) VALUES(1,'create');
INSERT INTO authorizations(authorized_user,operation) VALUES(1,'current');
INSERT INTO authorizations(authorized_user,operation) VALUES(1,'list');
```

This script just creates a database called seq and a user called "seq" with full privileges to the database. Then you create two tables. The first one is called authorized_users and contains all users who can do things to the sequence database. The second contains security information. The operation field contains the name of the operation permitted, so to get started you need to add a user called "admin," and provide this user with all operations available in the system at the moment. As you'll see later on, it's easy to create new operations, so this database design makes it easy for you to change later.

The second SQL script to run looks like Listing 9-2.

Listing 9-2. *seq.sql*

```
USE seq;

CREATE TABLE sequences (
        id int(11) DEFAULT NULL auto_increment PRIMARY KEY,
        name VARCHAR(255) NOT NULL,
        updated_at DATETIME,
        last_updated_by int(11),
        sequence_value int(30)
);
```

This script contains a name, which is what you'll mostly use to refer to it. You should probably make the name unique, but let's ignore that for the moment. The name updated_at is magic in Rails; if there is such a column it will be automatically set by Rails to the current timestamp each time Rails updates that field. Very handy. You'll also save a reference to who last updated the sequence, and the current value of it. In the design I've chosen here, the current value of the sequence is the next one to give a client.

Add these tables to your database:

```
< auth.sql mysql -u root -p
< seq.sql mysql -u root -p
```

After that, you're ready to get started on the Ruby parts of the engine.

A JRuby Sequence Engine

Because you want to let the EJB use Ruby code for the business logic, it makes sense to create the Ruby code first and test it in isolation, making sure it works correctly before trying to access it through a Java application server. You'll contain the Ruby engine code in one file, and it will use ActiveRecord, but not the rest of Rails.

So, begin by requiring the necessary code:

```
require 'rubygems'
require 'active_record'
require 'active_record/connection_adapters/jdbc_adapter'
```

After you've done that, you can establish a connection to the database, like this:

```
ActiveRecord::Base.establish_connection(
        :adapter  => 'jdbc',
        :driver   => 'com.mysql.jdbc.Driver',
        :url      => 'jdbc:mysql://localhost/seq',
        :username => 'seq',
        :password => 'Sekventially'
)
```

Then you can create ActiveRecord classes for your model:

```ruby
class AuthorizedUser < ActiveRecord::Base
  has_many :authorizations, :foreign_key => 'authorized_user'
end

class Authorization < ActiveRecord::Base
  belongs_to :authorized_user, :foreign_key => 'authorized_user'
end

class Sequence < ActiveRecord::Base
  belongs_to :last_updated_by, :class_name => "AuthorizedUser",
                               :foreign_key => 'last_updated_by'
end
```

As you can see, you need to specify foreign keys for all associations, because you didn't name them according to the Rails conventions. At the moment this code is bare, but you can still do most things with it. However, you'll add several helper methods to the Sequence class later.

At the moment, you'll instead create the main class that will be used for handling the sequences. I call it BBEngine:

```ruby
class BBEngine
  def initialize(uid, cred, method)
    log "inited: #{uid.inspect}, #{cred.inspect}, #{method.inspect}"
    unless authorized?(uid, cred, method)
      log "-- not authorized"
      raise "Not authorized"
    end
    @user = AuthorizedUser.find_by_uid(uid)
    @method = method.to_sym
  end

  private
  def log str
    $stderr.puts str
  end

  def authorized?(uid, cred, method)
    v1 = AuthorizedUser.find_by_uid_and_password(uid,cred)
    if v1 && (v = v1.authorizations.find_by_operation(method.to_s))
      (!v.respond_to?(:length)) || (v.length > 0)
    else
      false
    end
  end
end
```

Notice that you create a `log` method that you use in several places. Currently, you just print the log message to `stderr`, but later you should probably make this output go to a file instead. The `initialize` method takes a UID, a password, and a method name. It checks if the user can perform that method and then raises an error if not. Otherwise it just saves the information.

The only thing missing here is the central `invoke` method. It looks like this:

```ruby
def invoke(arg)
  log "-- invoked: #{arg.inspect}"
  case @method
  when :next: Sequence.next(@user,arg)
  when :last_updated: Sequence.last_updated(arg)
  when :last_updated_by: Sequence.last_updated_by(arg)
  when :reset: Sequence.reset(@user,arg)
  when :create: Sequence.ensure_exists(@user, arg)
  when :current: Sequence.current(arg)
  when :list: Sequence.find(:all).map{|s| s.name}
  else nil
  end
end
```

At the moment, none of these invocations will work, because you haven't added the necessary helper methods to the Sequence class yet. However, before you go ahead and do that, you should provide some way to test the sequences. At the bottom of the file, add this code:

```ruby
if __FILE__ == $0
  p BBEngine.new("admin","admin","create").invoke("seq1")
  ninv = BBEngine.new("admin","admin","next")
  p ninv.invoke("seq1")
  p ninv.invoke("seq1")
  p ninv.invoke("seq1")
  p BBEngine.new("olagus","admin","admin").invoke("seq1")
  p ninv.invoke("seq1")
  p BBEngine.new("admin","admin","last_updated").invoke("seq1")
  p BBEngine.new("admin","admin","current").invoke("seq1")
  p BBEngine.new("admin","admin","current").invoke("seq1")
  p BBEngine.new("admin","admin","current").invoke("seq1")
  p BBEngine.new("admin","admin","last_updated_by").invoke("seq1")
end
```

The code that compares $0 to the value of __FILE__ is a common Ruby idiom. It checks if the currently executing file is the program running, or has been required from some other program. It's common for Ruby libraries to add code such as this, which tests the implementation, if the code in question isn't used as a library.

So, finally you need to add the rest of the Sequence implementation. Let's start with the next method:

```ruby
def self.next(user, name)
  f = find_by_name(name)
  return f.next(user) if f
end

def next(user)
  transaction do
    ss = self.sequence_value
    self.sequence_value = ss+1
    self.last_updated_by = user
    self.save!
  end
  ss
end
```

You also add a helper method named next to the class that tries to find the sequence by name, and only in that case invokes the next method on it; otherwise the method returns nil. The next method itself starts a transaction, gets the current sequence_value, increments sequence_value, and sets the last_updated_by variable. It then saves the object using the "bang" version of save. This version will raise an error if something goes wrong, and the transaction will be rolled back.

The last_updated, last_updated_by, and current methods are similar to one another:

```ruby
def self.sattr(name, attr)
  f = find_by_name(name)
  return f.send(attr) if f
end

def self.last_updated(name)
  sattr(name, :updated_at)
end

def self.last_updated_by(name)
  x = sattr(name, :last_updated_by)
  x && x.uid
end

def self.current(name)
  sattr(name, :sequence_value)
end
```

They all use a helper method called `sattr`, which will try to find the sequence by name. `sattr` invokes the `attribute` method on it if so, and otherwise returns `nil`. You use this helper to succinctly implement several methods that are similar to one another:

```
def self.reset(user, name)
  f = find_by_name(name)
  return f.reset(user) if f
end
def reset(user)
  transaction do
    self.sequence_value = 0
    self.last_updated_by = user
    self.save!
  end
end
```

The `reset` method is close to the method called `next`, except that it doesn't have to return a value, which makes it slightly easier. Finally, the `ensure_exists` method creates the sequence if it doesn't exist, and otherwise does nothing:

```
def self.ensure_exists(user, name)
  f = find_by_name(name)
  return nil if f
  create(:name => name, :last_updated_by => user, :sequence_value => 0)
end
```

With all this in place, the sequence engine should be good to go. Make sure you have the MySQL drivers on your `CLASSPATH` and execute this command:

```
jruby bb_engine.rb
```

If all goes well, you should see the data from your command line test printed.

THE GLASSFISH APPLICATION SERVER

GlassFish is a new application server specifically targeted at the Java EE 5 specification (and EJB3). The project was started in 2005, and the first release was made in 2006. The code is developed in an open source development project driven by a core of Sun developers. The application server will be part of a commercial Sun application server eventually.

Several parts of the application server are based on other components. The persistence layer was donated from Oracle and is based on its highly popular TopLink system. The web container is based on Apache Tomcat, but adds a component called Grizzly, which provides high performance New Input/Output (NIO) code for scalability and speed.

At the time of writing, GlassFish v2 was still in development, but it might already have arrived when you read this.

Installation

To install GlassFish, download the latest stable release. This will probably come in the form of an executable JAR file that you should execute. When the program has finished running, you should enter the `glassfish` directory and run the `setup.xml` file with Ant:

```
ant -f setup.xml
```

After several pages of information have scrolled by, telling you what ports have been configured and so on, it's time to start the default domain, called `domain1`. Do this by running the `asadmin` command like this:

```
bin/asadmin start-domain domain1
```

As you can see from the output, a log file is created called `domains/domain1/logs/server.log`. This is the point to look if something goes wrong while trying to debug your application after deployment.

Management

At this point, the server is running and is ready to receive requests of all kinds. There is much more configuration to do to make GlassFish production ready, but you can easily find that information online. For the moment, you'll take a look at the management console available to you, so open up a web browser and visit `http://localhost:4848`. From this interface you can do all kinds of service management. You can deploy new beans, web applications, or enterprise applications, and also handle resource configuration of all kinds. You can do highly useful things, such as deploying new JDBC data sources, or search log files.

You won't really need all those functionalities in this chapter, but it's good to have them there. Instead, when we're talking about deploying beans, just copy the JAR file into `domains/domain1/autodeploy`, and GlassFish will try to deploy it automatically. You can check the status of your bean with the management console, but for simple deployment purposes, copy and wait is the way to go.

For other purposes—for example, if you need to shut down a domain—you should use the `asadmin` script, which has an excellent help mode that tells you what you can do with it.

A JRuby Bean Wrapper

After creating all the Ruby code necessary for the sequence engine, it's finally time to wrap the code in an EJB bean. You'll create a simple stateless session bean, with a separate business interface. Because you're using EJB3, you don't need any configuration at all. So, first of all, create the business interface (see Listing 9-3).

Listing 9-3. *com/bb/BBService.java*

```
package com.bb;

import javax.ejb.Remote;

@Remote
public interface BBService {
    Object invoke(String uid, String cred, String methodName, String argument);
}
```

As you can see, you need to attach the remote annotation to the interface, but except for that it's a simple interface. Notice how the arguments you provide to the `invoke` method match the information your sequence engine needs later on.

You'll take the enterprise bean in bits and pieces, to make it slightly more digestible. First, you need a package declaration and some imports:

```
package com.bb;

import java.io.PrintStream;
import java.io.IOException;
import java.io.FileOutputStream;

import java.util.List;
import java.util.ArrayList;
import java.util.Iterator;

import javax.annotation.PostConstruct;
import javax.annotation.PreDestroy;
import javax.ejb.Stateless;

import org.jruby.Ruby;
import org.jruby.RubyArray;
import org.jruby.RubyClass;
import org.jruby.RubyException;
import org.jruby.RubyKernel;
import org.jruby.RubyString;
import org.jruby.runtime.builtin.IRubyObject;
import org.jruby.runtime.Block;
import org.jruby.javasupport.JavaUtil;
import org.jruby.exceptions.RaiseException;
```

Most of these are JRuby classes that you need to handle. Because you need more low-level access, you can't really use JSR223 or BSF to access the Ruby engine. Instead, you'll work directly with the runtime:

```
@Stateless
public class BBServiceBean implements BBService {
    private Ruby engine;
    private RubyClass engineClass;
    private PrintStream out;
}
```

A `BBServiceBean` is marked by the stateless annotation, and implements the business interface. You keep track of a Ruby engine, the class for your engine, and an output stream that is where the standard output and standard error output from Ruby will go.

Because enterprise beans doesn't really follow the regular creation mechanisms of Java objects, you shouldn't add a custom constructor for initialization. Instead, you'll add a `PostConstruct` method and a `PreDestroy` method, so you can handle the instances of your objects. These are regular methods that you mark with annotations:

```
@PostConstruct
public void init() throws IOException {
    String jruby_home = "/usr/local/jruby";
    out = new PrintStream(
        new FileOutputStream(jruby_home + "/bbengine/log"));
    System.setProperty("jruby.home",jruby_home);
    System.setProperty("jruby.base",jruby_home);
    System.setProperty("jruby.lib",jruby_home + "/lib");
    System.setProperty("jruby.script","jruby");
    System.setProperty("jruby.shell","/bin/sh");
    this.engine = Ruby.newInstance(System.in, out, out);
    List loadPaths = new ArrayList();
    loadPaths.add(jruby_home + "/bbengine/lib");
    this.engine.getLoadService().init(loadPaths);
    RubyKernel.require(engine.getModule("Kernel"),
            engine.newString("bb_engine"),Block.NULL_BLOCK);
    this.engineClass = this.engine.getClass("BBEngine");
}


@PreDestroy
public void destruct() throws IOException {
    out.close();
    this.engine = null;
}
```

You're doing several important things here. First of all, the variable jruby_home should point to the JRuby installation you want to use. You could use the JRUBY_HOME environment variable, but in some situations you won't have that, so it's better to set it here explicitly. The only downside of doing it this way is that you can't use an existing JRUBY_HOME setting. However, that's easily added.

Second, place the sequence engine code in the directory JRUBY_HOME/bbengine/lib. This code creates a log file in JRUBY_HOME/bbengine/log, and needs to know the place the sequence code is located, so it can load the class it needs. Setting the jruby variables explicitly like this is only needed when you work with the JRuby engine manually. As you can see, you create a new instance of Ruby, with explicit input and output streams. You then create a new load path list, and initialize JRuby's load service with this. After you've done that, you can finally do the equivalent of "require 'bb_engine'", and then get a handle on the BBEngine class.

The destruct method just closes your out stream and removes the reference to the Ruby engine.

The only thing missing at this point is the invoke method, and it should look like this:

```
public Object invoke(String uid, String cred, String methodName, String argument) {
    try {
        IRubyObject u, p, m, a;
        if(uid != null) {
            u = engine.newString(uid);
        } else {
            u = engine.getNil();
```

```
        }
        if(cred != null) {
            p = engine.newString(cred);
        } else {
            p = engine.getNil();
        }
        if(methodName != null) {
            m = engine.newString(methodName);
        } else {
            m = engine.getNil();
        }
        if(argument != null) {
            a = engine.newString(argument);
        } else {
            a = engine.getNil();
        }

        IRubyObject inst = engineClass.callMethod(
              engine.getCurrentContext(),"new", new IRubyObject[]{u,p,m});
        IRubyObject res = inst.callMethod(
              engine.getCurrentContext(),"invoke", a);
        if(res instanceof RubyString) {
            return res.toString();
        } else if(res.isNil()) {
            return null;
        } else if(res instanceof RubyArray) {
            List arr = new ArrayList();
            for(Iterator iter = ((RubyArray)res).iterator();iter.hasNext();) {
                arr.add(iter.next());
            }
            return arr;
        }
        return res.toString();
    } catch(RaiseException re) {
        RubyException rr = re.getException();
        if(rr != null) {
            out.println("RubyException: " + rr.inspect());
            rr.printBacktrace(out);
        } else {
            out.println("RaiseException: " + re.toString());
        }
        return null;
    }
}
```

This method is long, but it doesn't do much. First, you guard against RaiseExceptions, so you can print them out in full, and return null. Half the code then goes to checking each argument for null, and creating a Ruby string for it if it isn't null. Then you create a new instance of the BBEngine class, and send it the correct parameters. Finally, you invoke "invoke" on the BBEngine instance, with the last argument. You then need to handle the result. In this case, the return value can be either a Ruby string, nil, or a Ruby array. In the case of an array, you need to turn each item in it into the Java equivalent, which you do implicitly by iterating over it.

Now you're finished enough to compile the code. To do this, you need the jruby.jar file and the API JAR for Java Enterprise Edition (Java EE) 5. If your source code is in src, and the libraries are in lib, you can compile your code like this:

```
mkdir -p build
javac -cp lib/jruby.jar:lib/javaee.jar -d build src/org/bb/BBService*.java
```

If all goes well, you should now have the corresponding class files in your build directory. To make a JAR file that you can deploy in GlassFish, you also need all the dependencies packaged into the same JAR as these class files. To do this, first copy your mysql JAR into the build, then follow these commands:

```
cp $JRUBY_HOME/lib/asm-2.2.3.jar build
cp $JRUBY_HOME/lib/asm-commons-2.2.3.jar build
cp $JRUBY_HOME/lib/backport-util-concurrent.jar build
cp $JRUBY_HOME/lib/jline-0.9.91.jar build
cp $JRUBY_HOME/lib/jruby.jar build
cd build
jar cf ../bbservice.jar .
cd ..
```

At this point, you should have a file called bbservice.jar in the current directory. Deploy this according to the instructions in the sidebar "The GlassFish Application Server," and make sure no exceptions show up in the log for your domain.

Now the application is deployed, but it would sure be nice to be able to see that it works as well. So, you're going to create a small JRuby script that lets you test operations against the service. But first, you need a wrapper that adds some things to the CLASSPATH before you execute jruby (see Listing 9-4).

Listing 9-4. *runjr*

```
#!/bin/sh

GLASSFISH=/usr/local/glassfish
DOMAIN=${GLASSFISH}/domains/domain1
export CLASSPATH=${CLASSPATH}:${GLASSFISH}/lib/appserv-rt.jar
export CLASSPATH=${CLASSPATH}:${GLASSFISH}/lib/j2ee.jar
export CLASSPATH=${CLASSPATH}:${GLASSFISH}/lib/j2ee-svc.jar
export CLASSPATH=${CLASSPATH}:${GLASSFISH}/lib/javaee.jar
export CLASSPATH=${CLASSPATH}:${DOMAIN}/autodeploy/bbservice.jar

jruby $*
```

In this script, you need to add the correct path to your GlassFish installation, and also to the place where your `bbservice.jar` file is located. Now that you have all the `CLASSPATH` variables you need, you can create a small script to use the service. This is exceedingly easy:

```
require 'java'

import javax.naming.InitialContext

ic = InitialContext.new
x = ic.lookup("com.bb.BBService")
x.invoke("admin","admin","create","seq1")
puts x.invoke("admin","admin","next","seq1")
puts x.invoke("admin","admin","next","seq1")
puts x.invoke("admin","admin","next","seq1")
```

If everything goes well, this should print 0, 1, and 2 on separate lines. As you can see, the only thing you need to do is to import the `InitialContext` (which is the class you use to talk to JNDI services in Java). Then you create a new instance of it and look up the stateless session bean implementing the business interface called `com.bb.BBService`. That's all; everything else is taken care of by Java and the GlassFish runtime.

Summary

In this short chapter, we looked at how to wrap JRuby inside an enterprise layer. There are still lots of things left to be done to make it really enterprisey, but this is a good start to provide easy services. When you really need enterprise services you should drop out to Java, but in most situations this code is small compared to the actual business rules and business contracts. If these can be implemented in Ruby, they should be. You reap the benefits of using Ruby in those areas where change is most likely, and business code is always subject to change.

As you've also seen, it's an easy task to get started wrapping Ruby in EJBs, so go ahead and experiment with the code and see if you can improve it. In later chapters we'll also look at how to tie this EJB code in with JMX, to allow unprecedented management and control over your application.

But first, we need to create the Rails application that uses this EJB. As you saw here, it's easy to connect to these services, so we're not building a large application. In fact, in terms of code, this application is the smallest.

CHAPTER 10

∎∎∎

An EJB-Backed Rails Application

In the last chapter we managed to create an Enterprise JavaBean that uses JRuby for its implementation of features. In this manner we've separated the concerns of implementing the business rules from all the other concerns existing outside of the business logic. In this chapter we'll continue with this application by creating a web interface to this functionality, called Big Brother. The web interface is simple by design. The point is to show how you could use an enterprise resource from a Rails application in a simple and useful way. In most cases, this interaction should only need to happen in a few places in your application, and making the architecture of your web application reflect this makes the whole endeavor much simpler.

Because this application is small, we'll also take the opportunity to check out a few ways we can make use of Java Management Extensions (JMX), which is a Java technology for managing Java applications. Some of the features of JMX will enable you to look at memory and thread statistics of your application, without having to write any code for this. All these capabilities are part of the core Java platform nowadays, and your application will get the same benefits just by running on the JVM.

However, JMX also allows you to implement some useful things for your application. We'll take a look at how you can do this, both for the server parts and for the client Rails application.

WHAT IS JMX?

Java applications always need to be controlled and managed in different ways. Usually, the application developer creates custom code to accomplish this for his or her application, or the framework used provides some way of handling resources. The problem with this approach is that as soon as you want to use two libraries together, you have two separate ways to manage these libraries. If you want to connect larger applications with each other, this situation quickly becomes intractable.

Cue JMX. JMX was defined by JSR 3, one of the first and longest running JSRs. The specification provides tools for managing and monitoring applications, system objects, resources, devices, service oriented networks, and almost any kind of system you want to connect it to. The core of JMX is called MBeans, and can be simple or complicated, depending on your needs.

Application servers have supported JMX since J2EE 1.4, and JMX became part of the Java platform from version 5.0. If you need this support on earlier versions, you can download libraries to provide it.

The support offered by MBeans is divided into different categories: attributes, operations, and notifications. There are five types of MBeans: Standard, Dynamic, Model, Open, and Monitor. We'll just use Standard MBeans in this chapter, because they're the simplest. The largest distinguishing factor between the different types is the level of control you have over descriptions of the services in the bean. For Standard beans, all this information is gathered at runtime by the use of introspection of interfaces, while the other bean types can explicitly describe themselves.

You need to register MBeans with an MBeanServer. You can do this in several different ways, either by doing it programmatically or by providing a so-called M-Let, which is an XML description of an MBean to be deployed. Once deployed in an MBeanServer, MBeans can be reached by MBean clients. There are two types of clients: generic or specific. The specific clients work explicitly with the operations they know the server provides, while generic clients can discover things at runtime, and let you decide how to invoke operations.

JConsole is a good example of both specific and generic operations. The specific parts of it are what allow you to see the memory and thread usage of a Java application. Because that information is provided by specific MBeans in Java, and JConsole knows how to use them, it can provide nice graphs of this information. On the other hand, you can also look at attributes and invoke operations on user-defined MBeans in JConsole, which is the generic part.

The EJB Client Revisited

First of all, let's take a closer look at the EJB client you created in the last chapter. It looked like this:

```
require 'java'

import javax.naming.InitialContext

ic = InitialContext.new
x = ic.lookup("com.bb.BBService")
p x.invoke("admin","admin","create","seq1")
p x.invoke("admin","admin","next","seq1")
```

Now, to understand what's happening here, it's important to know how this code can connect to the correct GlassFish instance, find the EJB you want, and send the invoke calls to it. In the case of GlassFish, these things are easy to explain. You needed to create a wrapper script for invoking your application; in that wrapper you added a few paths to the CLASSPATH. The most important of these is $GLASSFISH/lib/appserv-rt.jar. This file contains all Java classes you need to connect to the GlassFish server. It also contains a file called jndi.properties. When a new instance of javax.naming.InitialContext is created, it will try to find a file with that name on the CLASSPATH, and use the properties in it to configure itself. You can override this behavior by sending in explicit parameters to the InitialContext constructor, but in this case you don't need to. The GlassFish jndi.properties points out the correct JNDI implementation to use, and which server and port to connect to.

The next stage is InitialContext.lookup. In this case, I decided not to give the service bean an explicit name, so it will be deployed with the same name as the service interface used. I could have decided on a custom name as an attribute to the Stateless annotation if I wanted to, and then I would've written that in the lookup call instead.

After the server has found and instantiated the stateless session bean, the Java object that you get is a local proxy implementation of the business interface. In fact, because JRuby uses dynamic proxy instances to interact with Java objects, the x variable points to a proxy implementation of a proxy implementation that points to a server-contained proxy implementation to a proxy implementation. That's quite neat. A wise man once said, "All problems can be solved by one more layer of indirection," and that's exactly what's happening here.

If you need to change some of the parameters for GlassFish, you can either change the jndi.properties file or provide other parameters to the constructor call. I recommend sending explicit parameters, and looking up on the GlassFish home page exactly what properties to set for the effect you want to achieve.

Creating the Application

You know the drill by now, I hope. Begin by creating a new Rails application. (I called mine bbapp, but that doesn't matter.) Next, append the require to jdbc_adapter inside the environment.rb file. Also, make sure you've created a new MySQL database for the project, and added this configuration to the database.yml file. At this point you'll once again create a simple authentication system, but this time you need some more data in the user table. The database will be simple though, because authentication is all you'll use it for.

Begin by doing a model for it:

```
jruby script/generate model User
```

Then, go ahead and edit the migration for it. It should end up like this:

```
class CreateUsers < ActiveRecord::Migration
  class User < ActiveRecord::Base; end

  def self.up
    create_table :users do |t|
      t.column :username, :string
      t.column :password, :string
      t.column :name, :string
      t.column :service_username, :string
      t.column :service_password, :string
    end

    User.create :username => 'admin',
                :password => 'admin',
                :name => 'Administrator',
                :service_username => 'admin',
                :service_password => 'admin'
  end

  def self.down
    drop_table :users
  end
end
```

As you can see, you've added a name field, and fields for the username and password to provide to the EJB service. Migrate this application to the latest version and create a scaffold for the user model:

```
jruby -S rake db:migrate
jruby script/generate scaffold User
```

In fact, the scaffold you've generated for the user will be left almost exactly like it is. The only things you'll change are parts of the view pages, and the layout for it. However, you should remove the show action, and all mention of it in the views generated. Before you can do that, you need to have authentication available for your users. Open app/controllers/application.rb and change it:

```
class ApplicationController < ActionController::Base
  # Pick a unique cookie name to distinguish our
  # session data from others'
  session :session_key => '_bbapp_session_id'

  before_filter :authentication, :except => [:login]

  private
  def authentication
    unless session[:user_id] &&
                      (@user=User.find_by_id(session[:user_id]))
      flash[:notice] = "Please log in"
      redirect_to(:controller => 'auth', :action => 'login',
                                      :into => url_for(params))
    else
      @loggedin = true
    end
  end
end
```

This is the same model you've used before. As such, you shouldn't be surprised that you now need to generate an AuthController:

```
jruby script/generate controller Auth login logout
rm app/views/auth/logout.rhtml
```

Implementing login and logout shouldn't come as a surprise either:

```
def login
  if request.post?
    if user = User.find_by_username_and_password(
                      params[:username],params[:password])
      session[:user_id] = user.id
      redirect_to params[:into] || {:controller => 'users'}
      return
    else
      flash[:error] = "Wrong username or password"
    end
```

```
    end
    @into = params[:into]
  end

  def logout
    session[:user_id] = nil
    redirect_to url_for(:action => 'login')
  end
```

The login.rhtml view is simple:

```
<h2>Please login with your username and password</h2>

<%= start_form_tag %>
<%= hidden_field_tag 'into', @into %>
<table width="400">
  <tr>
    <td>Username:</td><td><%= text_field_tag 'username' %></td>
  </tr>
  <tr>
    <td>Password:</td><td><%= password_field_tag 'password' %></td>
  </tr>
  <tr>
    <td colspan="2" align="right"><%= submit_tag 'Login' %></td>
  </tr>
</table>
<%= end_form_tag %>
```

After this is in place, you need to change the list.rhtml file for the UserController, because it shouldn't show passwords:

```
<h1>Listing users</h1>

<table width="500">
  <tr>
    <th>Username</th>
    <th>Name</th>
    <th>Service user</th>
  </tr>

<% for user in @users %>
  <tr>
    <td><%=h user.username %></td>
    <td><%=h user.name %></td>
    <td><%=h user.service_username %></td>
    <td><%= link_to 'Edit', :action => 'edit', :id => user %></td>
    <td><%= link_to 'Destroy', { :action => 'destroy',
              :id => user }, :confirm => 'Are you sure?',
                         :method => :post %></td>
```

```
    </tr>
<% end %>
</table>

<%= link_to 'Previous page', {
    :page => @user_pages.current.previous } if
                    @user_pages.current.previous %>
<%= link_to 'Next page', {
    :page => @user_pages.current.next } if
                    @user_pages.current.next %>

<br />

<%= link_to 'New user', :action => 'new' %>
```

Now you need a layout and some actual functionality, and then you'll be finished with the application. Before that, though, remove the file public/index.html and add this row to the routes so that the users controller will be the first a user sees, after logging in:

```
map.connect '', :controller => "users"
```

Call the layout bb and begin by copying the file public/stylesheets/shoplet.css, from the first project, into the file public/stylesheets/bb.css. With that in place, create the layout file app/views/layouts/bb.rhtml:

```
<!DOCTYPE html PUBLIC "-//W3C//DTD XHTML 1.0 Transitional//EN"
        "http://www.w3.org/TR/xhtml1/DTD/xhtml1-transitional.dtd">

<html xmlns="http://www.w3.org/1999/xhtml" xml:lang="en" lang="en">
<head>
  <meta http-equiv="content-type" content="text/html;charset=UTF-8" />
  <title>Big Brother: <%= controller.action_name %>
                        <%=h params[:controller]%></title>
  <%= stylesheet_link_tag 'bb' %>
  <%= javascript_include_tag :defaults %>
</head>
<body>
  <table width="100%" height="100%">
    <tr>
      <td width="250" height="800" class="leftMenu"
                            align="center" valign="top">
        <h2>Big Brother</h2>
        <br/>
        <% if @loggedin %>
        <p>Logged in as:<br/><%= h @user.name %></p>
        <ul style="text-align: left;">
          <li><%= link_to 'Sequences', {:controller => 'sequences'},
                  :class => 'adminLink' %></li>
          <li><%= link_to 'Users', {:controller => 'users'},
                  :class => 'adminLink' %></li>
```

```
        </ul>
        <br/>
        <p><%= link_to 'Log out',
                    :controller=>'auth',:action=>'logout'%></p>
        <% end %>
      </td>
      <td class="main" valign="top">
        <p style="color: green"><%= flash[:notice] %></p>
        <p style="color: red"><b><%= flash[:error] %></b></p>

        <%= yield  %>
      </td>
    </tr>
  </table>
</body>
</html>
```

As you can see, you've added a SequencesController, links to your other controllers, and also a logout link. Proceed by adding this line to the UsersController and AuthController:

```
layout "bb"
```

You can then go ahead and try the application, add some users, and generally look around before you start creating the interface to the sequences.

Creating a Small Sequence Library

To get your connection with the sequence service functional, you need to create a small client library to use it. This doesn't need to be complicated at all. The only thing you have to remember is to set the CLASSPATH so that the Rails application can find the needed classes, just as with the test client you wrote before. You can use the same approach: creating a runjr script that you use instead of JRuby.

You should place the file you create in lib/sequence_manager.rb, and you'll take it piecemeal. First, take care of your initial needs:

```
import javax.naming.InitialContext

SequenceData = Struct.new :name, :value,
                          :last_updated, :last_updated_by
```

You need to import an InitialContext, and also create a structure that will contain the data returned by some of the SequenceManager methods. As you might notice, this structure contains exactly the data you have about a sequence in the service database. The actual SequenceManager contains a few real methods, and several methods that mostly provide easy access. First, the basic class definition looks like this:

```
class SequenceManager
  include Singleton
```

```
  def initialize
    ic = InitialContext.new
    @connection = ic.lookup("com.bb.BBService")
  end
end
```

Including the module Singleton means that there can only ever be one instance of this SequenceManager in the same Rails process. This is to make it easy to handle the InitialContext connection. You don't want more than one of those, because they're expensive. The initialize method just creates a context, looks up the bean, and saves this as the @connection instance variable.

As might be obvious, you need to invoke all the methods you want to call on the server in the same manner, with the service_username and service_password. To make all this invocation easier, add a with_user method that takes care of this:

```
private
def with_user(user, method, arg)
  @connection.invoke(user.service_username,
                     user.service_password,method,arg)
end
```

This method makes the real call, sending the method and argument along. Now, the first two operations you need to support are list and get:

```
def list(user)
  with_user(user,'list',nil)
end

def get(id, user)
  s = SequenceData.new
  s.name = id.to_s
  s.value = with_user(user,'current',id.to_s)
  s.last_updated = with_user(user,'last_updated',id.to_s)
  s.last_updated_by = with_user(user,'last_updated_by',id.to_s)
  s
end
```

The get method does several invocations. This isn't best practice for Enterprise JavaBeans, but it works for us right now. You can handle the rest of the methods generically; because these methods all follow a simple pattern, you can just generate the methods:

```
%w(reset next create).each do |n|
  define_method n.to_sym do |id, user|
    with_user(user,n,id.to_s)
  end
end
```

Finally, because it's cumbersome to get the instance of the singleton, you'd like to have these methods available on the `class` object too, so you can just call it directly. To do that, you generate methods on the `class` singleton object, which calls `instance` and then calls the current method on the object returned from `instance`:

```
class << self
  def list(user)
    instance.list(user)
  end

  %w(get reset next create).each do |n|
    define_method n.to_sym do |id, user|
      instance.send n.to_sym, id, user
    end
  end
end
```

You need to handle `list` differently, because it doesn't take an `id` argument. The other methods all follow the same pattern, though. Now you have everything to make access to this EJB easy and convenient. Let's get on with doing the Rails side of things for it too!

Sequence Controller and Views

You've created a library to handle your remote access to the enterprise bean. The only thing left is creating something that uses it. So, let's create a `SequencesController` and the corresponding views:

```
jruby script/generate controller Sequences index list
                                            show reset next create
rm app/views/sequences/reset.rhtml
rm app/views/sequences/next.rhtml
rm app/views/sequences/create.rhtml
```

You'll design the mutating methods to do their mutation and then redirect back to the current point, because it doesn't make any sense to have separate pages for these. This controller should use the `bb` layout, and you need to have the `index` action redirect to the `list` action. Further, you should protect the mutating operations so they only can be reached by POST:

```
layout "bb"

def index
  list
  render :action => 'list'
end
```

```
# GETs should be safe
# (see http://www.w3.org/2001/tag/doc/whenToUseGet.html)
verify :method => :post, :only => [ :reset, :next, :create ],
       :redirect_to => { :action => :list }
```

The rest of the actions are simple:

```
def list
  @sequences = SequenceManager.list(@user)
end

def show
  @sequence = SequenceManager.get(params[:id], @user)
end

def reset
  SequenceManager.reset(params[:id], @user)
  flash[:notice] = "Have reset sequence '#{params[:id]}'."
  redirect_to :action => :show, :id => params[:id]
end

def next
  val = SequenceManager.next(params[:id], @user)
  flash[:notice] = "Next for '#{params[:id]}': #{val}."
  redirect_to :action => :show, :id => params[:id]
end

def create
  if params[:id]
    SequenceManager.create(params[:id], @user)
    flash[:notice] = "Ensured sequence '#{params[:id]}' exists"
  end
  redirect_to :action => :list
end
```

You make sure that the actions that change the current value of a sequence report this in the flash. Except for that, there's nothing to this controller.

The views aren't much more complicated. The first one, list, should look like this:

```
<h1>Sequences</h1>

<ul>
  <% for seq in @sequences %>
  <li>
```

```
    <%= link_to h(seq), {:action => 'show', :id => seq},
                    :class => 'adminLink' %>
  </li>
  <% end %>
</ul>

<h2>New sequence</h2>

<%= start_form_tag :action => 'create' %>
  <p><label for="id">Name:</label> <input type="text"
                                    name="id" id="id"/></p>
  <%= submit_tag "Create" %>
<%= end_form_tag %>
```

You have the form for creating a new sequence in the same page that lists all sequences, because it just contains one small part. The only wrinkle in this list is that you don't have any pagination of the results, which means you'll get all results in one page, regardless of how many there are. On the other hand, there shouldn't be that many sequences available at that.

To show a sequence, you use the `show.rhtml` view:

```
<h1>Sequence: <%= h @sequence.name %></h1>

<p><b>Current: </b> <%= h @sequence.value %></p>
<p><b>Last updated: </b> <%= h @sequence.last_updated %></p>
<p><b>Last updated by: </b> <%= h @sequence.last_updated_by %></p>

<%= link_to 'Next', { :action => 'next',
                        :id => @sequence.name },
                    :method => :post %> |
<%= link_to 'Reset', { :action => 'reset',
                        :id => @sequence.name },
                    :method => :post %><br/><br/>

<%= link_to 'Back', :action => 'list' %>
```

Here, you also allow the sequence to be incremented or reset.

Now you have every piece in place, and you should try the application out. Just start up Mongrel with your wrapper script that puts the needed files on the CLASSPATH.

As you might notice, using an EJB back end imposes some constraints on your application, but you don't have to jump through large hoops to get it working. In the next section you'll see how to improve your application by adding management capabilities implemented in JMX to it. Figure 10-1 shows what a typical sequence can look like when you've taken a few numbers from it.

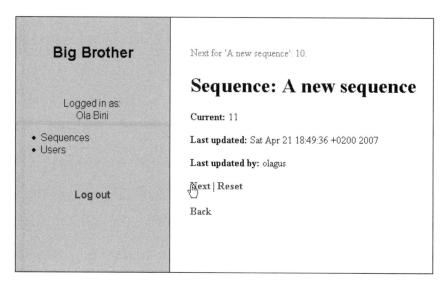

Figure 10-1. *Administrating a sequence from the Big Brother application*

JMX for the Server

At this point, you've made the Sequence service available as an EJB and also through the Rails interface you built for it. Another way to give this access would be through a simple JMX MBean. Because it can use the same EJB beneath the covers, you can easily create a bean that uses it. First of all, you need to have an MBean interface. You can see the code for it in Listing 10-1. Because you're doing a simple MBean, the only requirement for the interface is that it ends with MBean. Add this file to your bbservice project.

Listing 10-1. *src/com/bb/mbean/SequenceManagerMBean.java*

```
package com.bb.mbean;

public interface SequenceManagerMBean {
    Object invoke(String uid, String cred,
                String methodName, String argument);
}// SequenceManagerMBean
```

As you can see, you have the same operation as the EJB. Next, you create an implementation of this interface that uses the enterprise bean (see Listing 10-2).

Listing 10-2. *src/com/bb/mbean/SequenceManager.java*

```java
package com.bb.mbean;

import java.util.List;

import javax.naming.InitialContext;
import javax.naming.NamingException;

import javax.management.MBeanServer;
import javax.management.MBeanServerFactory;
import javax.management.ObjectName;

import com.bb.BBService;

public class SequenceManager implements SequenceManagerMBean {
    private BBService service;

    public SequenceManager() throws NamingException {
        InitialContext ic = new InitialContext();
        service = (BBService)ic.lookup("com.bb.BBService");
    }

    public Object invoke(String uid, String cred,
                                    String methodName,
                                    String argument) {
        return service.invoke(uid,cred,methodName,argument);
    }

    public static void main(String[] args) throws Exception {
        List servers = MBeanServerFactory.findMBeanServer(null);
        MBeanServer server = (MBeanServer) servers.get(0);
        SequenceManager sm = new SequenceManager();
        ObjectName on =
                new ObjectName("UserDomain:Name=SequenceController");
        server.registerMBean(sm,on);
        while(true) {}
    }
}// SequenceManager
```

This code does three things. First, the constructor creates an InitialContext and looks up the BBService, in the same way as all the other EJB clients. Second, the invoke method just passes the invoke call on to the enterprise bean. Third, the main method tries to find an already existing MBean server, create a new SequenceManager, and register it to the server. After that, the main method loops, because the MBean is the real point of this particular application. In a real-world situation, the MBean would probably be there to manage something else.

Compile these two files in the same way as described before, and package everything inside the bbservice.jar again. Then, create a new file called runjava that contains the same CLASSPATH settings as the runjr script. However, instead of invoking JRuby, it should invoke java, like this:

```
java -Dcom.sun.management.jmxremote $*
```

This allows the main code to work correctly; if you don't provide this property, no Java JMX server will be started by default. With this file created, you can start it like this:

```
./runjava com.bb.mbean.SequenceManager
```

You can then switch to another window and start jconsole. Choose the process running SequenceManager and attach to it, and choose the tab called "MBeans." There should be an entry in the tree chooser that says "UserDomain." Fold it up, and open the entry "Sequence-Controller" and then "Operations." Here you'll just see the invoke operation. Provide any parameters you'd like and press the "invoke" button. You should get a window telling you the result of the operation back. For example, type **admin**, **admin**, and **list** in the first boxes; this should give you all sequence names available. Or, create a new sequence and increment it.

The interesting thing about this small management application is that it's incredibly easy to create something powerful such as this, and you can add on it to provide everything you need to handle your application in a programmatic manner. You can add attributes that control everything about your application, and the MBean framework lets you update this information and change it anytime you like, through a standard interface such as JConsole. Or, if you have deployed your application in GlassFish or JBoss, you can use their standard web interfaces for the same thing.

Simple JMX Access to Rails

Now that you've seen how you can use JMX on the server side to control your operations, it's time to see how to take control of a Rails application. The basics of doing this are simple, and you already have most of the pieces needed. After that, the only thing stopping you is your imagination. However, right now you'll just provide an MBean that allows you to connect to a Rails process and execute anything you want, much like the script script/runner that's available in all Rails applications. You'll let this code reside in the bbservice project too, because the bbapp application needs to refer to this JAR file anyway (see Listing 10-3).

Listing 10-3. *src/com/bb/rails/RailsOperationMBean.java*

```
package com.bb.rails;

public interface RailsOperationMBean {
    String runner(String command);
}// RailsOperationMBean
```

This MBean takes a command as a `String`, and returns a `String` that describes the result of this operation. The implementation looks like the one in Listing 10-4.

Listing 10-4. *src/com/bb/rails/RailsOperation.java*

```java
package com.bb.rails;

import java.util.List;

import javax.management.MBeanServer;
import javax.management.MBeanServerFactory;
import javax.management.ObjectName;

import org.jruby.Ruby;
import org.jruby.runtime.builtin.IRubyObject;

public class RailsOperation implements RailsOperationMBean {
    private Ruby runtime;
    private int number;
    private static int runtimes = 0;

    public RailsOperation(IRubyObject obj) throws Exception {
        this.runtime = obj.getRuntime();
        synchronized(RailsOperation.class) {
            this.number = runtimes++;
        }

        List servers = MBeanServerFactory.findMBeanServer(null);
        MBeanServer server = (MBeanServer) servers.get(0);
        ObjectName on = new ObjectName(
                    "Rails:Name=OperationController,Number=" +
                            this.number);
        server.registerMBean(this,on);
    }

    public String runner(String command) {
        return runtime.evalScriptlet(command).callMethod(
                runtime.getCurrentContext(),"inspect").toString();
    }
}// RailsOperation
```

Now, as I said before, you've already seen everything that happens in this class. You have a static field containing a number of runtimes in the same process. This is usually not many, but if you deploy with Rails integration, it might be more than one. The constructor of this class takes an `IRubyObject`. You don't care what object that is; you just use it to get at the JRuby runtime, so you can save it. You use the current number to save away the current instance in the MBean server with a generated object name, based on the number this instance has. The `runner` method implementation just calls `evalScriptlet` with the command as the argument, then invokes the Ruby method "inspect" on the result, and finally calls toString() on the result. This results in something readable in all cases, because inspect should always return readable String representations.

When you've compiled these files and added them to the bbservice.jar file, there are only two more things to do. First, open up the runjr file and add this setting somewhere in it:

```
export JAVA_OPTS=-Dcom.sun.management.jmxremote
```

That way there will be a JMX MBean server available for you. Finally, open config/environment.rb, and add this at the bottom:

```
com.bb.rails.RailsOperation.new(self)
```

Because you don't care about which IRubyObject you send in to the constructor of RailsOperation, you use the current self, which is bound to be an object that the JRuby runtime won't automatically convert into something else. In this way, you make sure that the MBean gets registered at startup of a new Rails instance, and that this will only happen once for each Rails instance. If you do this in production, make sure that this won't lead to a memory leak somewhere. Depending on your deployment scenario, this could cause huge amounts of memory to be leaked. The proper way to avoid this is to save the runtime reference in a WeakReference, and once that WeakReference returns null, deregister the MBean from the MBean server. You can easily find how to do all that in the JavaDoc for Java.

Now it's time to start up the Rails application and try the MBean out. After the application has started, run jconsole. Navigate to MBeans, and find the Rails entry in the left pane. Within it you will have OperationControl, one or more numbers, and beneath each number an entry called "operations." Go to one of these, and you'll see the runner operation in the right pane. Here you're free to try any valid Ruby code out. Because you have the whole Rails application available, you can use it to add a new authorized user, test the sequence manager, or whatever else you might feel like. To try it out, find out the names of all your users:

```
User.find(:all).map(&:name)
```

On my current installation, this returns the String '["Administrator", "Ola Bini"]'. If you want to list sequences, just do it the same way as you would from the controller:

```
SequenceManager.list(@user)
```

This gives you a nasty-looking printout of each struct instance for every sequence, but you get the idea.

Of course, letting access such as this lie around is a good way to get cracked, so make sure you read up on how to secure your JMX server. Usually, providing local Java management access doesn't require a username and password, but this would be a good idea for setting up access to a remote server. When you finally decide to put it into production, making access locked to specific IP addresses is also a good measure.

Summary

In this chapter we first completed the Big Brother application, writing Ruby code that accesses an EJB and uses the result in different ways. Because this code is incredibly easy to write in Ruby, it didn't take much space, and the resulting application was also compact. We also took a quick look at JMX, what it is, and how to connect it to another Java program.

In the last section, we created a small JMX class that allowed us to execute anything we wanted inside the context of a Rails application. Doing it the way we did is the easiest technique. It would have made more sense in a production app to expose some common methods as zero-argument procedures, and that's probably how MBeans for Rails should be used in production. One of the things that Rails doesn't do for you is empty the session, and providing a zero-argument MBean operation that empties the session store by running a simple Ruby script could be a good idea. Other things you can do include creating more advanced MBeans, using the monitoring API to get real-time information on access to what's currently happening. It would be easy to replace the ActiveRecord `execute` method, letting an MBean see in real time the amount of queries executed or other data like that.

In short, the only limitation is your imagination. JMX holds the promise of being incredibly useful for Rails applications. Not only do you get everything for your custom beans, you can also use the standard JConsole application to monitor memory, CPU, and thread usage in a friendly and intuitive user interface.

That leaves the hard question of deployment. We haven't talked about it yet, so we'll spend a complete chapter looking at different ways to do it, and which way is recommended.

CHAPTER 11

■■■

Deployment

Deploying Rails applications has traditionally been somewhat of a pain. The current status in the Ruby community is that there are tools that help, but it's still not as fun as the rest of developing a Rails application. One of the major selling points for JRuby on Rails is that it makes deployment much easier, as well as managing the application after it's up and running. You saw some of those capabilities at the end of the last chapter, and you'll see more of these benefits as we go along.

However, to understand the choices we have when deploying Rails applications, we'll first do a whirlwind tour of the possibilities. I'll describe most of the available solutions for regular Ruby on Rails applications, and then we'll take a look at the alternatives for JRuby. Some overlap and some don't, but I'll describe each alternative separately, because the details are somewhat different, even for similar approaches.

The final part of the chapter will show you the two recommended approaches: the best practices for handling JRuby on Rails applications. I'll show you two different solutions; which one you prefer depends on where you come from. As a Ruby on Rails developer, you'll probably be more comfortable with the pack of Mongrels you deploy inside one JVM. As a Java developer, you'll feel right at home bundling the application as a WAR file and deploying inside of Tomcat. I'll also detail the pros and cons of these two variations, what you should think about when doing it, and how to make it happen in practice.

Several of the JRuby solutions showcased in the tour will have some advantages over the other ways, but in all those cases, one specific detriment makes this solution unmanageable in the generic case. For example, Rails-asyncweb can give you great speed, at the cost of using a nonstandard web container, with not many documentation and management hooks. However, if you need speed, it's unparalleled. For convenience, WEBrick or Mongrel are good solutions, but they don't scale and shouldn't be used in production like you use them while doing development.

Deployment is overall one of the harder practical problems in development today. There is no easy way, and you need to evaluate your options and come to a good conclusion for yourself. This chapter can help you with that.

When I need a Rails application to display how the different solutions work, I tend to use Shoplet, because it's a small application that still uses most of the features of JRuby on Rails. In some cases, it will be interesting to show how to handle Java dependencies; in those cases using the JDBC JAR files as examples will be the norm.

Deploying Ruby on Rails

As mentioned in the introduction, deployment of regular Ruby on Rails applications comes in several different forms. The question of how to best handle deployment is something of a fashion issue, so at any point in time, you'll find almost all people recommending the same approach. The reason for this is that the evolution of best practices goes fast in the Rails world. Currently, the last solution (pack of Mongrels) is the preferred way to handle regular Rails applications. It's easy to change deployment solutions, though, because most Rails organizations use Capistrano to handle the actual deployment. By changing what Capistrano recipes are used, you can also change the deployment method easily. I won't cover Capistrano here; there are good tutorials on the Net and books describing how to accomplish these things.

Some of the solutions provided here will also work with JRuby, but we'll look independently at these in the next section.

WEBrick

The simplest way of handling a Rails application is to handle it the same way you do when developing it: start a WEBrick server and be done with it:

```
ruby script/server webrick -e production
```

This solution is probably one of the worst ones, along with the CGI one. WEBrick is highly useful for testing your application during development. It's small, it's pure Ruby, and it's already installed on all Ruby machines. This makes it straightforward to handle. On the other hand, it's written in pure Ruby, which means the performance could be much better. In fact, WEBrick is slow. It also has a tendency to hang and stop responding after a while. For these reasons, it works fine for short-lived development runs, and possibly also for running automated test suites. However, for real-world deployment, you need another solution.

CGI

Because the Rails framework is developed in a shared-nothing style, and all states should be put in either the model or the session, this means you could theoretically start a new Rails instance for each request that arrives. Because of this, you can use Rails with raw CGI. Code exists in Rails for this, and you can set up and configure Apache to handle all requests by sending them to the Rails CGI dispatcher. This isn't good for anything. CGI is a protocol that puts all information to the CGI program within environment variables, and then executes it. Because it starts Rails and loads all libraries for each request, it is incredibly inefficient and slow. You'll usually wait several seconds for each web page to show. For this reason, CGI isn't a useful technology for Rails, except when doing proof-of-concept implementations. In fact, CGI was the first protocol JRuby on Rails handled, because that was the easiest way of getting something working.

FastCGI

Due to all the problems with CGI, and the need for a similar solution that can be put behind a regular web server, FastCGI was developed. It was initially created to make PHP programs more efficient, but there are handlers for several languages, Ruby among them. On a basic level, FastCGI does things the same way as CGI, except that it starts Rails instances beforehand. It then doesn't tear them down at the end of a request, but uses them again. This allows you to put a web server such as Apache or LightTPD in front of Rails, and get good performance. FastCGI can be tricky to get working, due to Apache and LightTPD being hard to configure, but once it works it's fast. For a long time, this was the main solution to deployment of Rails applications.

The major problem with FastCGI is that the connectors are a little flaky. The Apache support has been known to cause large problems, with FastCGI processes getting hung, eating your CPU, and other bad things. Another problem is getting it all working together; the components are tightly tied to each other when finally configured correctly, which means it's easy to cause everything to fail by changing one small detail.

Because FastCGI uses a native C extension to function, JRuby has no support for it at the moment. That's bound to change as soon as someone decides FastCGI is important enough to create a Java extension for.

What both CGI and FastCGI have going for them is that you can configure them not to serve static files, but to let the enclosing web server handle these files. In those situations, no Ruby code will run for fetching an image, style sheet, or cached rendering of a view. This can give a huge performance improvement, because evaluating Ruby in the call chain always has some impact on performance.

Mongrel

A few years back, a hacker named Zed Shaw decided that WEBrick wasn't a good enough web server for Ruby. He spent some time trying to come up with a better solution, and the result was Mongrel: a good web server written mostly in Ruby with a small C extension for handling the parsing of requests. Mongrel 1.0 was released in conjunction with Rails 1.2 in the beginning of 2007. Mongrel is widely believed to be much faster than WEBrick, and is also a good standalone library for creating smaller web applications. In many places, Mongrel has replaced WEBrick as the server of choice for Rails development. Because it is fast to start and easy to configure in standalone mode, this means you get a better and faster web server for your Rails development, all for free.

For smaller web applications, you can also use Mongrel in standalone mode to serve Rails applications in production. If you know that the site traffic will be small, and there is no huge demand on scalability, Mongrel is usually good enough. It's also easy to get going; you can just start it with `script/server` and it runs flawlessly.

Pack of Mongrels

To solve the scalability problem with Mongrel, the standard solution is to deploy a "pack of Mongrels." This is made easy by a small plug-in for Mongrel called mongrel_cluster that lets you start several Mongrel instances on the same machine with consecutive port numbers. The other side of this is usually a load balancer of some sort. The two most common real world deployments use Apache and Pound. With the Apache solution, you configure the web server to handle all static content, and then use the module called `mod_proxy_balancer`, which balances requests between all the available Mongrels. The beauty of this solution is that if your needs grow, or if your site gets popular, you can just add more Mongrel instances, on the same or another computer. The Apache front end then load balances over all the new Mongrels with a reloading of the configuration file. This means you can just "throw hardware" at the scalability problem.

Pound is a standalone load balancer that's also easy to configure and get going with Mongrel and Rails. The benefits are mostly the same as with Apache, but Pound is lightweight compared to Apache. However, if you already have Apache knowledge in your organization, or need to handle more than one web domain from the same place, Apache is usually the way to go. This has been the best practice for Rails deployment for more than six months (this is a long time in the Ruby community).

Deploying JRuby on Rails

In the last section you saw a plethora of variations on how to deploy a Rails application with regular Ruby. In fact, JRuby adds several new possibilities, while still retaining almost all the original versions. The only deployment scenario that currently doesn't work with JRuby is FastCGI; a FastCGI interface exists for Java, but no one has done the work of integrating it with JRuby on Rails. That seems to be a significant thing to do, and probably wouldn't offer any benefits over the current solutions. Because even the same deployment scenarios are more or less different compared to Ruby, we'll take a quick look at these scenarios in the JRuby version too.

WEBrick

As you've seen in many of the previous chapters, using WEBrick during development usually works well with JRuby. However, for deployment, it suffers from exactly the same problems as WEBrick on regular Ruby: it's slow and unstable, having a tendency to stop responding. Except for the most noncritical applications, you shouldn't use WEBrick for deployment in JRuby.

CGI

Because CGI doesn't depend on network connection in any real degree, and you can get it working using another web server, it's a good solution for bootstrapping a new implementation to Rails functionality. That was exactly how the JRuby team got basic Rails support up and running, long before the network subsystems were in place. Using it this way was useful, but no one would deploy it like that. Just like loading regular Rails on each CGI request, doing the same with JRuby would be prohibitive; Rails takes a long time to load, and you also have to add the hit of loading the Java Virtual Machine to that, which always takes some time. In conclusion, using CGI is not worth the trouble or performance hit in any situation.

Mongrel

Mongrel has a native extension written in C, which is one of the reasons it's faster than WEBrick. This extension has been ported to Java, which means you can use Mongrel from JRuby and give a JRuby on Rails application many of the same advantages as Mongrel with regular Ruby. You can use it in standalone mode, as well as set up a pack of Mongrels with a load balancer in front of them. A small variation is useful for Mongrel running in JRuby: when setting up a pack of Mongrels, it can be inefficient to just start several Java runtimes. What you can do instead is run the Mongrel instances in the same JVM with different JRuby runtimes. In this way, you get all the good points of Mongrel, while still saving memory and startup time. You can find the exact syntax for doing this by running the `mongrel_cluster` command in JRuby.

GoldSpike (Rails Integration)

The main JRuby deployment scenario is usually that you want to create a WAR file and deploy it in a J2EE web container. GoldSpike provides this functionality for you in an easy package. You install Rails integration as a plug-in, and get hold of several Rake tasks, including `war:standalone:create`. By invoking these, you can package the complete Rails application inside a WAR file, which you can drop into Tomcat, Jetty, GlassFish, or any other compliant Java web container. GoldSpike automatically takes care of creating more runtimes to handle requests; it also uses the Java session store by default. This means that if your web container supports clustering or session affinity in the base system, your Rails application can take advantage of this too. Further, you can also configure lots of parameters, changing the default GoldSpike handling of requests, sessions, and which libraries should be added to the `CLASSPATH`.

We'll take a closer look at GoldSpike later in the chapter, because this is the proper way to deploy most JRuby on Rails applications, giving you the full benefits of the Java platform.

Grizzly

When the creators of the GlassFish Application Server project needed a New Input/Output (NIO)-capable HTTP front end, they decided to create Grizzly. Grizzly is a framework that makes it easy for you to take advantage of some of the good things in the Java NIO libraries. A Rails integration service for Grizzly has been created, and can be installed as a Gem (called `grizzly-rails`). When installed, it lets you start Rails applications with the `grizzly_rails` command, much like `mongrel_rails`. The advantage over GoldSpike is that by using NIO and asynchronous sockets, Grizzly has the potential to perform much better for certain kinds of applications.

GlassFish v3 currently ships with the Ruby on Rails libraries for Grizzly.

Rails-asyncweb

AsyncWeb is a capable HTTP front end, written in Java. Its explicit purpose is to do away with traditional, blocking request processing and use a new asynchronous model to achieve much higher performance. This means that standard Java servlets doesn't run in it, but on the other hand you can write custom components for AsyncWeb that look much like their servlet counterparts. In 2006, Naoto Takai created Rails-asyncweb, which is an AsyncWeb "servlet" that wraps a JRuby runtime, handling Rails dispatching through it. The main advantage of using AsyncWeb for Rails deployment is much the same as with Grizzly: you do away with the compatibility layer and gain higher throughput with a massively scaling front end. Rails running through AsyncWeb has been shown to be between five to ten times as fast as alternatives.

It is also easy to use:

```
cd your-reals-app
rails-asyncweb .
```

If you need high performance, you should try AsyncWeb, and see if it meets your demands. You'll have to weigh the advantage of speed against using an unconventional web front end, which will be harder to handle in final deployment. For some people this tradeoff makes sense, and for others not.

Retty

Retty is a simple Rails plug-in, based on the Java web containers Jetty and GoldSpike. It was created by Jon Tirsen and can be installed from Google Code:

```
jruby script/plugin install http://retty.googlecode.com/svn/trunk/plugins/retty
```

When you've installed the plug-in, you can start a Jetty server that handles Rails requests with this command:

```
jruby -S rake retty:run
```

Jetty is a small and fast web container, and running smaller Rails applications in this way makes for the best parts of a Rails application and embedding a real Java web server. You can use Retty for deploying smaller standalone applications without a problem, and it can also easily be used in a pack.

Best Practice JRuby on Rails Deployment

You've now seen a multitude of available ways to deploy your JRuby on Rails application. Most of these might fit a specific situation fairly well, but among all these I would recommend just two options. In my mind, these are the best practices. Actually, I would favor the WAR approach over the Mongrel approach too, but if you're unfamiliar with the Java platform, that might make it hard to handle. In this situation, starting a pack of Mongrels in the same JVM is a handy substitute to mongrel_cluster.

A Pack of JVM Mongrels

As you saw in the introduction to different approaches, you can use Mongrel in standalone mode for smaller applications, but where it shines is when you start several and use a real load balancer in front of them. The problem with this approach on the Java platform is that you don't want to start several JVMs, because they are slow to start and resource heavy. JRuby sports the option of starting a JRuby server and spinning off new runtimes for each request that arrives on that port. By using that capability, you can start several Mongrel instances in the same JVM. The Mongrel service uses a simple protocol, sending strings to the port in question. For example, you invoke the mongrel_rails command by simply sending the string mongrel_rails. Every parameter you can give to the standalone version of JRuby can be sent to the jruby server (except for those that give parameters to the JVM). At the moment, it's not possible to selectively kill runtimes in the JRuby server, because this can introduce severe resource problems, contention between threads, and other problems. The only way to kill the Mongrels is to kill the JRuby server itself. However, this fits nicely with the way you'd use it to handle a pack of Mongrels.

First of all, you must make sure to have the mongrel_jcluster Gem installed. This is almost exactly like mongrel_cluster, but instead of starting separate processes, mongrel_jcluster starts several JRuby instances in the same JVM, using the JRuby server system. After you've installed the Gem and created your application, it's time to configure your clustering configuration. You do this by running the mongrel_rails command with several parameters describing the configuration:

```
jruby -S mongrel_rails jcluster::configure -e production -p 4000 -c .
                  -N 4 -R 20202 -K yourVerySecretKey
```

This creates a configuration file called `config/mongrel_jcluster.yml`, which contains the parameters you specified on the command line. The ones I've provided earlier are the most important ones: describing which environment the cluster should run, and the first port to listen on (the rest of the ports will be sequential from the first one). The -n parameter says how many Mongrels to start, -R which port JRuby Server should listen on, and -K the secret key for this JRuby server. In other words, this configuration will start four Mongrels within JRuby, listening on 4000, 4001, 4002, and 4003 for Rails applications in the current directory.

Table 11-1 shows the available parameters for the `configure` command.

Table 11-1. *mongrel_jcluster Parameters*

Parameter	Description
-e, --environment	Describes the environment in which to run the Mongrel application.
-p, --port	The first port Mongrel should bind to (defaults to 3000).
-a, --address	The local IP address to listen on.
-l, --log	The log file to write Mongrel log messages.
-c, --chdir	The directory of the Rails application to run.
-t, --timeout	The amount of seconds to wait before timing out a request.
-m, --mime	Points to a YAML file that lists additional MIME types.
-r, --root	The document root of the application (defaults to "public").
-n, --num-procs	The number of processor threads to use.
-B, --debug	Enable debugging mode (takes no parameters).
-S, --script	Load the given file as an extra configuration script.
-N, --num-servers	The number of Mongrel servers to start (defaults to 2).
-C, --config	Path to the jcluster configuration file (defaults to "config/mongrel_jcluster.yml").
-R, --jport	The local port where the JRuby server should start (defaults to 19222).
-K, --jkey	The secret key used for authenticating to the local JRuby server.
--user	User to run as.
--group	Group to run as.
--prefix	The Rails prefix to use (for subhosting a Rails application).

All these parameters are associated with simple configuration keys in the configuration file. So, after you've created the configuration, you can start the cluster of Mongrels like this:

```
jruby -S mongrel_rails jcluster::start
```

Now, when this command is finished, you'll need to wait a little longer so that all the processes have started. You can take a look at the files `jrubyserver.*.log-files`, and see when the Mongrels have started. After that, it's easy enough to try them out directly if you want. Just remember, if you try to look at the default Rails page, viewing the properties of the installation, this won't work when running in production mode. This is an expected artifact of the production mode, and doesn't work on regular Ruby either.

If you need to stop the servers, that's as easy as doing this:

```
jruby -S mongrel_rails jcluster::stop
```

Do this to restart:

```
jruby -S mongrel_rails jcluster::restart
```

When your Mongrel instances have started, the next step is to put an Apache HTTP server in front of it. I assume you've already compiled Apache 2.2, and compiled support for mod_proxy, mod_proxy_http, and mod_proxy_balancer into it.

After you've installed Apache, to configure it to use load balancing proxy support, you should edit httpd.conf. First, you need to load the modules in question:

```
LoadModule proxy_module modules/mod_proxy.so
LoadModule proxy_http_module modules/mod_proxy_http.so
LoadModule proxy_balancer_module modules/mod_proxy_balancer.so
```

After you've done that, you should create a cluster directive:

```
<Proxy balancer://shopletcluster>
  BalancerMember http://127.0.0.1:4000
  BalancerMember http://127.0.0.1:4001
  BalancerMember http://127.0.0.1:4002
  BalancerMember http://127.0.0.1:4003
</Proxy>
```

This is where you add different components to your cluster. They don't have to be located on the same machine, and you can also choose to separate proxying between two different machines. Just type in the different addresses.

The next step is to create a VirtualHost that uses this balancer. You also want to have a balancer-manager, so you can handle the proxy balancing in real time from the web. Begin by adding that:

```
<Location /balancer-manager>
  SetHandler balancer-manager
</Location>
```

With this in place, you can visit http://localhost/balancer-manager and get much valuable information about your current load, and also change and administrate many settings. The VirtualHost itself needs to pass these proxy requests:

```
<VirtualHost *:80>
  ServerName shoplet
  ProxyRequests off
  ProxyPass /balancer-manager !
  ProxyPass / balancer://shopletcluster
  ProxyPassReverse / balancer://shopletcluster
</VirtualHost>
```

Now you can start up your application, and everything should just work if you access http://localhost/. You may use different Mongrels each time, but you don't notice that because Rails doesn't care. You should add some security to the `balancer-manager`, by the way. As is, anyone can change your proxy balancing settings, which can't be good.

Make WAR with Java

As mentioned in the whirlwind tour, you install GoldSpike as a plug-in in the Rails application you want to use it from, and then use one of several Rake targets provided to package everything into a nice WAR file. The file will be self containing, providing all the JRuby libraries, and will also package everything in your Rails application. Further, you can configure it to include external JAR dependencies if needed. If you need to handle more complicated situations, you can change most of the workings of GoldSpike by editing a file called `config/war.rb`.

After you've created the WAR file, you can deploy it directly into a compliant web container. You'll use Tomcat for this purpose, but it could be done in GlassFish, Jetty, or any other container.

The first step in creating a JRuby on Rails WAR file is to install the plug-in. Enter the application's home directory:

```
cd shoplet
jruby script/plugin install -x
  svn://rubyforge.org/var/svn/jruby-extras/trunk/rails-integration/plugins/goldspike
```

The `-x` command links the plug-in directly to the remote repository, so that when you update from version control, the plug-in will also be updated. If your Rails application isn't in Subversion you should remove the `-x` flag, though, because it won't work in that case.

After you've installed the plug-in, you should configure the application. In most cases, you don't need to do much, but for all cases where you use JDBC connections in your code, you should make sure to package the JAR file within it. You do this in the `config/war.rb` file:

```
maven_library 'mysql', 'mysql-connector-java', '5.0.4'
```

You can add any library known to Maven in this way to the WAR file generated. You don't need to package JRuby, though, because the standard packaging in GoldSpike will include all these things. This is all you need to have the WAR file working. You build it by running this command:

```
jruby -S rake war:standalone:create
```

This command shows you some output describing what's currently happening; you can see what Gems are added to the archive and also what libraries get added by default. This finally generates a file named the same as the current application; for example, `shoplet.war`. The final step in all these schemes is to deploy the WAR file in a web container. This is the nice part. Provided you have an installed Tomcat, Jetty, or GlassFish installation, you can just copy the WAR files to their respective `autodeploy` directories, and the Rails application will get started inside the server. You can use all the regular Java management tools from these web containers to handle the Rails application. As you saw in the last chapter, it's easy to add even more support for management to the Rails application.

The DSL in the `war.rb` file can be done in two different ways, but I'm just going to describe the recommended way here.

war_file FILENAME

By default, the WAR file generated for a Rails application will be named after the Rails application in question. In some cases, this is not optimal. This parameter allows you to easily change this file name:

```
war_file 'mephisto123.war'
```

exclude_files FILENAME

By default, GoldSpike tries to include almost all the files in a Rails directory inside the WAR file. This isn't necessarily what you want, so you can use exclude_files to specify which parts you don't want to include. The parameter should be a String, which can contain globbing patterns:

```
exclude_files './config/database.yml.local'
exclude_fails './log/*'
```

servlet CLASSNAME

In some situations, you might want to override the default RailsServlet used to dispatch into Rails. In those cases you need to use the servlet parameter, naming a Java class to use. The easiest way to make this work would probably be to subclass org.jruby.webapp.RailsServlet, which is the default servlet. You need to make sure that the class named is on the CLASSPATH inside the WAR file; the easiest way to do this is to use maven_library or include_library:

```
servlet 'org.jruby.webapp.FancierRailsServlet'
```

compile_ruby BOOLEAN

GoldSpike can try to compile all Ruby files before packaging them. This demands that all files in your project are supported by the JRuby compiler. In this case, the WAR file won't contain any Ruby source (except for the views), but instead the Ruby functionality will be found in Java class files. The default at the moment is false.

```
compile_ruby true
```

add_gem_dependencies BOOLEAN

In some situations, you might not want all the dependencies of all your Gems being included in the WAR file. If you set this to false, only the Rails Gems are included in the WAR file. The default is true, and you must make sure that the code has some way of getting at these dependencies in another way if you set it to false.

```
add_gem_dependencies false
```

keep_source BOOLEAN

When `compile_ruby` is set to `true`, you can specify that you still want the WAR file to include the Ruby source too. The only situation where this might be useful is for looking at the source on the server to find errors. It can also be useful for following backtraces when something goes wrong. Overall, if you compile Ruby, it's usually not a problem leaving the sources out. The default is `false`.

```
keep_source true
```

add_gem NAME, VERSION

Because GoldSpike has no way of knowing which Gems you need for your application, you need to add these manually. Depending on the setting of `add_gem_dependencies`, you might not have to specify that many Gems here. The version string is a standard RubyGems version, which means you can specify major version, minor version, and if it should be equal to or larger than the version provided.

```
add_gem 'RedCloth', '= 3.0.4'
```

datasource_jndi BOOLEAN

Set this to `true` if the application uses JNDI as a data source for database connections. The default is `false`. If it's set to `true`, you also need to provide a `datasource_jndi_name`.

```
datasource_jndi true
```

datasource_jndi_name NAME

If you're using a JNDI data source to provide database connection for the application, you need to specify the JNDI name that's to be used, so that GoldSpike can provide a resource definition for this:

```
datasource_jndi_name "jdbc/fooDataSource"
```

include_library NAME, PROPERTIES

If you need to include a specific Java library, there are two ways to do it: you use either `include_library` or `maven_library`. Use `maven_library` when the JAR file is in some Maven repository. When you have the file in your file system, you should use `include_file`. Now, the name is the part of the JAR file except for version information. Properties should be a map containing both `:version` and `:locations`. Locations can either be a string or an array of strings, each detailing paths to the JAR file:

```
include_library 'foobar', :version => '1.2.3-snapshot',
                          :locations => 'lib/java/foobar.java'
```

maven_library GROUP, NAME, VERSION

The easiest way to add a Java library to your Rails application is to define it as a Maven library. When you've done that, GoldSpike will just download the library from a Maven repository for you. Simple and handy. You need to specify the group, name, and version:

```
maven_library 'mysql', 'mysql-connector-java', '5.0.4'
```

Deploying the WAR File

As you have a finished WAR file, let's take a few seconds to look at the options for deployment you have. If you already have a Java web container or application server lying around, that would be a first choice. Otherwise, several options work well that are also available as open source. The most obvious of these are Tomcat, Jetty, GlassFish, Geronimo, and JBoss. What they all have in common is that it's incredibly easy to deploy into them; you usually can just put a WAR file into their respective autodeployment directories, and the application server takes care of the rest.

In fact, to be able to deploy a Rails-in-a-WAR, the only real requirement is that the application server must unpack the WAR archive somewhere. Rails is file centric, and won't work at all unless it's unpacked.

Of all the available choices you can make, I would recommend using Tomcat for deployment. If you need other enterprise resources, running Tomcat within JBoss is a solution that has been tried and true for a long time. GlassFish and Geronimo have some interesting new features, but at the time of writing they aren't production quality and won't be for a while.

To reinforce the recommended approach, we'll walk through packaging and deploying in Tomcat.

If you have Tomcat installed, you can skip this step; otherwise, download it from `http://tomcat.apache.org/download-60.cgi`. You just need to have core distribution. If you're on Linux or Mac OS X, take the appropriate package and unpack it somewhere (I'm unpacking it into ~/system/tomcat). If you're on Windows, download the installer and run it. Make sure to start it (usually by running $TOMCAT_HOME/bin/startup.sh or $TOMCAT_HOME/bin/startup.bat), and navigate to `http://localhost:8080` to see that it works (see Figure 11-1).

Figure 11-1. *The standard Tomcat start page*

After that, it's time to add the GoldSpike plug-in to your application:

```
jruby script/plugin install -x
   svn://rubyforge.org/var/svn/jruby-extras/trunk/rails-integration/plugins/goldspike
```

As mentioned earlier, you need to add your database driver to a `war.rb` file (see Listing 11-1).

Listing 11-1. *config/war.rb*

```
maven_library 'mysql', 'mysql-connector-java', '5.0.4'
```

Once that's done you can just create the WAR file by running this:

```
jruby -S rake war:standalone:create
```

Figure 11-2 shows you what the output of that command looks like.

Figure 11-2. *Creating a WAR file with GoldSpike*

If your Tomcat is started, you can now deploy the application by copying it into Tomcat's webapps directory:

```
cp shoplet.war $TOMCAT_HOME/webapps
```

Look in the file $TOMCAT_HOME/logs/localhost.TODAYS-DATE.log, where TODAYS-DATE is today's date, until you see Runtime 0 loaded. At that point you should be able to navigate to localhost:8080/shoplet. You need to add some products, because this is the production environment. So, the first place you should visit is localhost:8080/shoplet/products and add some new products (see Figure 11-3).

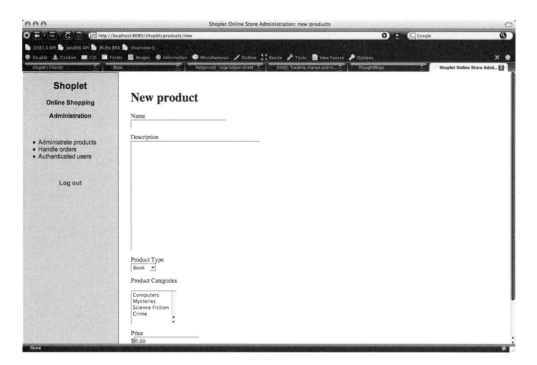

Figure 11-3. *The Shoplet application running on Tomcat*

Right now you have Rails running in a production environment with two runtimes loaded by default. More will be added if concurrent requests arrive that need it. If you want to deploy this solution into production, you should probably add an Apache front end to this package, but that's not entirely necessary.

Summary

This chapter has focused solely on the hard question of deployment. It's difficult to do the subject justice, especially because what's in vogue for deployment shifts from month to month in the Rails world. Nonetheless, packaging JRuby on Rails applications into WAR files ideally won't be as short lived. It seems to be a wonderful solution to the problem, and the flexibility and power you get from it is unsurpassed compared to other solutions. That said, if Mongrel is your thing, JRuby can handle that, too. However, if you have a free choice, I'd say that GoldSpike is the recommended solution.

In the next project, we'll take a look at some other services that are usually an important part of the enterprise. There we'll see how to integrate all those things that you traditionally have to use Java for, into a great solution where Rails is used sometimes and Java at other times.

PROJECT 4

∎∎∎

A Library System (LibLib)

Web Services with JRuby

With this chapter we begin work on the final project in this book. Without doubt, it will be the most complex application described in this book, and not all code will be written out because that would take too much space. You can download the full source code from the Source Code/Download area of the Apress web site at http://www.apress.com.

In the applications we've created so far, we've had the luxury of writing most of the code ourselves. Things are not always so easy in the real world, and we'll now take a closer look at specific ways to interoperate with other language systems, primarily using web services and Java Messaging Service (JMS).

Web services will be the first focus, though, and we'll quickly see how easy some parts of interoperating can be with Ruby. However, in the end it makes more sense to use the Java solutions to get hold of the stability and reliability of these implementations.

Web services have been a staple of the enterprise world for a long time. With the appearance of the REST protocols, some of this has changed, but there are still many SOAP services in the world. For a long time, the S in SOAP meant "simple," but this has now changed. Working with the whole web service stack can be extremely complicated without the right tools to help. I won't take the WS-* approach too far in this chapter; I'll just look at what you need to do to get started with web services that are exposed on the Internet. If you want to create your own web service, you're probably better off using REST, and Rails has extremely good support for REST. A sidebar about REST is included at the end of the chapter, but that is all I'll say about REST in this book, because nice documentation of Rails and REST exists in other places.

Like the description of XML libraries earlier, we'll develop standalone programs in this chapter, and generalize into a library that can be dumped into a Rails application later. The web service chosen as an example is Amazon Web Services (AWS). This has both advantages and drawbacks; it's a mature system with an incredible amount of operations (but we'll only use a small subset in this chapter). It's available for free as a developer service, and it's a useful service. The largest drawback is that because it's so complicated, dynamically generating calls to it is not feasible. For that reason, I'm going to show a simpler version of dynamically generating web service code, so we can still discuss how to accomplish that.

First of all, we need to take a look at the project we're developing.

The LibLib System

Project 4 will be a library system called LibriLiberation, or LibLib for short. What makes it an interesting challenge is that there is an existing legacy system that takes care of all book information and also part of the borrowing data. The only current way to interoperate with this system is through a custom data format sent through a message queue. A JMS interface to this queue exists, so that Java systems can use the legacy data. The legacy system doesn't have any concept of users; it just associates an identifier with a borrowing, and it's up to the library systems to handle this identifier.

What makes the situation more complex is that each library will have its own instance of the Rails web application running (because this information should only be available on the intranet in each library). The main goal of the Rails installation is to provide a web system that runs on all computers in each library. You can search for books there, you can add yourself as a new borrower, and you can also see some information about yourself and the books you've borrowed.

As I mentioned, each library system wants to have its own Rails application and separate databases with user and administrator information. To avoid having to replicate this information across all libraries all the time, replication messages are sent using JMS topics when there is need for them. In this way, a new library can be opened without having to change the existing instances of the application.

Communication between libraries is opened up when a user who already has an account at another library walks into a library where he or she hasn't been before. When this happens and the user tries to log in to loan a book, the LibLib instance will send out a general request for information, and will update its own records if the user is found in any other system. Otherwise, it will require the user to create a new identity in the system.

The third usage of the LibLib system is as an administrative user interface for adding and removing books, and also for handling users. The admin interface is local to each library, but new books added to the system will be available in the central legacy system so that searches from other libraries can see it. At the moment there is only one way to add a new book to the system, and that is through importing the information from Amazon and "buying" it. (In fact, you won't buy anything from Amazon right now; it suffices to just extract the information through AWS and add this to the legacy database.)

So, to recap, you have these moving parts:

- A legacy system containing book information for each library.

- A JMS system that allows communication between the legacy system and the different LibLib instances.

- One LibLib instance for each library, containing the following:

    - One database with user, administrator, and borrowing information.

    - A user interface, allowing book browsing, borrowing, and the addition of new users.

    - An administrative interface, allowing user and book administration.

I won't show you the legacy system code at all. The only thing visible will be the JMS interface that you interact with, and in fact that's how legacy interaction usually works: it gets hidden behind a simple interface of some kind, which just makes all the strange details happen automatically. In the downloadable code I'll implement the legacy system in simple Java, but it could just as well have been a mainframe running VAX/VMS behind it.

We'll take a closer look at the other parts in the next two chapters, but for now we'll concentrate on the communication with AWS to allow importing book information into our system.

Amazon Web Services

Amazon has extensive resources available in its systems, and you can access almost all of them through several exposed web services interfaces. You can access most of the functionality either through SOAP or REST. (If you have any choice, you should use REST, but that doesn't let me show you how to work with SOAP from Ruby.) You'll be using a specific service called KeywordSearch, which allows you to fetch information about books based on search information. What you get back from such a keyword search is enough to fill in the information in your legacy system, so that is all you'll be using. In fact, if you ever find yourself wanting to create a bookstore, you could do it all with web service calls to Amazon. Everything is there, even payment gateways.

In fact, Amazon has several resources that don't pertain specifically to business transactions either. For example, the Amazon Elastic Compute Cloud (EC2) provides scalable virtual private servers, and the Amazon Simple Storage Service provides web-hosted storage for applications. The part containing the core business services is called Amazon E-Commerce Service (ECS). ECS has gone through four different revisions, and all are more or less different from one another. Due to a problem with SOAP4R, you won't use ECS 4 (the latest version); the ECS 4 WSDL specification isn't correctly handled currently. Ideally this will have been remedied at the time you read this, though, but for now you'll use ECS 3 both for the Ruby code and the Java code (even though the Java code can handle ECS 4).

To use ECS, you'd have to buy a license from Amazon. However, because you're just doing development right now, that isn't needed. Instead, you can just go to http://aws.amazon.com and sign up for a Web Services account as a developer. You can't do everything with this account, but it provides enough capabilities so you can search for books and develop most applications. After you've created the account, you need to find your AWS Access Key ID. You can do this by clicking the button "Your Web Services Account," choosing "AWS Access Identifiers," and logging in. You should replace my placeholder with your key in all places, or your code won't work.

If nothing else is noted in the text, all the code displayed can be run as is, from either Ruby or JRuby. The SOAP4R library currently works well with both implementations, and you won't use any Java features right now. Of course, when we turn to using Java classes for SOAP, this changes.

Also, a Ruby/Amazon library exists that wraps these operations and makes them much more usable. However, once again, that wouldn't help you when looking at SOAP services.

SOAP4R

SOAP4R is an implementation of a library that supports SOAP 1.1 and WSDL for Ruby. It is WS-I compliant. It was first released in 2000 and has been distributed with Ruby for quite some time now. It hasn't seen any significant updates in a while, but is pretty stable where it's at right now. It was written by Hiroshi Nakamura, and can be a little hard to get right sometimes. One thing to keep in mind is that the error messages you get might not always be so useful. In that case, it always helps to turn on wire dumping, which lets you see the XML documents going out and coming in as they are, without any parsing or processing. Because SOAP4R only supports SOAP 1.1, it can be limiting when trying to use it against new web services that use more advanced features. There are also ways in which SOAP4R breaks unexpectedly for valid input. I've run into one case where an object contained a property called "not", which broke SOAP4R completely. In the same manner, using multipart MIME documents seems to fail consistently.

Despite this, SOAP4R is highly useful both in development and production. It allows you to consume web services much more easily than with any other language, and the malleability of the Ruby language helps the implementation a lot. Also, when problems arise it can often be simple to find them yourself and fix them. On the other hand, some limitations are hard to get around. For example, SOAP4R doesn't like multipart MIME data very much, and the only solution I've found to that problem is to strip all multipart data from the SOAP response before SOAP4R sees it.

The WSDL support is quite nice, allowing you to generate both server and client stubs from a WSDL file. If the WSDL isn't too complicated, you can generate this information at runtime too. There is support for XML Schema, but it's not complete. Further, SOAP4R doesn't support generating WSDL at this point.

SOAP4R also can handle both SSL communication and authentication using either HTTP BASIC or SSL authentication through the underlying transport layer. You can also do some low-level things with SOAP if you feel the need to, working outside WSDL and other communication protocols. You probably won't be compatible with other implementations while doing this, but the library still makes it easy.

Dynamic Generation

It can be easy to call a web service with a dynamic language. (In fact, this specific technique also works in Java, but through entirely different means.) In some situations you would want the ability just to call a web service directly, specifying its WSDL address, and then be finished with it. SOAP4R supports this for simple structures, but breaks down when you need to have custom objects as parameters. The AWS KeywordSearch is implemented to take a single argument that is a Data Transfer Object, making the dynamic generation break down in SOAP4R. Because of this, we'll instead look at a simple stock quote service, which happens to be the canonical SOAP example:

```
require 'soap/wsdlDriver'

wsdl = 'http://services.xmethods.net/soap/urn:xmethods-delayed-quotes.wsdl'
driver = SOAP::WSDLDriverFactory.new(wsdl).create_rpc_driver
puts 'Stock Price: %.2f' % driver.getQuote('MSFT')
```

If all goes well, this little snippet will output "Stock Price: 1.01." (At the time of writing it outputs 30.58, so I guess that number is wishful thinking.)

Let's take a quick look at what is going on here. First of all, if you aren't familiar with WSDL, it stands for Web Services Description Language, and is an XML dialect specifically designed to describe web services, the available actions, and what arguments they take and return. It's a complicated language, and if you're lucky you'll never have to understand or use it directly.

You begin by doing a require on the file soap/wsdlDriver.rb, which provides all the functionality you need to create a SOAP client based on WSDL. The URL to the WSDL file points to a free service hosted by XMethods, providing delayed quote information. You then create a new WSDLDriverFactory with the URL to the file, and then create a Remote Procedure Call (RPC) driver from the factory. That's all you need to do. The dynamic nature of Ruby takes care of the rest, so that when you call the method getQuote with "MSFT" as the argument, SOAP4R will find the description of the getQuote RPC method call in the WSDL file, will see that it takes one argument that matches what you sent, and then will generate an XML SOAP file containing this information. It will send this document to an endpoint described in the WSDL, and that endpoint will generate an answer based on the information you sent in. This answer will get embedded in a SOAP response XML format and will be sent back to your system. SOAP4R will again use the information in the WSDL file and unmarshal the XML data, extracting the return value of the method call you executed. This will result in returning a float value representing the current stock quote of MSFT to your program, which you then format and print.

As mentioned earlier, this solution works well for a major part of all web services that exist. Most systems take parameters that are easy to handle, and when this is the case SOAP4R will always let you call that service dynamically. Doing all this computation at runtime can be a major performance bottleneck, so even in this case you might be better off using another solution.

Using Stubs

Arguably the best way to invoke WSDL services is to use a code generator that reads the WSDL file and then generates proxy stubs that invoke the SOAP call correctly. One of the reasons that this model is superior is because SOAP4R can't handle all types of calls dynamically. For example, a call to AWS requires the code to be pregenerated, because the calls need an argument that is a complex type.

It is still easy to accomplish this with SOAP4R, though, using the wsdl2ruby.rb command. Unfortunately, this utility part of SOAP4R isn't available in the Ruby core distribution, so you need to install the soap4r Gem. This adds the wsdl2ruby.rb file into your bin directory. Create an empty directory and execute this command in it:

```
jruby -S wsdl2ruby --type client
    --wsdl http://soap.amazon.com/schemas3/AmazonWebServices.wsdl
```

The output of this command will generate three different files. These files are called AmazonSearch.rb, AmazonSearchDriver.rb, and AmazonSearchServiceClient.rb. The file AmazonSearch.rb contains information about all the complex types this web service supports. Because Amazon's web services are large, there are many classes in this file. The AmazonSearchDriver.rb file contains mappings between service endpoint information and the model classes. Finally, the AmazonSearchServiceClient.rb file contains some example code showing how to use this web service. You'll create a new file from scratch in this directory, called amazon1.rb (see Listing 12-1).

Listing 12-1. *amazon1.rb*

```
require 'pp'
require 'rubygems'
require_gem 'soap4r'
require 'AmazonSearchDriver.rb'

endpoint_url = ARGV.shift || AmazonSearchPort::DefaultEndpointUrl
obj = AmazonSearchPort.new(endpoint_url)

obj.wiredump_dev = STDERR if $DEBUG
```

```
devtag = "XXXXXXXXXXXXXX" #REPLACE WITH YOUR OWN AWS ID

keywordSearchRequest = KeywordRequest.new("Ruby", "1",
                                            "books", nil, "lite", devtag)
pp obj.keywordSearchRequest(keywordSearchRequest).
        details.map{|d| [d.productName, d.authors]}
```

Here you're doing some more things, making this code a little clunkier. On the other hand, you get some nice capabilities, and it performs way better. Further, this code works with Amazon, which the other approach wouldn't have.

First of all, you require the pp library, which stands for "pretty print." This allows you to present a much more readable view of the information you fetch. Because you create the stubs with wsdl2ruby.rb from a Gem, you need to use the same Gem to run this, to make sure there are no incompatibility problems. Finally, you require the AmazonSearchDriver, which gives you the AmazonSearchPort class.

Also, you allow a customized endpoint to be added to the arguments to this program, but if it's not used you just provide the default endpoint URL. The capability to use different endpoints for the same stubs makes it easy to have one environment for development and one for production, because you can just switch the endpoint URL used.

You use the AmazonSearchPort class to call remote methods on the Amazon service. If someone provides the -d flag to the Ruby interpreter, you also dump everything that happens to STDERR. This allows you to inspect the XML being generated and sent. You need to insert your own AWS development tag where noted. Then you create a KeywordRequest object, which holds all the parameters that you want to send to the call. You're interested in the keyword Rails, and page 1. You want to search among everything with type "books", and you want the smaller result version. That's almost all there is to it. You call details on the result, fetch the book name and author names, and print this in a nice way.

That's how simple it is to consume an Amazon web service. Of course, Amazon is one of the web services that work well with SOAP4R. In other circumstances (or if you want to use ECS 4) you might not be so lucky. In those cases, SOAP4R breaks down and it's hard to fix in certain cases. That's where it would be useful to have Java implementations of SOAP and WSDL available . . .

SOAP with Java

There are several good frameworks for working with both server- and client-side SOAP and WSDL in Java. Among the open source ones, Axis and XFire are highly regarded. We'll use XFire, because it's easy to use, fast, and incredibly compliant. It supports most of the standards (SOAP, WSDL, WS-I Basic Profile, WS-Addressing, and WS-Security), and the SOAP stack is good. It supports pluggable bindings to several different services, such as Plain Old Java Objects (POJOs), XMLBeans, Java Architecture for XML Binding (JAXB), and Castor. It can also use different transports, such as HTTP, JMS, Extensible Messaging and Presence Protocol

(XMPP), and In-JVM—SOAP4R only supports HTTP. It also can generate both client and server stubs. Overall, it's a well rounded package for working with web services, and indicative of the differences between Ruby libraries and Java counterparts. Because several competing (and all good) SOAP frameworks exist, it means you don't have to stay with XFire if it proves problematic for some reason. To illustrate this principle, halfway through writing this section I decided to switch from XFire to Axis, because XFire doesn't support the RPC/Encoded type needed by AWS. However, because the XFire dynamic client code is extremely readable, I'll use that to illustrate dynamic generation of code.

To use XFire, you need to have Commons Logging on your CLASSPATH, and also WSDL4J, which you can download from http://www.ibiblio.org/maven/wsdl4j/jars. You also need Apache WS-Commons, which you can download here: http://ws.apache.org/commons/XmlSchema/download.cgi. Also, download JDOM 1.0 from http://www.ibiblio.org/maven/jdom/jars and Commons HTTPClient from http://www.ibiblio.org/maven/commons-httpclient/jars. Commons HTTPClient requires Commons Codec from http://www.ibiblio.org/maven/commons-codec/jars.

Dynamic Generation

XFire shares the same problem as SOAP4R regarding generating arbitrarily nested objects as arguments. Because that's the case, we'll instead implement a small web service client that fetches the conversion rates between two currencies. This code won't look too different from the SOAP4R code, in fact:

```
require 'java'
require 'xfire-all-1.2.6.jar'

import org.codehaus.xfire.client.Client

client = Client.new(java.net.URL.new(
        "http://www.webservicex.net/CurrencyConvertor.asmx?WSDL"))

results = client.invoke("ConversionRate", ["USD","SEK"].to_java)

puts 'Conversion rate: %.2f' % results[0]
```

This code depends on you having the xfire-all-1.2.6.jar file in the current directory. Modify as needed. You require 'java' to get hold of the JRuby Java integration features and then import the XFire Client class. You then create a new Client based on a URL object that points to the WSDL file in question. Notice that the WSDL you're using here points to a Microsoft .NET assembly. Isn't that bridging the gaps? Using Ruby to drive Java classes to communicate with a .NET service—neat.

You then invoke the method ConversionRate and send it a primitive Java array containing the two currencies you want to get the rate for. You need to explicitly turn the Ruby array into a primitive Java array using to_java. What you get back from the invoke call is always an array, because a web service can return more than one value. Here you just use the first value and print it in a formatted style.

Notice the fact that using this code through JRuby made it almost as painless as using the SOAP4R version. You can improve the experience, though. After you've imported the Client class, use this code:

```
class Client
  def method_missing(name, *args)
    self.invoke(name.to_s, args.to_java)
  end
end
```

You can now replace the invocation code with this:

```
results = client.ConversionRate("USD","SEK")
```

The code looks almost exactly like the corresponding SOAP4R code would look. It's a powerful concept to be able to add handling for Ruby method processing to Java objects in this way, and it makes it dead easy to create usable APIs, even when the original Java library is cumbersome. So, what's still wrong here? Well, we can't invoke the Amazon services with this code either . . . Let's see what XFire gives us for stubbing.

Using Stubs

Just as with SOAP4R, it usually makes sense to create static stubs for invocation in Java. In Java this is even more true, due to the high cost of reflection and dynamic invocation of methods. In contrast with XFire, you add the needed files to the CLASSPATH instead, because JRuby will handle the XML parsing a bit strangely otherwise. You need to have commons-discovery.jar on your CLASSPATH. Finally, you need jaxrpc.jar from the Axis distribution:

```
java org.apache.axis.wsdl.WSDL2Java
      'http://soap.amazon.com/schemas3/AmazonWebServices.wsdl'
```

This command generates a directory called com/amazon/soap that contains all Java classes needed. The next step is to compile all these files:

```
javac com/amazon/soap/*.java
```

When this has been done, you can finally proceed to use the classes to implement a simple service:

```
require 'java'
require 'pp'

$CLASSPATH << '.'

devtag = "XXXXXXXXXXXXXXXXXX" #REPLACE WITH YOUR OWN AWS ID

port = com.amazon.soap.AmazonSearchServiceLocator.
                new.getAmazonSearchPort
req = com.amazon.soap.KeywordRequest.new(
              "Ruby", "1", "books", "", "lite", devtag, nil, nil, nil)

pp port.keywordSearchRequest(req).
      details.map{|d| [d.productName, d.authors.to_a]}
```

As you can see, this code is similar to what you used when generating stubs with SOAP4R. The big difference here is that this code is backed by Java, performs better, and supports many more features than SOAP4R. You do need to jump through some additional hoops to get everything to work seamlessly here. You first add the current directory to the CLASSPATH used by JRuby. This feature can be handy but doesn't work for all kinds of classes (database drivers and XML drivers, for example). You then use the AmazonSearchServiceLocator to get a port for the Amazon search. This additional layer of indirection means that Axis can generate arbitrarily complex Web Services clients, including those that include more than one port and service. When you have the port, you create a KeywordRequest, exactly like in SOAP4R and then call the method keywordSearchRequest on the port object. You fetch the details collection and map this. The only thing you need to add here is a call to to_a on the authors array, because you get back a primitive Java array from the authors call, and that doesn't display as well.

If you run the SOAP4R version and the Axis version side by side, you shouldn't see any difference in the output at all (except possibly a warning about attachment support not turned on from Axis).

What's interesting with this approach is that you could, if you wanted, begin by implementing everything in Ruby and try different things out. Then, when you want the more stable and better-performing SOAP version you go ahead and generate the Java stubs instead and switch the implementations. Because these two versions are almost exactly the same, this works well in practice.

As usual when working with Java libraries, you need to have many JAR files on your CLASSPATH. This can get messy and unwieldy, and sometimes it's hard to find clashes between libraries. However, in the end it still works out well. Even better, you can approach the problem like I did, by first trying one implementation and seeing if it has what it takes, and if not, switching to something else. In the Java world alternatives always exist. When wrapping these libraries in an expressive language such as Ruby, it means that you can switch Java libraries easily—especially if you've created a DSL layer around the Java code to make it even easier to use. Several JRuby applications use this approach; for example, the RMagickJr Gem wraps the Java2d libraries instead of using a native implementation of ImageMagick. If something goes wrong, RMagickJr can always change to another implementation of these algorithms, and the clients need never see anything different.

Using Java for SOAP and XML services is always a good choice, because the Ruby support is sometimes lacking. Even more important, the Java libraries are usually rock solid. In many cases the reference implementations are written in Java, which means that you can achieve a higher level of compliance than would ever be possible using Ruby. There's much talk about Ruby being a good glue language, meaning that most applications consist mostly of libraries glued together with some business logic. Ruby excels in this, and JRuby makes it even better by making it possible for you to glue Java libraries to Ruby libraries and Ruby business code.

Creating a Small Book Library

The first step to packing all this up into one usable bundle is to create a JAR file containing the Axis-generated stubs you created earlier. Just package all those class files into a file called amazon.jar. After this, you're ready to create a small library that you can use from a Rails application or another Ruby script to fetch relevant book information from Amazon, based on a keyword.

There isn't that much to this library, but it will give a little more Rubyesque access to this book information. Without further ado, take a look at Listing 12-2.

Listing 12-2. *book_service.rb*

```ruby
require 'java'
require 'amazon.jar'

module BookService
  DEVTAG = "XXXXXXXXXXXXXXXXXX" #REPLACE WITH YOUR OWN AWS ID
  PORT = com.amazon.soap.AmazonSearchServiceLocator.
                         new.getAmazonSearchPort
  KeywordRequest = com.amazon.soap.KeywordRequest

  Book = Struct.new(:name, :authors, :isbn, :image_url, :price, :publisher)

  class Book
    def self.from_info(info)
      new(info.productName,
          info.authors.to_a,
          info.asin,
          info.imageUrlSmall,
          info.ourPrice,
          info.manufacturer
          )
    end
  end

  def self.find(keyword)
    values = []
    index = 1
    val = nil
    while !val || val.length == 10 && index < 11
      req = KeywordRequest.new(keyword, index.to_s,
                         "books", "", "lite", DEVTAG, nil, nil, nil)
      val = PORT.keywordSearchRequest(req).details
      values += val.to_a
      index += 1
    end rescue nil
    into_books(values)
  end

  private
  def self.into_books(val)
    val.map{|v| Book.from_info(v) }
  end
end

if __FILE__ == $0
  p BookService.find("jruby on rails")
end
```

The code begins by including the `amazon.jar` file you created earlier. When you've done that, you can go ahead and create your `AmazonSearchPort` within the module, and assign that to a constant, so you never need to create such an object again. You also need to import the `KeywordRequest` class so you can work more easily with this when creating keyword searches.

A `Struct` called `Book` is created so you have somewhere to save all the information. You also need a helper method that will create new `Book` objects from the `ProductInfo` object that's contained in the result's `details` array. Just go ahead and extract the interesting information from this object and call `new` on the `Book` object, returning it at the same time.

The `find` method is the central part of this module; it takes a keyword and returns an array of `Books`. We'd like to fetch all books in one go, but that doesn't seem possible, so you have to iterate until there are no more pages to fetch. You can see this either by the fact that the list returned is not ten items long, or an exception is thrown. On both these conditions, you `rescue nil` and call `into_books`, which turns a native array of Java `ProductInfo` objects into `Book` objects in a regular Ruby `Array`.

Finally, if the current file executing is this, we try to find books mentioning JRuby on Rails (this only returns the book you're holding at the moment, but when you read it, ideally this situation will have changed).

This is all there is to using a Java web service from Ruby. It's intuitive and nice, and it makes building SOA applications doable, if not fun.

REST

The latest vogue in web services is not really a technology, but rather a few guidelines about how to do useful but simple web services. The original term comes from a paper by Roy Fielding, written in 2000. *REST* stands for Representational State Transfer, and the idea is to use the underlying transport layer to make the communication more intuitive for both developers and machines.

The main way this applies to current web services is through web services consumed over HTTP. That isn't necessarily all there is to REST, but it's certainly where most code is written. The way REST looks at the world is through resources. Everything is resources, and you do things to these resources. When using HTTP, REST uses the HTTP verbs to make resource management easy to handle. As a concrete example, say you want to fetch information about a specific blog post. You'd do a `GET /posts/1` request. If you want to add a new post, you do `PUT /posts`, and provide a simple XML representation of the information to add in the request body. Updating an entry works the same way; just use something like `POST /posts/1`, providing the data to be updated. `DELETE /posts/1` is also obvious.

The main difference between REST web services and old school RPC web services using SOAP and other systems is that RPC usually exposes an object with operations that you can invoke on it. REST generalizes this to talking about resources, and doing a small set of operations—usually CRUD—on these resources. This makes them easier to reason about and usually also to understand. Other benefits are that you usually don't need to send as much information, and most of the communication is understandable by humans.

Rails has good support for REST web services, both consuming and producing them. In fact, using the helpers that Rails provides, you can easily do web services that act and look exactly like ActiveRecord models, and the code for these ActiveResource models is as simple as those for ActiveRecord.

REST also shows up in other places. For example, JavaBeans can be described as using a REST protocol. Also, the ATOM publishing protocol is considered to be "RESTful" in design.

It can be argued that the right way to do SOA would be to use REST interfaces between small, focused applications. This would make it easier to have the different services communicate among one another, doing away with high-ceremony angle brackets. It also makes it easier for external clients, because they can choose which parts of the services they are interested in, and don't need to concern themselves with other resources or operations. It allows services to be more focused on the business logic while retaining (and improving) the flexibility of web services.

Summary

In this chapter we've seen several ways to use web services. Since their introduction many years back, they've resurfaced all over the place, and they're now an integral part of many applications on the Web. Even though some of the current services are converted to a REST style, many parts of the infrastructure will still depend on SOAP, WSDL, WS-I, and other protocols that are cumbersome to use and hard to implement.

In those circumstances it makes sense to use the best implementation you can find, to avoid more trouble than necessary. We've seen that SOAP4R leaves something to be desired, instead of being counted among the better implementations. By turning to Java implementations instead, we made it much easier to use web services safely.

In the next chapter we'll do a deep dive into Message-Oriented Middleware (MOM)—specifically, message queues that allow us to talk to legacy services. We'll also take a serious look at some of the parts of the LibLib application, looking closely at the architecture.

CHAPTER 13

■ ■ ■

JRuby and Message-Oriented Systems

You can interact with legacy systems in three major ways: with web services, with Message-Oriented Middleware (MOM), and with binary socket communication. It's common to add a thin layer of web services or MOMs over a binary-based legacy system, so in practice that's what we'll be working against. We looked at web services in the last chapter; this chapter will be devoted to MOMs, with some help from the Java Messaging Service (JMS). To drive the point home about a cumbersome interface, the legacy system described will have an inconvenient binary protocol—well, not inconvenient, but bad enough.

First of all, we'll take a closer look at what a MOM can incorporate and why large organizations like to use them. (MOMs are highly useful for several domains, in fact—not just for legacy systems.) After that, I'll describe in some detail the protocol of the legacy system, but I won't provide the code for it here. (You can download the code from the Source Code/Download area at `http://www.apress.com`, and you have to do that to be able to run these examples, unless you decide to implement this interface yourself.)

I'll show you a library called ActiveMessaging, which has some nice features. We won't be using it in this chapter, because the support for JRuby isn't fully fleshed out at the time of writing. Instead, we'll use the JMS libraries directly. This isn't as painful as it sounds, but there's lots of boilerplate code to set up Java objects in this chapter, due to our use of JMS directly. Also, make sure that you have a GlassFish installation handy, because that application server will be used for all examples.

After that, we'll quickly look at what there is to know about using JRuby and message-driven beans (MDBs) together, and finally we'll create two libraries. The first one will help us connect to the legacy system, and also retrieve answers from it. The second library will allow communication between several Rails servers; this example will show situations where a MOM can be useful, especially if there's no way to have a shared database between instances of Rails.

We'll use both these libraries as is in the LibLib Rails application we'll build in the next chapter. They'll be tuned to the demands of this application, and not used as general libraries right now.

It's important to keep in mind that message-based systems can simplify certain problem domains significantly, but they also have a tendency to become a golden hammer. Queues and Topics can be a part of many types of distributed applications, but it's rare to need them at the core of the application. They add considerable power, but also some complexity, especially in deployment.

What Is MOM?

We need to begin by taking a look at the concept of MOM. MOM stands for Message-Oriented Middleware, and the name is used to group together a wide range of libraries and applications that enable inter-application communication. This communication is usually asynchronous. RPC, CORBA, and other systems that enable synchronous execution of code in a distributed way are not classically called MOM. There are two basic variations on the message orientation: either you can use message queues, or you can use a system of broadcast or multicast messages. In fact, most modern MOM servers include both those variations because they're useful for different purposes. When talking about message queues, the name "queue" is usually used; when talking about broadcast or multicast, the most common term used is "topic."

Middleware has traditionally been used in many situations for legacy integration; for example, where an old mainframe system should be connected to modern PCs over a network. Usually, the difference between the mainframe and the PCs necessitates that the integrator creates adapters in both the mainframe and the PCs. Using a middleware system, where all the logic that connects to the mainframe is contained, and where the middleware also handles communication with the PCs, makes the implementation much easier on both sides. That's because the mainframe doesn't have to be changed, and the software in the PCs isn't constrained by limitations of the mainframe. Of course, the PC software usually needs to adapt to an asynchronous programming model, but that's usually worth the effort, especially because modern windowing systems are all message-based anyway.

MOM servers and libraries usually provide many services based around the message passing. Many of these can be important, and a real MOM is not usable for a real application if it doesn't feature most of these. Persistent messages are central. This means that one application can register interest in a topic, and the MOM then saves away all messages for this application, even if that application isn't online at that moment. This is close to how e-mail works, so it shouldn't come as a surprise. A MOM can also guarantee that a message will never get lost. If it cannot be delivered, there are usually many ways of describing how the sender or the MOM should handle this. Further, many MOM systems include advanced support for rollback of different degrees, which means that you can sometimes integrate your MOM system with databases using two-phase commit, and get transactional safety all over the system. Of course, that's a major feature that most applications don't often need.

MOM services don't necessarily need to be located in one server. In fact, they're at their most useful when you have hundreds of MOM servers, all routing messages among each other to different applications and services that need them.

Further, a MOM can also transform messages as it goes. Once again, all these functionalities are close to e-mail in concept. What makes the transformations extra practical is that in many cases the MOM provider also provides good graphical tools for dragging and dropping transformations.

Before we get into the legacy system, a few concepts need to be clarified, because they're often used when talking about MOMs. I'll use the vocabulary of JMS to make things easier.

First of all, a message is divided into a header and a body. The header contains lots of information, and can also contain user-provided properties. In larger systems, it can be useful to route and direct messages based on their properties. The body of a message can contain most things, but in Java there are some restrictions on what kind of data you can send.

Broadly, you can send a dictionary of data, you can send a serialized Java object as data, or you can send text messages as data. All these versions provide easy support for sending all kinds of information, but the text message is arguably the easiest way to send information. You can also send empty messages that only contain header data.

Both queues and topics are called *destinations* (which isn't true, because the destination of a message is the endpoint, which is the code handling the message). Systems that send messages are called *producers* and systems that get messages are called *consumers*. There are also more specific words that are only used in connection with a specific type of destination. A *publisher* is a producer for a topic, and a *subscriber* is a consumer for a topic. For a queue, the producer is called a *sender*, and the consumer is called a *receiver*. You can guess the major difference between a topic and a queue from the names of the actors. In a topic, a publisher can publish something, and all subscribers to that topic will get that message. In the same way, there can be more than one publisher for the same topic. A queue can also have more than one receiver, and more than one sender. The difference is that only one receiver will receive the same message. As seen earlier, a topic multicasts messages to all subscribers for that topic, while a queue delivers one message at a time to receivers. This feature of queues makes it mostly useful to have one receiver and many senders. Of course, there are situations where more than one receiver can be considered useful too.

The Legacy System

As the previous chapter described, the LibLib system will contain several Rails servers revolving around a central legacy system. Communication with this legacy system will go through a JMS system, where requests are sent to a queue and responses will be published to a topic. That means that the Rails application servers will need to keep track of a transaction ID so they can associate a response with the corresponding request. It's also important to note when reading this code that you'll use a MOM only for its legacy integration; you'll work around the asynchronous features of it into a regular method call framework.

This description will be divided into two parts. First we'll take a brief look at the binary data system that will be used by all communication, and then we'll look at the actual operations that are available to use. In a real-world situation you'd probably have to read a spec or existing client code (in the worst case, COBOL) to find out what this format is.

I hope this description will be a little more readable than either of those alternatives, especially because the format is designed to not be too hard for you.

The binary data format understands three different things: strings, lists, and integers. I'll use a variation on the Java generics syntax to specify what a specific call looks like. For example, `LIST<STRING, LIST<STRING, INTEGER>, INTEGER>` is a list of entries, where the first part of the entry is a string, the second part is a list of string and integer after each other, and finally an integer.

In the binary format, a list can be a maximum of 255 entries long. The list begins with one unsigned byte specifying the length, and then the entries of the list. Because the different data formats are predefined, and the content of each entry in a list is also predefined, there's no need for any kind of separator between entries. When one entry is finished, the next one begins.

A `String` works the same way. `Strings` can't be more than 255 characters long either, and the binary format is first the byte describing the length, then the actual contents of the strings.

Finally, integers are packed into two bytes. The maximum integer in the system is 65,535. The first byte is the higher bytes of the integer, and the second byte is the lower 255 values. For example, say you have the specification LIST<STRING, INTEGER>. Take a look at this binary example (where each tag represents one byte):

```
<2><5><72><101><108><108><111><0><42><5><87><111><114><108><100><3><24>
```

It's equal to a list containing "Hello", 42 as its first entry and "World", 792 as its second entry.

The system provides many different operations for you to use, and the application you'll build uses most of these. Shortly, I'll describe all available operations and the data format of the requests and responses. The mutating operations usually don't return any response, except when they create a new ID for an entry when the response is returned. The format for data uses the data types from earlier, but prepended by a descriptive name and a colon separating the name from the type, such as LibraryID:INTEGER.

The actual data contents of the request begin with one byte identifying which operation is requested.

Add Library

This operation creates a new library entry in the legacy system. You should only do this when a new Rails instance is set up for a new library. The ID of the newly created library is returned.

- *Operation ID*: 0

- *Request*: LibraryName:STRING

- *Response*: LibraryID:INTEGER

Remove Library

Removes the selected library from the legacy system. There are no checks in place that stop this from happening, even if there are still references to the library in other places. The library data is removed, but entries pointing to it aren't touched.

- *Operation ID*: 1

- *Request*: LibraryID:INTEGER

- *Response*: Nothing

Get Library Name

To get hold of the name of a library that you have the ID for, you can use this service. Provided you submit a valid ID, this service returns the name of that same library. Otherwise there is no return value at all.

- *Operation ID*: 9

- *Request*: LibraryID:INTEGER

- *Response*: LibraryName:STRING

Add Book Description

A book description contains the data the legacy system is interested in knowing about a book, which in this case is title, authors, and the ISBN number. Using this method doesn't mean you have any books matching the description, just that you might want to create instances of the description.

- *Operation ID*: 2

- *Request*: `Title:STRING Authors:LIST<Author:STRING> ISBN:STRING`

- *Response*: `BookDescriptionID:INTEGER`

Remove Book Description

This operation removes the specified book description from the system. Make sure that there are no instances of this book available in the system, otherwise the system might crash.

- *Operation ID*: 3

- *Request*: `BookDescriptionID:INTEGER`

- *Response*: Nothing

Get Book Description

This operation fetches all book information available from the database for a specific book description ID, and returns that information. That includes the regular information about a book, but also information about which instances are available, which are borrowed, and at which libraries they are.

- *Operation ID*: 10

- *Request*: `BookDescriptionID:INTEGER`

- *Response*: `BookDescriptionID:INTEGER Title:STRING`

    - `Authors:LIST<Author:STRING> ISBN:STRING`

    - `Instances:LIST<InstanceID:INTEGER LibraryID:INTEGER InLibrary:INTEGER>`

Add Book Instance

To add a new book instance, call this operation with the book description ID to add, and the ID of the library to add it to.

- *Operation ID*: 4

- *Request*: `LibraryID:INTEGER BookDescriptionID:INTEGER`

- *Response*: `InstanceID:INTEGER`

Remove Book Instance

This operation removes a book instance from the database.

- *Operation ID*: 5

- *Request*: `InstanceID:INTEGER`

- *Response*: Nothing

Lend Book Instance

To lend a specific book instance to someone, call this method. The legacy system doesn't keep track of who lends what; it just keeps track of whether a book instance is lent or not. You can call this operation on an already lent book; that makes no difference. So, the user of these operations should do all checking that needs to be done.

- *Operation ID*: 6

- *Request*: `InstanceID:INTEGER`

- *Response*: Nothing

Return Book Instance

This operation is exactly like lending a book, but the inverse. As with lending, the legacy system doesn't check anything, and you can return a book instance that hasn't been lent to anyone.

- *Operation ID*: 7

- *Request*: `InstanceID:INTEGER`

- *Response*: Nothing

Search

Searching is the final operation. It's the one that the clients of the legacy system probably will use the most, because this is the only way to find books when you don't have an instance ID for them. You can search on title or author, but there's no way to specify that both should be `true`. Even if you specify values, the operation will be `OR`, not `AND`. You can make the searches match many cases by using % before, after, or around the search string. The result is a list of book descriptions.

- *Operation ID*: 8

- *Request*: `TitleSearch:STRING AuthorSearch:STRING`

- *Response*: `Results:LIST<BookDescriptionID:INTEGER`

    - `Title:STRING Authors:LIST<Author:STRING> ISBN:STRING`

    - `Instances:LIST<InstanceID:INTEGER LibraryID:INTEGER InLibrary:INTEGER>>`

ActiveMessaging

Before we start talking about how to implement the connectivity with the legacy system, I want to mention ActiveMessaging. A13G started out as a Rails integration library for regular Ruby applications that wanted to talk to MOM systems. It did this by creating several customized adapters for servers such as Amazon and WebSphere MQ. It also had an adapter for a protocol called Streaming Text Orientated Messaging Protocol (STOMP). STOMP is a MOM protocol in pure text, which makes it easy to create new servers, carriers, and clients for it. It's a lightweight protocol that a few systems support. ActiveMQ is one of those, and ActiveMQ provides adapters to get STOMP connected to JMS systems. So, ActiveMessaging allows regular Ruby applications to connect to JMS servers, through an intermediate ActiveMQ server.

There are a few problems with the way ActiveMessaging works for regular Ruby. First of all, setting it up can be hard to get right, because there are many moving parts and many connections that can go wrong. It's also not as well-performing as it could be without all those middlemen. Finally, due to implementation limitations in the protocols used, you have to start up a separate "poller" process to be able to receive messages into the application.

This all changed with JRuby. A JMS adapter for ActiveMessaging that runs on JRuby was easy to write and is now available for download. I would use it in this chapter, but the adapter hasn't been fully integrated into A13G yet, so I'll just show you how it might possibly look.

First of all, ActiveMessaging installs as a plug-in. When you've installed it, you need to add a configuration file called `config/broker.yml` that contains username and password information for the different environments. Here's an example for the development part. It looks much like the `database.yml` file, but configures which MQ brokers should be used instead:

```
development:
    adapter: jms
    username: guest
    password: guest
```

Second, you need to define which destinations you're interested in, and provide friendly names for these. You do that in a file called `config/messaging.rb`:

```
ActiveMessaging::Gateway.define do |s|
  #s.connection_configuration = {:reliable => true}
  #s.queue :orders, '/queue/Orders'
  #s.processor_group :group1, :order_processor

  s.queue :hello_world, '/queue/HelloWorld'
end
```

This creates a new local name called `hello_world` that points to the queue that can be found at the name `/queue/HelloWorld`.

When you need to send information to such a queue, you usually need to do it from a controller. The best way to do that is first to include the ActiveMessaging libraries at the top of the code:

```
require 'activemessaging/processor'
include ActiveMessaging::MessageSender
```

When you have this as part of your controller, publishing or sending a new message is as easy as this:

```
publish :hello_world, "<say>Hello World!</say>"
```

You can add header information and customizations if needed, but there isn't more to it. "Processors" handle the other side of the story—receiving messages. You can find these in the directory called app/processors—created when installing the ActiveMessaging plug-in. An example processor can look like this:

```
class HelloWorldProcessor < ApplicationProcessor
  subscribes_to :hello_world

  def on_message(message)
    $stderr.puts "HelloWorldProcessor received: " + message
  end
end
```

A processor follows the pattern of ActiveRecord, and allows you to specify which messaging resources this processor should use. What's interesting is that only the configuration needs to change if you change provider or adapter. This makes ActiveMessaging highly useful for tying Rails applications into MOM systems.

JRuby and Message-Driven Beans

As the second sidetrack on our track to a message-driven application, we'll take a quick look at using JRuby with J2EE MDBs. In fact, the legacy system is implemented as a pure Java MDB, so you'll soon see how interaction with such an MDB works. The second way to use JRuby with MDBs is by doing the same as you did with a stateless session bean in Chapter 9. A simple MDB that doesn't do anything at all looks like this in Java:

```
package com.book;

import javax.jms.Message;
import javax.jms.MessageListener;
import javax.annotation.Resource;
import javax.ejb.MessageDriven;
import javax.ejb.MessageDrivenContext;

@MessageDriven(mappedName = "TheQueueOrTopicName")
public class AMessageDrivenBean implements MessageListener {

    @Resource
    private MessageDrivenContext mdc;

    public AMessageDrivenBean() {
    }

    public void onMessage(Message msg) {
    }
}
```

So, to create an MDB, the class needs to implement `MessageListener`, and you need to provide the `MessageDriven` annotation. The `MessageDriven` annotation takes as the argument `mappedName`, which defines which queue or topic this MDB should listen to. You can also use the `Resource` annotation to inject the `MessageDrivenContext` into the application, if you need to get hold of any services the container provides.

The `onMessage` method itself gets called each time a new message arrives. So, with this implementation, you can handle JRuby just as you did in the stateless session bean. Create the instance in the constructor, and do calls to it in the `onMessage` implementation. I won't show this, because that code is identical to what you did in Chapter 9.

A Library for Legacy Interaction

The first thing you need for your legacy interaction is some Java code to make things easier. This will be a thin wrapper around some of the legacy interactions, and there won't be much Java code to talk about. First, create an interface (see Listing 13-1).

Listing 13-1. *com/liblib/LegacyMessageHandler.java*

```java
package com.liblib;

public interface LegacyMessageHandler {
    void handle(String id, String msg);
}
```

This interface contains what you're interested in knowing about a message that arrives. It provides the transaction ID for it, and the actual text message inside. You'll implement this from Ruby later on.

You can find the actual connection code in a class that's unsurprisingly named `LegacyConnector`. I've separated the code into different segments—one for each method, to facilitate easier discussion. First, create the empty class and include the contents of Listing 13-2.

Listing 13-2. *com/liblib/LegacyConnector.java*

```java
package com.liblib;

import javax.naming.Context;
import javax.naming.InitialContext;
import javax.jms.Message;
import javax.jms.MessageListener;
import javax.jms.Connection;
import javax.jms.Destination;
import javax.jms.TextMessage;
import javax.jms.Topic;
import javax.jms.Queue;
import javax.jms.MessageConsumer;
```

```
import javax.jms.Session;
import javax.jms.MessageProducer;
import javax.jms.ConnectionFactory;

public class LegacyConnector implements MessageListener {
    private Topic returnTopic;
    private Queue requestQueue;
    private ConnectionFactory topicConnectionFactory;
    private ConnectionFactory queueConnectionFactory;

    private Connection returnConnection;
    private Session returnSession;
    private MessageConsumer cons;

    private LegacyMessageHandler handler;
}
```

You need several classes imported for this code. First, you need several member variables. This connector takes care both of sending requests, and handling return messages, but it won't connect requests and responses. That's up to your Ruby connection code.

The constructor is the code that does most of the work, handling connecting everything to JNDI:

```
public LegacyConnector() throws Exception {
    java.util.Hashtable properties = new java.util.Hashtable(2);
    properties.put(Context.PROVIDER_URL,"iiop://127.0.0.1:3700");
    properties.put(Context.INITIAL_CONTEXT_FACTORY,
                "com.sun.appserv.naming.S1ASCtxFactory");

    Context ctx = new InitialContext(properties);
    topicConnectionFactory = (ConnectionFactory)ctx.
                            lookup("TopicConnectionFactory");

    returnTopic = (Topic)ctx.lookup("LibLibRes");
    returnConnection = topicConnectionFactory.
                                createConnection();
    returnSession = returnConnection.
            createSession(false, Session.AUTO_ACKNOWLEDGE);

    cons = returnSession.createConsumer(returnTopic);
    cons.setMessageListener(this);

    queueConnectionFactory = (ConnectionFactory)ctx.
                            lookup("QueueConnectionFactory");
    requestQueue = (Queue)ctx.lookup("LibLibReq");
}
```

The constructor creates an InitialContext with some customized settings.

These settings allow you to connect to a JMS server running on the local machine. If you try to use this code with any other JMS provider, you'll need to change your settings accordingly.

The code first creates the Context, then uses that Context to look up a connection factory for creating Topic connections. The Context is also used to look up the Topic called LibLibRes.

The code creates a connection from the factory, and a session from the connection. Finally, the session is used to create a consumer, and you set the message listener for the consumer to this. You also look up a connection factory for queues, and the queue named LibLibReq. At that point the constructor is finished.

```
public void send(String id, String msg) {
    Connection connection = null;
    try {
        Destination dest = (Destination) requestQueue;
        connection = queueConnectionFactory.createConnection();
        Session session = connection.createSession(
                        false, Session.AUTO_ACKNOWLEDGE);
        MessageProducer producer = session.createProducer(dest);
        TextMessage message = session.createTextMessage();
        message.setIntProperty("TransactionID",
                            Integer.parseInt(id));
        message.setText(msg);
        producer.send(message);
    } catch(Exception e) {
        e.printStackTrace();
    } finally {
        if(connection != null) {
            try {
                connection.close();
            } catch(Exception e) {}
        }
    }
}
```

The send method takes a transaction ID and the text message to send. It creates a new queue connection, a session for this connection, and then a producer. After all that, you use the session to create a TextMessage, on which you set the Transaction ID and text, and then send it with the producer. Finally, you need some cleanup code and exception handling.

The actual code to handle incoming messages is incredibly easy:

```
public void onMessage(Message msg) {
    try {
      handler.handle(""+msg.getIntProperty("TransactionID"),
                        ((TextMessage)msg).getText());
    } catch(Exception e) {
        e.printStackTrace();
    }
}
```

The method onMessage just extracts the transaction ID from the received message, and calls the handler with the ID and the text of the message.

Finally, the last real method is setHandler, which allows you to customize the handling of messages by implementing the LegacyMessageHandler interface. The actual connection to the result topic isn't turned on until a valid handler exists for it.

```
public void setHandler(LegacyMessageHandler handler)
                throws Exception {
    this.handler = handler;
    returnConnection.start();
}
```

The static initializer block in the next code snippet is there because the JMS code for GlassFish generates copious amounts of logging to the console on several different loggers. This code just goes through all the loggers in the system, shutting them off. Obviously, if something is wrong, you'll need to remove it.

```
static {
    // Shut off annoying logging
    for(java.util.Enumeration<String> enm = java.util.logging.
            LogManager.getLogManager().
            getLoggerNames();enm.hasMoreElements();) {
        java.util.logging.Logger.getLogger(
            enm.nextElement()).setLevel(
                java.util.logging.Level.OFF);
    }
}
```

Finally, the main method just sets up a handler that prints information received, and then sends a message:

```
public static void main(String[] args) throws Exception {
    LegacyConnector cc = new LegacyConnector();
    cc.setHandler(new LegacyMessageHandler() {
            public void handle(String id, String msg) {
                System.err.println("HANDLE(" + id +
                            ", " + msg.length() + ")");
            }
        });
    cc.send("123","\u0000\u0004Test");
}
```

You should package this as a JAR file called liblib-connector.jar. To run the test code in the main method, you need to invoke the call with several things on your CLASSPATH. I usually create a script that looks something like Listing 13-3.

Listing 13-3. *run*

```sh
#!/bin/sh

CLASSPATH=${CLASSPATH}:${GLASSFISH}/lib/appserv-admin.jar
CLASSPATH=${CLASSPATH}:${GLASSFISH}/lib/appserv-rt.jar
CLASSPATH=${CLASSPATH}:${GLASSFISH}/lib/appserv-ws.jar
CLASSPATH=${CLASSPATH}:${GLASSFISH}/lib/javaee.jar
APP=${GLASSFISH}/lib/install/applications
CLASSPATH=${CLASSPATH}:${APP}/jmsra/jmsra.jar
CLASSPATH=${CLASSPATH}:${APP}/jmsra/imqjmsra.jar
CLASSPATH=${CLASSPATH}:${APP}/jmsra/imqbroker.jar
CLASSPATH=${CLASSPATH}:${GLASSFISH}/imq/lib/imq.jar
CLASSPATH=${CLASSPATH}:${GLASSFISH}/imq/lib/jms.jar
CLASSPATH=${CLASSPATH}:liblib-connector.jar

java $*
```

Then you can invoke the class by doing this:

```
./run com.liblib.LegacyConnector
```

To stop the application you need to use Ctrl+C, because the listener won't quit on its own.

Now that we've looked at the Java parts of the connector, we need to see the code that ties it all together. We'll take it piece by piece, beginning with the header of the file. Open up a file called liblib_connector.rb and put liblib-connector.jar in the same directory:

```ruby
require 'java'
require 'liblib-connector.jar'

BookDescription = Struct.new :id, :name, :authors, :isbn, :instances

module LegacySystem
end
```

All your code will live in the LegacySystem module, except for the book description. The first thing you need to do within the LegacySystem module is to import some classes that you want to use, and create some handy things:

```ruby
LegacyConnector = com.liblib.LegacyConnector
LegacyMessageHandler = com.liblib.LegacyMessageHandler

Connection = LegacyConnector.new
Transactions = {}
@@current_trans_id = 0

class RubyHandler
  include LegacyMessageHandler
```

```
  def handle(id, msg)
    Transactions[id.to_i] = msg
  end
end
```

```
Connection.handler = RubyHandler.new
```

First, you include the two Java classes you created earlier. Then, you create a new instance of the LegacyConnector. You create a constant to hold the current transactions, and a class variable to hold the current transaction counter. You also need to implement LegacyMessageHandler; you do this by including it in RubyHandler and implementing the handle method. The implementation is dead simple: you just add the data to the Transactions hash. Finally, you create an instance of this handler and set the handler of the Connection to it.

You need some constants that correspond to the different operations. To make it easier for yourself, transform these constants into Strings, so they can be easily concatenated:

```
OP_ADD_LIB = 0.chr
OP_REM_LIB = 1.chr
OP_ADD_BOOK_DESC = 2.chr
OP_REM_BOOK_DESC = 3.chr
OP_ADD_BOOK_INST = 4.chr
OP_REM_BOOK_INST = 5.chr
OP_LEND_BOOK_INST = 6.chr
OP_RET_BOOK_INST = 7.chr
OP_SEARCH = 8.chr
OP_GET_LIBRARY_NAME = 9.chr
OP_GET_BOOK_DESCRIPTION = 10.chr
```

You also need some helper methods to aid you when packing and unpacking data. The first one you need is sleep_until, which waits for a message to appear in the Transactions hash, or timeout:

```
def self.sleep_until(tid)
  ix = 0
  until (msg = Transactions[tid]) || ix > 10
    sleep 1
    ix += 1
  end
  msg
end
```

Packing and unpacking integers is easily done with these helpers:

```
def self.pack_int(i)
  ((i>>8)&255).chr + (i&255).chr
end
```

```
def self.unpack_int(i)
  i[1] + (i[0] << 8)
end
```

Packing a String is also easily accomplished. Here's a one-letter method to make the code more compact:

```
def self.s(str)
  pack_string(str)
end

def self.pack_string(str)
  str.size.chr + str
end
```

I could arguably have put these methods on the String and Fixnum objects, but I chose to do it this way instead. That's because the data types used for representing things could change; then the method names could still be there, but we would use other implementations.

```
def self.a_s(arr)
  pack_array_of_string(arr)
end

def self.pack_array_of_string(arr)
  arr.size.chr + arr.map{|str| s(str) }.join('')
end
```

Finally, packing an array of Strings is easy: use the map method on the array, transform each String to its packed counterpart, and then join them together with the length of the array prepended.

That concludes the helper methods. We can now continue to take a look at the different operations provided. First, here's the helper to add a library:

```
def self.add_library(name)
  tid = @@current_trans_id += 1
  Connection.send(tid.to_s, OP_ADD_LIB + s(name))

  msg = sleep_until(tid)

  Transactions.delete(tid)

  unpack_int msg
end
```

You first create a new transaction ID, then send the operation and the name with the Connection object. You then wait until you get an answer, delete the transaction from Transactions, and return the unpacked integer that represents the ID of the new library. Removing a library is even easier, because you don't expect a return value:

```
def self.remove_library(id)
  tid = @@current_trans_id += 1
  Connection.send(tid.to_s, OP_REM_LIB + pack_int(id))
end
```

Getting the name of a library is also simple. You just pack the ID of the library you want the name for, and then unpack the name by taking all characters in it, except for the first:

```
def self.get_library_name(id)
  tid = @@current_trans_id += 1
  Connection.send(tid.to_s, OP_GET_LIBRARY_NAME + pack_int(id))

  msg = sleep_until(tid)

  Transactions.delete(tid)

  msg[1..-1]
end
```

Adding a new book description takes some more code, but not much. Your helper methods easily handle the complication of sending an array of strings:

```
def self.add_book_description(desc)
  tid = @@current_trans_id += 1
  Connection.send(tid.to_s, OP_ADD_BOOK_DESC +
             s(desc.name) + a_s(desc.authors) + s(desc.isbn))

  msg = sleep_until(tid)

  Transactions.delete(tid)

  unpack_int msg
end
```

Removing a book description looks like removing a library, and you should probably refactor them into each other later on:

```
def self.remove_book_description(id)
  tid = @@current_trans_id += 1
  Connection.send(tid.to_s, OP_REM_BOOK_DESC + pack_int(id))
end
```

Here's how to add a new instance of a book:

```
def self.add_book_instance(libid, descid)
  tid = @@current_trans_id += 1
  Connection.send(tid.to_s, OP_ADD_BOOK_INST +
             pack_int(libid) + pack_int(descid))

  msg = sleep_until(tid)

  Transactions.delete(tid)

  unpack_int msg
end
```

Removing, lending, and returning an instance are all the same:

```ruby
def self.remove_book_instance(id)
  tid = @@current_trans_id += 1
  Connection.send(tid.to_s, OP_REM_BOOK_INST + pack_int(id))
end

def self.lend_book_instance(id)
  tid = @@current_trans_id += 1
  Connection.send(tid.to_s, OP_LEND_BOOK_INST + pack_int(id))
end

def self.return_book_instance(id)
  tid = @@current_trans_id += 1
  Connection.send(tid.to_s, OP_RET_BOOK_INST + pack_int(id))
end
```

You have two operations left to support: search and get book description. Get book description is the more simple of those:

```ruby
def self.get_book_description(id)
  tid = @@current_trans_id += 1
  Connection.send(tid.to_s, OP_GET_BOOK_DESCRIPTION + pack_int(id))
  msg = sleep_until(tid)

  Transactions.delete(tid)
  id = unpack_int(msg[0..1])
  msg = msg[2..-1]
  nm_len = msg[0]
  name = msg[1..nm_len]
  msg = msg[(nm_len+1)..-1]
  authors = []
  len2 = msg[0]
  msg = msg[1..-1]
  len2.times do
    a_len = msg[0]
    auth = msg[1..a_len]
    msg = msg[(a_len+1)..-1]
    authors << auth
  end
  is_len = msg[0]
  isbn = msg[1..is_len]
  msg = msg[(is_len+1)..-1]
  len3 = msg[0]
  msg = msg[1..-1]
  instances = []
  len3.times do
    instid, libid, lended = unpack_int(msg[0..1]),
```

```
                        unpack_int(msg[2..3]),
                        unpack_int(msg[4..5]) == 0
    msg = msg[6..-1]
    instances << {:book_instance_id => instid,
                  :library_id => libid,
                  :lended => lended }
  end
  BookDescription.new(id.to_i, name, authors, isbn, instances)
end
```

This code isn't too clean; there's probably a DSL just waiting for you to find it in here. However, the workings of this code are procedural and simple. You first unpack the ID of the book description, then the name. You fetch the length of the array of authors and then fetch each author name. After that, you get the ISBN and then walk through the list that provides instance information about this book description. Finally, you create a new BookDescription object containing this information.

The search method looks like this:

```
def self.search(name, author)
  tid = @@current_trans_id += 1
  Connection.send(tid.to_s, OP_SEARCH + s(name) + s(author))
  msg = sleep_until(tid)
  Transactions.delete(tid)
  unpack_search_list msg
end
```

It uses the unpack_search_list method, which is much like the get_book_description method. That's because it needs to do the same thing, but repeatedly. The only difference is that this method unpacks more than one entry and returns a list of BookDescription objects:

```
def self.unpack_search_list(msg)
  len = msg[0]
  msg = msg[1..-1]
  all = []
  len.times do
    id = unpack_int(msg[0..1])
    msg = msg[2..-1]
    nm_len = msg[0]
    name = msg[1..nm_len]
    msg = msg[(nm_len+1)..-1]
    authors = []
    len2 = msg[0]
    msg = msg[1..-1]
    len2.times do
      a_len = msg[0]
      auth = msg[1..a_len]
      msg = msg[(a_len+1)..-1]
      authors << auth
    end
```

```
      is_len = msg[0]
      isbn = msg[1..is_len]
      msg = msg[(is_len+1)..-1]
      len3 = msg[0]
      msg = msg[1..-1]
      instances = []
      len3.times do
        descid, libid, lended = unpack_int(msg[0..1]),
                                 unpack_int(msg[2..3]),
                                 unpack_int(msg[4..5]) == 0
        msg = msg[6..-1]
        instances << {:book_description_id => descid,
                      :library_id => libid,
                      :lended => lended }
      end
      all << BookDescription.new(id.to_i, name,
                                 authors, isbn, instances)
    end
    all
  end
end
```

Finally, if you want to test this Ruby code, you can use this test code at the end of the file:

```
if __FILE__ == $0
  id = LegacySystem.add_library("FooLib")
  id2 = LegacySystem.add_library("BarLib")
  LegacySystem.remove_library(id)
  bid = LegacySystem.add_book_description(
          BookDescription.new(nil, "Practical Stuff",
                  ["Ola Bini", "Arnold Donner"], "123443545"))
  LegacySystem.add_book_instance(id2, bid)
  mid = LegacySystem.add_book_instance(id2, bid)
  LegacySystem.add_book_instance(id2, bid)
  LegacySystem.lend_book_instance(mid)
  require 'pp'
  pp LegacySystem.search("%","%")
end
```

It creates two new libraries, removes one, adds a book description and some instances, lends an instance, and then searches and pretty prints the result. From this, you see how to work with the library. To invoke the script, create a script called jrun, which looks exactly like the run script created earlier, but replace the word java with jruby in it. Then you can try the application out. Remember that you need to kill the process explicitly with Ctrl+C.

That's the grand total of integration with the legacy library. As you can see, it isn't too painful to hide a binary protocol behind a nice Ruby API. You'll be able to use this library directly from your Rails application in the next chapter to provide library services for the LibLib application.

Inter-Rails Communication

You've now seen one approach to using JMS for communication through Ruby. In this part you'll create a library that Rails applications (or other Ruby applications for that matter) can use to send one another messages on a Topic. It will be specific to the LibLib application, but it could well be generalized into something like ActiveMessaging (or you could just use ActiveMessaging when it's finished).

For these examples to work, you need to add two Topics to your GlassFish installation. You can do this by visiting the administration page at localhost:4848. There you can look at the Resources heading, and there add new JMS resources. You should add a TopicConnectionFactory, a QueueConnectionFactory, and two Topics named LibraryInformationReq and LibraryInformationRes. You need to read the documentation for the legacy system's source code to see what more needs to be created for the legacy system to work.

The code is pure Ruby, but uses some Java libraries. Open up a file called liblib_communication.rb:

```ruby
require 'java'
module LibLib
  module Communication
    Hashtable = java.util.Hashtable
    Context = javax.naming.Context
    InitialContext = javax.naming.InitialContext
    Session = javax.jms.Session
    MessageListener = javax.jms.MessageListener

    class ResponseListener
      include MessageListener
      def onMessage(msg)
        ::LibLib::Communication::handle_response(msg)
      end
    end

    class RequestListener
      include MessageListener

      def onMessage(msg)
        ::LibLib::Communication::handle_request(msg)
      end
    end
  end
end
```

You'll put more code into the Communication module later on, after the RequestListener class. As you can see, you import the needed Java classes and create two Ruby classes that are MessageListeners. The onMessage method just dispatches to the handle_response and handle_request methods on the Communication module. You need a way of killing logging until you start using this application together with the other JMS application, so you do that as you did in Java:

```
def self.kill_logging
  enm = java.util.logging.LogManager.log_manager.logger_names
  while enm.hasMoreElements
    java.util.logging.Logger.getLogger(
            enm.nextElement).level = java.util.logging.Level::OFF
  end
end
```

Obviously, the code is a little more readable in Ruby format.

You'll create two consumers, so add a helper method for doing that:

```
def self.create_consumer(ctx, name, listener_class)
  dest = ctx.lookup(name)
  conn = @conn_factory.create_connection
  session = conn.create_session(false, Session::AUTO_ACKNOWLEDGE)
  consumer = session.create_consumer(dest)
  listener = listener_class.new
  consumer.setMessageListener(listener)
  conn.start
  return dest, conn, session, consumer, listener
end
```

This code expects there to be an instance variable called @conn_factory before the method gets called. It creates the connection, session, and listener; adds the listener to the consumer; and starts the connection, finally returning all values of interest to the caller.

A user of this library should call the start message to get everything going:

```
def self.start
  @current_id = 0
  properties = Hashtable.new(2)
  properties.put(Context::PROVIDER_URL,"iiop://127.0.0.1:3700")
  properties.put(Context::INITIAL_CONTEXT_FACTORY,
            "com.sun.appserv.naming.S1ASCtxFactory")
  ctx = InitialContext.new(properties)
  @conn_factory = ctx.lookup("TopicConnectionFactory")

  @req, @req_conn, @req_session, @req_cons, @request_listener =
      create_consumer(ctx, "LibraryInformationReq", RequestListener)

  @res, @res_conn, @res_session, @res_cons, @response_listener =
      create_consumer(ctx, "LibraryInformationRes", ResponseListener)
end
```

The start method creates a counter for the current ID, sets the same properties as you saw in the Java code, creates a Context, looks up a connection factory, and then creates two consumers: one for requests and one for responses. Because you need to hold on to those variables, you save them as instance variables with a given naming scheme.

The next part of the library is the ability to send a message. You can either send a request message or a response message. Both these variations are almost exactly the same:

```
def self.send_msg(session, dest, id, headers, txt)
  prod = session.create_producer(dest)
  msg = session.create_text_message
  msg.setIntProperty("TransID", id)
  msg.setIntProperty("LibraryID", $CURRENT_LIBRARY_ID)
  headers.each do |k,v|
    msg.setStringProperty(k,v)
  end
  msg.set_text(txt)
  prod.send(msg)
end

def self.request_msg(id, *args)
  send_msg(@req_session, @req, $CURRENT_LIBRARY_ID*10_000+id, *args)
end

def self.response_msg(*args)
  send_msg(@res_session, @res, *args)
end
```

The only difference here has got to do with the transaction ID. In this kind of communication, it is important for receivers not to handle messages from themselves. That's why you use the $CURRENT_LIBRARY_ID global, which contains the unique library identifier. Each Rails instance must have its own value in that global. In that way, the TransactionID can be unique among instances, and different instances can also recognize messages from themselves. The reason you don't have the same code in response_msg is that the ID you send when doing a response already has the library ID information baked into it; you want to return this message to the library it originated from.

There are obviously other ways of doing this too, but in this way many libraries can take part of information if they want, and the structure can be cleanly multicast in all directions.

The handle_response method is simple and reminiscent of the way you handled responses from the legacy system:

```
Responses = {}
def self.handle_response(msg)
  tid = msg.getIntProperty("TransID")
  (Responses[tid % 10_000] ||= []) <<
          msg.getText if tid/10_000 == $CURRENT_LIBRARY_ID
end
```

You need to unwrap the transaction ID from the library ID, and also make sure that you only handle responses that are meant for you to handle.

The way you handle requests will include some model classes from the Rails application you'll build in the next chapter. If you want to test it out, just stub this code out, and write some debugging statements here instead:

```
def self.handle_request(msg)
  tid = msg.getIntProperty("TransID")
  # Don't handle messages from ourself
  unless tid/10_000 == $CURRENT_LIBRARY_ID
    username, password =
      YAML::load(msg.getText).values_at(:username, :password)
    if (auth = Authentication.find_by_username_and_password(
                            username, password))
      if (borr = Borrower.find_by_authentication_id(auth.id))
        ret = { :auth => {'username' => auth.username,
                          'password' => auth.password},
                :borrower => {'name' => borr.name},
                :borrowed => [] }
        for bbook in borr.borrowed_books
          ret[:borrowed] << {
            'book_description_id' => bbook.book_description_id,
            'library_id' => bbook.library_id,
            'book_instance_id' => bbook.book_instance_id}
        end
        response_msg(tid, {}, ret.to_yaml)
      end
    end
  end
end
```

In this code, you first need to check if it is a request from yourself. In that case, you ignore it. Otherwise you YAML::load the text of the message and extract the values of username and password, try to find authentication information for this data, and then try to find a Borrower for the information. If you find this information, you put together a response that includes the username, the password, the borrower's name, and information about all the books this person has borrowed. This message is then sent with the response_msg method in YAML format.

The helper method next_tid creates a new transaction ID for you:

```
def self.next_tid
  c, @current_id = @current_id, ((@current_id + 1) % 10_000)
  c
end
```

Finally, the Rails application uses the find_borrower method to get information from other libraries about the Borrower:

```
def self.find_borrower(username, password)
  tid = next_tid
  request_msg(tid, {}, {:username => username,
                        :password => password}.to_yaml)
  sleep 2
  responses = Responses.delete(tid)

  return nil unless responses

  data = {:auth => {}, :borrower => {}, :borrowed => {}}
```

```
  for rdata in responses
    response_data = YAML::load(rdata)
    data[:auth] = response_data[:auth] if
        data[:auth].blank? && response_data[:auth]
    data[:borrower] = response_data[:borrower] if
        data[:borrower].blank? && response_data[:borrower]
    for bdata in response_data[:borrowed]
      data[:borrowed][bdata['book_instance_id']] = bdata
    end
  end
  data
end
```

This method takes the borrower's username and password and tries to find information about him or her from other libraries. It first creates a new tid, then sends a request_msg with the username and password as YAML. It returns nil if new responses arrive; otherwise it unpacks all responses into a Hash data structure that the caller can use.

This is the final method in the library. The only thing more that's needed is a small test driver to make it possible to test the code:

```
if __FILE__ == $0
  LibLib::Communication::kill_logging
  $CURRENT_LIBRARY_ID ||= (ENV["LIBLIB_ID"] || 82).to_i
  LibLib::Communication::start
  LibLib::Communication::request_msg(123,
      {"hello" => "goodbye", "goodnight" => "today"},
      "this is a test message")
  LibLib::Communication::response_msg(123,
      {"hello" => "goodbye", "goodnight" => "today"},
      "this is a test message")
end
```

You first kill logging, then create a $CURRENT_LIBRARY_ID from an environment variable, or fall back on the value 82 otherwise. The communication is started, and one request and one response is sent. You need to stub out handle_request and handle_response for this to work correctly while running in standalone mode.

Summary

In this chapter we've seen both the value and the complication of using a message-oriented system. Because the paradigm is different from what we're used to in regular programming, it might take some time getting everything correct. It's also important to use the middleware correctly, and not abuse it for doing things it clearly shouldn't do. To reiterate, when you need communication between several distributed parties, where some or all code will be changed, added to, or removed from, it makes sense to use a messaging system to handle this.

Messaging gives you lots of flexibility for accomplishing things that would be hard without it. The Java libraries for JMS are useful, but they look even better when wrapped in a small layer of Ruby.

CHAPTER 14

■ ■ ■

The LibLib Rails Application

In the last two chapters, we've looked at how to use web services to interact with Internet services, at how to use them to find out book information from Amazon.com, and also how to work with messaging systems both to talk to legacy systems and also to control communication between Rails applications. In this chapter we'll finally put all this together into one Rails application. The resulting user interface won't be that large, but the underlying code is complex in some cases because we need to communicate with things that we usually don't work with from Rails.

However, as we'll see, using Rails gives us the advantage of nice database integration and user interface handling. This leaves the responsibility of writing the business logic in our hands, and lets us avoid getting bogged down with the clutter of web applications. The application will knit together the libraries we worked with in the two earlier chapters with some logic. LibLib will provide a primitive user interface for Borrowers, allowing Borrower information to be shared between LibLib instances, and also to interact with the underlying legacy database system.

Using JMS for communication between Rails instances means that the system administrators can take control of security, allowing specific proxy servers to send along certain JMS messages, but nothing else. In short, doing this communication with messaging gives them more flexibility to make the system secure and easy to handle from their side.

We'll begin by looking at the database and the model, and also how to make different Rails instances have different properties, while using the same code base. (In fact, it's not a very clever trick, but it works well.) Both the database and the model will be simple, so they won't take much time. After that, we'll spend most of the time looking at the views and the controllers. Because we spent two whole chapters writing the three libraries we'll be using, most of the controller code will just be using these.

The user interface is divided into three broad parts: one area where Borrowers can look at books, lend books, and return books; one area where Librarians can add new books and book instances, and also remove them and administrate librarians; and finally the area where both Librarians and Borrowers can log in and log out. Most of these will be interleaved with one another in the code and user interface, but those three areas of functionality are what will be in the application.

We'll spend little time on the looks of the application; in this case it's the functionality and pulling together of several different resources that's interesting. By using JRuby as an enabler, we'll be able to accomplish some powerful things using Java as the platform and Ruby as the glue.

Before we begin, make sure that you understand what the code in the previous chapters does, because all the functionality in this chapter will depend on what we've already built. Some of that code was complicated due to the inherent complexity in handling messaging systems and web services. LibLib will put an easy face on the underlying mess, but doing that will cost us some while implementing it. The code in LibLib will be a lot larger than the other projects, but we've worked through most of that code in the last chapters.

The Database

To begin with, create the new Rails application by running `jruby -S rails liblib`. You know the score by now. Also make sure to add the `require` of `jdbc_adapter` to `environment.rb`. Once that's done, you can go ahead and configure a database. Give it a name such as `liblib_development`, with username "liblib" and password "liblib." You'll change this in a bit, but right now it's good enough. Further, make sure the database is there. You won't migrate anything in it at this stage, but sometimes Rails makes funny things happen when no database is available.

After you've created and configured the database, you need to create some models and migrations. As I mentioned in the chapter introduction, the actual model for LibLib isn't that complicated:

```
jruby script/generate model Authentication
jruby script/generate model Librarian
jruby script/generate model Borrower
jruby script/generate model BorrowedBook
```

Now, the `Librarian`, `Borrower`, and `BorrowedBook` models are obvious in what they represent, but `Authentication` isn't as easy. Simply put, `Authentication` contains the username and password of either a `Borrower` or a `Librarian`, or both. So, it's the object that's used for authentication, and you can share this authentication between a `Borrower` and a `Librarian` if you want.

The migration for `Authentication` is more or less what you would expect:

```
class CreateAuthentications < ActiveRecord::Migration
  class Authentication < ActiveRecord::Base; end
  def self.up
    create_table :authentications do |t|
      t.column :username, :string
      t.column :password, :string
    end
    Authentication.create :username => 'admin', :password => 'admin'
  end
  def self.down
    drop_table :authentications
  end
end
```

You need to bootstrap by creating a simple authentication for `admin`. The actual database table is just two strings and the regular Rails ID.

The second migration is `CreateLibrarian`, which only is a list of `Authentications` that have access to administrate the library:

```
class CreateLibrarians < ActiveRecord::Migration
  class Authentication < ActiveRecord::Base; end
  class Librarian < ActiveRecord::Base; end
  def self.up
    create_table :librarians do |t|
      t.column :name, :string
      t.column :authentication_id, :integer
    end
    Librarian.create :name => 'Administrator',
          :authentication => Authentication.find_by_username('admin')
  end
  def self.down
    drop_table :librarians
  end
end
```

You also added a `name`, for good measure, and also made sure that there is at least one `Librarian` from the beginning, so you can create more of them later on. Notice that you need to define both an `Authentication` model and a `Librarian` model within the migration, so that you have access to them. You can't use the class created in `CreateAuthentications`, because that one was confined to the scope of that class, and it's even possible that the Rails migration engine tears down everything between different parts of the migration.

The `Borrower` migration is almost the same as the `Librarian` one, except that you don't need to create any initial `Borrower`; it will be possible for `Borrowers` to register their own accounts later on:

```
class CreateBorrowers < ActiveRecord::Migration
  def self.up
    create_table :borrowers do |t|
      t.column :name, :string
      t.column :email, :string
      t.column :authentication_id, :integer
    end
  end
  def self.down
    drop_table :borrowers
  end
end
```

Finally, here's the model that represents the borrowed books of a `Borrower`:

```
class CreateBorrowedBooks < ActiveRecord::Migration
  def self.up
    create_table :borrowed_books do |t|
      t.column :book_description_id, :integer
      t.column :library_id, :integer
```

```
      t.column :book_instance_id, :integer
      t.column :borrower_id, :integer
    end
  end
  def self.down
    drop_table :borrowed_books
  end
end
```

The reason you have some more information in this table is not that you need it, but because you don't have to hit the legacy system as often with this information. It would have sufficed with just the book_instance_id and the borrower_id, but memory is cheap these days.

There isn't much more to the database you need, because most of the information is stored in the legacy system anyway.

Deploying More Than One Rails Instance

If you need to deploy more than one Rails instance, and have these work as separate entities that can communicate and interact with one another, you need a strategy for deployment. Deployment gets harder when you want to run more than one instance on the same machine, using different databases and ports, and the instances are communicating with one another. However, the solution is simple. Because Ruby allows you to use environment variables to change the behavior of your system, you can use the variables at startup to decide which database you want to use and similar information.

To allow this kind of flexibility, open up config/environment.rb and add a line like this at the top of the file:

```
LIBLIB_INSTANCE = ENV["LIBLIB_INSTANCE"] || "1"
```

This is a counter. The instance ID can be anything really, just something that identifies the Rails instance, and can be used for generating a working database connection string. To use this information, you can create a database.yml file that looks like this:

```
development:
  adapter: jdbc
  driver: com.mysql.jdbc.Driver
  url: jdbc:mysql://localhost/liblib<%=LIBLIB_INSTANCE%>_dev
  username: liblib<%=LIBLIB_INSTANCE%>
  password: liblib<%=LIBLIB_INSTANCE%>
test:
  adapter: jdbc
  driver: com.mysql.jdbc.Driver
  url: jdbc:mysql://localhost/liblib<%=LIBLIB_INSTANCE%>_test
  username: liblib<%=LIBLIB_INSTANCE%>
  password: liblib<%=LIBLIB_INSTANCE%>
production:
  adapter: jdbc
  driver: com.mysql.jdbc.Driver
```

```
url: jdbc:mysql://localhost/liblib<%=LIBLIB_INSTANCE%>_prod
username: liblib<%=LIBLIB_INSTANCE%>
password: liblib<%=LIBLIB_INSTANCE%>
```

You use the `LIBLIB_INSTANCE` string to determine both which databases to use, and the username and password used to connect to these. Now, make sure you have at least the databases `liblib1_dev` and `liblib2_dev` defined, with usernames "liblib1" and "liblib2" for each, with the same password. You'll be trying the application out with two instances running on the same machine like this.

You can customize the `LIBLIB_INSTANCE` variable by setting the `LIBLIB_INSTANCE` environment variable before you start the Rails instance. On Linux and Mac you can do this like so:

```
export LIBLIB_INSTANCE=2
```

Or you can do this:

```
setenv LIBLIB_INSTANCE 2
```

On Windows you would do it either in the "System" preferences, on the "Advanced" tab, under "Environment Variables," or you can execute this command:

```
set LIBLIB_INSTANCE=2
```

In all these cases, the value will get interpolated into the Rails application. While you're at it, you should probably use the same technique to customize the library ID for each Rails application. Add this to the `environment.rb`:

```
$CURRENT_LIBRARY_ID = (ENV["LIBLIB_ID"] || 82).to_i
```

Because the ID should be numeric for your legacy integration code to work correctly, you need to call `to_i` on the resulting value, just to make sure.

With all this in place, you can always change the behavior of the application before starting it. Not only can you do it manually, but it's easy to add this information to the start script that you'll be using to invoke the Rails application (because you still have all those Java JAR dependencies that need to be on the `CLASSPATH` when starting).

Creating the Model

As we talked about earlier, there isn't much to the model, so I'll just present it without adornment here. Here's the `Authentication` model:

```
class Authentication < ActiveRecord::Base
  validates_presence_of :username, :password
  validates_uniqueness_of :username
end
```

It makes sure that both username and password are provided, and also that you don't provide a username that's already in use. Other than that, it's your basic garden-variety model.

The `Borrower` and `Librarian` models are in the same vein:

```
class Librarian < ActiveRecord::Base
  belongs_to :authentication
```

```
    def is_borrower?
      Borrower.find_by_authentication_id(self.authentication.id)
    end
end
class Borrower < ActiveRecord::Base
  belongs_to :authentication
  has_many :borrowed_books
  def is_librarian?
    Librarian.find_by_authentication_id(self.authentication.id)
  end
end
```

A Librarian belongs to a specific Authentication, and so does a Borrower. A Librarian can possibly be a Borrower too, and the easy way of checking is to see if there is a Borrower attached to an Authentication. In the same manner, the easiest way to find out if a Borrower is a Librarian is just to check if there is an authentication for it. A Borrower also has many borrowed_books, and each one of these looks like this:

```
class BorrowedBook < ActiveRecord::Base
  belongs_to :borrower
end
```

That's all the actual model you need. Of course, the BookDescription you'll be passing along will act like a model, and a few other objects will too, but you count those as libraries, not as models in this case.

Views and Controllers

In this section, you'll finally create all the support structure needed for your application to get finished. That means creating controllers and views that glue the application together. I've tried to keep the responsibilities reasonably separated, but there will be some leak through. Specifically, I'll try to view the final code for each part instead of going back and revising it afterward for the next part. That means you'll see some authentication code under the "Layout" heading, for example.

The first step is to create all the controllers you're going to need, so all those chores are out of the way. You're going to use five different controllers, named AuthController, AmazonController, BookController, BorrowerController, and LibrariansController. Generate each with actions as specified, by using these commands:

```
jruby script/generate controller auth blogin llogin logout
jruby script/generate controller amazon index search import
jruby script/generate controller book index book
              add_instance remove_instance
              add_description remove_description search lend ret
jruby script/generate controller borrower index list
              remove create_librarian new create
jruby script/generate controller librarians index
              list add create_borrower remove
```

```
rm -rf app/views/auth/logout.rhtml app/views/amazon/index.rhtml
rm -rf app/views/book/index.rhtml app/views/book/add_instance.rhtml
rm -rf app/views/book/remove_instance.rhtml
rm -rf app/views/book/add_description.rhtml
rm -rf app/views/book/remove_description.rhtml
rm -rf app/views/borrower/create.rhtml app/views/borrower/remove.rhtml
rm -rf app/views/librarians/create_borrower.rhtml
```

With this in place, you're ready to start adding some content. The first step is to create a start script, though. Something like what you've used before will work fine (see Listing 14-1).

Listing 14-1. *jr*

```
#!/bin/sh
GLASSFISH=/path/to/your/glassfish
CLASSPATH=${CLASSPATH}:liblib-connector.jar
CLASSPATH=${CLASSPATH}:${GLASSFISH}/lib/appserv-rt.jar
CLASSPATH=${CLASSPATH}:${GLASSFISH}/lib/appserv-ws.jar
JMSRA=${GLASSFISH}/lib/install/applications/jmsra
CLASSPATH=${CLASSPATH}:${JMSRA}/jmsra.jar
CLASSPATH=${CLASSPATH}:${JMSRA}/imqjmsra.jar
CLASSPATH=${CLASSPATH}:${JMSRA}/imqbroker.jar
CLASSPATH=${CLASSPATH}:${GLASSFISH}/lib/imq.jar
CLASSPATH=${CLASSPATH}:${GLASSFISH}/lib/appserv-admin.jar
CLASSPATH=${CLASSPATH}:${GLASSFISH}/imq/lib/jms.jar
CLASSPATH=${CLASSPATH}:${GLASSFISH}/lib/javaee.jar
LIBLIB_INSTANCE=1
LIBLIB_ID=42
jruby $*
```

This script makes sure that this is the first LibLib instance, and that the ID of this library in the legacy system database is 42. Change your values to match, but make sure that the legacy system has an entry matching the value you choose.

Layout

The first step in getting your application working is to get a layout set up. In this case you want to have the same layout for every page in the system, which means that you can create a file that looks like Listing 14-2.

Listing 14-2. *app/views/layouts/application.rb*

```
<!DOCTYPE html PUBLIC "-//W3C//DTD XHTML 1.0 Transitional//EN"
      "http://www.w3.org/TR/xhtml1/DTD/xhtml1-transitional.dtd">
<html xmlns="http://www.w3.org/1999/xhtml" xml:lang="en" lang="en">
  <head>
    <meta http-equiv="content-type"
        content="text/html;charset=UTF-8" />
    <title>LibLib</title>
```

```erb
    <%= stylesheet_link_tag 'liblib' %>
</head>
<body>
<table width="100%" height="100%">
  <tr>
    <td width="250" height="800" class="leftMenu"
                  align="center" valign="top">
      <h2>LIBLIB</h2>
      <ul>
        <li><%= link_to 'Search for books',
                       :controller => 'book' %></li>
        <% if @a_librarian %>
          <li><%= link_to 'Administrate librarians',
                :controller => 'librarians' %></li>
          <li><%= link_to 'Administrate borrowers',
                :controller => 'borrower', :action => 'list' %></li>
          <li><%= link_to 'Add new books from Amazon',
                :controller => 'amazon' %></li>
        <% end %>
        <% if !@a_librarian %>
          <li><%= link_to 'Log in as Librarian',
                :controller => 'auth', :action => 'llogin' %></li>
        <% end %>
        <% if !@a_borrower %>
          <li><%= link_to 'Log in as Borrower',
                :controller => 'auth', :action => 'blogin' %></li>
        <% end %>
      </ul>
      <% if @a_librarian %>
        <p><i>Logged in as Librarian:</i><br/>
        <b><%= h @a_librarian.name %></b>
            (<%= @a_librarian.authentication.username %>)</p>
      <% end %>
      <% if @a_borrower %>
        <p><i>Logged in as Borrower:</i><br/>
        <b><%= h @a_borrower.name %></b>
            (<%= @a_borrower.authentication.username %>)</p>
      <% end %>
      <% if @a_librarian || @a_borrower %>
        <p><%= link_to 'Log out',
                :controller=>'auth',:action=>'logout'%></p>
      <% end %>
    </td>
    <td class="main" valign="top">
      <p style="color: green"><%= flash[:notice] %></p>
      <p style="color: red"><%= flash[:error] %></p>
      <%= yield  %>
```

```
        </td>
      </tr>
    </table>
  </body>
</html>
```

There isn't anything new in this file. Note the fact that you check the existence of @a_librarian and @a_borrower to see if they're logged in. Further, you only provide a logout link if one or both of them is there. The reason I didn't use the instance name @librarian or @borrower is that the default names for Rails get in the way when creating new instances of these models. Most of the links provided are for Librarians, because Borrowers can't do that much. Of course, you could provide a way for them to look at their current borrowed books, but we won't do that in this chapter. You could add many further extensions to LibLib if you wanted. Most of them are easy to do, due to our infrastructure that gives access to much of the back-end system.

You also need to change your application controller so that the @a_librarian and @a_borrower instance variables are available if the person is logged in. The file app/controllers/application.rb should look like this:

```
class ApplicationController < ActionController::Base
  session :session_key => '_liblib_session_id'
  before_filter :try_borrower
  protected
  def authenticate_librarian
    unless session[:librarian_id] &&
        (@a_librarian = Librarian.find_by_id(session[:librarian_id]))
      redirect_to :controller=>'auth',
        :action=>'llogin', :into=>url_for(params)
    end
  end
  def try_librarian
    @a_librarian = Librarian.find_by_id(
        session[:librarian_id]) if session[:librarian_id]
  end
  def try_borrower
    @a_borrower = Borrower.find_by_id(
        session[:borrower_id]) if session[:borrower_id]
  end
end
```

You have three different filters and one before_filter declaration. The before_filter invokes try_borrower for all pages. You don't do the same thing for try_librarian, because there are a few cases where you don't want to do try_librarian (specifically those cases where a Librarian needs to be logged in). The method authenticate_librarian will be used from several controllers, so it makes sense to share the implementation. The actual implementation is the same thing you've seen before; it uses the session value librarian_id—if it exists—to find the Librarian. Otherwise it redirects to the llogin method (standing for librarian login, as compared to blogin) on the Auth controller.

The two `try` filters check if the session contains a `librarian_id` and a `borrower_id`, and try to find them from the database in that case.

Finally, to get the layout fully working, you also need to add a style sheet, in the file `public/stylesheets/liblib.css`. This is the same style sheet that you used in the earlier applications, so just copy it from the Shoplet application to the new name.

Searching and Looking at Books

The first part to implement should reasonably be the functionality to list and search books. Lending and returning should be a part of this also, but because you don't implement authentication until later, you'll skip those parts too, by just putting links for them in the code, which you provide functionality for later.

The first step, before you start creating the book listing code, is to make sure this is what gets seen when first visiting the application. So, remove `public/index.html` and change `config/routes.rb` to include this:

```
map.connect '', :controller => "book"
```

Next, open up `book_controller.rb`, and first of all add the filters that need to be in place for authentication to work, later:

```
before_filter :authenticate_borrower, :only => [:lend, :ret]
before_filter :authenticate_librarian, :only => [:add_instance,
            :remove_instance, :add_description, :remove_description]
before_filter :try_librarian, :only => [:index, :search, :book]
```

You only require authentication to be in place for certain specific operations, as you can see, and you try to add librarian information for the `index`, `search`, and `book` actions.

The `index` action just delegates to the `search` action:

```
def index
  search
  render :action => 'search'
end
```

The `search` action looks like this:

```
def search
  if params[:searching]
    @search = params[:search]
    @results = LegacySystem.search("%#@search%","%#@search%")
  end
end
```

Because you want to use the same view for search, regardless if searching has been done or not, you just add the `@search` and `@result` instance variables if a search has been requested. Usually you would have checked if the request was a `POST` or `GET` to discern if it's a search, but because searches should be idempotent it makes sense to have them be `GET` too, so you can give out URLs for a specific search.

The actual searching just uses the LegacySystem module directly, calling the search method. You add percentage signs before and after the search string to make sure you don't try to match complete strings when searching. Of course, it would be easy to add a small feature so you can search on either title or author but not both.

The view for the search action should look like Listing 14-3.

Listing 14-3. *app/views/book/search.rhtml*

```
<h1>Book search</h1>
<p>Search for book:
<% form_tag({}, :method => :get) do %>
  <%= text_field_tag 'search', @search %>
  <%= hidden_field_tag 'searching', 'true' %>
<% end %>
<% if @results %>
  <% if @results.empty? %>
    <p>No books found</p>
  <% else %>
    <%= render :partial => 'book_result', :collection => @results %>
  <% end %>
<% end %>
<br/>
<%= link_to 'Add new book',
      :action => 'add_description' if @a_librarian %>
```

First you provide a simple form that also sets the searching parameter to true. You fill in the text field with the previous search, if one exists. Further, if the @results instance variable exists, you know that you should view search results. The actual results are displayed using a partial called book_result. Finally, you also add a link to make it possible to add a new book description if you're a Librarian.

The book_result partial is simple. You don't use tables for this display, so the only things you need are the title, authors, and a link to more information (see Listing 14-4).

Listing 14-4. *app/views/book/_book_result.rhtml*

```
p><b><%=link_to book_result.name,
        :action => :book, :id=>book_result.id%></b> by
<%= book_result.authors.join(", ") %> (<%=book_result.isbn%>)</p>
```

Because you know that each entry in the list of results will be a BookDescription struct (which you created in the last chapter), you can just ask it for name, ID, authors, and ISBN and display the information. The link points to the book action, which displays one specific book with some more data and options available.

Before we look at the book action and view, let's briefly see what the add_description button does (in book_controller.rb):

```
def add_description
  redirect_to :controller => 'amazon'
end
```

Because adding a new book requires you to import it from Amazon.com, this action just redirects the `Librarian` to the `AmazonController`.

Viewing a book is a tad complicated, for the simple reason that you need to collate the instance information into something useful for the viewer. Preferably, you should be able to see how many books are available at each library, and only see a link to lend a book if it's possible to lend the book in the current library.

```ruby
def book
  @book = LegacySystem::get_book_description(params[:id].to_i)
  instances = @book.instances
  @sorted = { }
  instances.each do |cc|
    curr = (@sorted[cc[:library_id]] ||=
              [LegacySystem::get_library_name(cc[:library_id]), 0, 0])
    curr[1] += 1
    if !cc[:lended]
      curr[2] += 1
      if cc[:library_id] == $CURRENT_LIBRARY_ID
        @lendable_here = cc[:book_instance_id]
      end
    else
      if cc[:library_id] == $CURRENT_LIBRARY_ID
        @returnable_here = true
      end
    end
  end
end
```

The first step is to get the book description for the specified ID. That's the easy part. Then, you have the code to sort the instances. Each entry in the sorted hash has a key that's the library ID, and a value entry that's a three-entry array. The first part of the array is the library name, the second is how many instances of the book that library has, and the final number is how many books are in the library and not lent. You compile this information by walking through each book instance, creating a new entry for the library it belongs to the first time you see it, getting the library name through the legacy system, and then incrementing the value of books in that library. Then you check whether the book is not lent; in that case, you increment the second value. Finally, you check if the book isn't lent and if the library ID you are working with right now is the same as the library this Rails instance is working for. In that case, you set the `@lendable_here` instance variable to the instance ID that's available. In this way, you save two pieces of information in the same place: first, that this book can be lent from this library, and which instance ID is available. If more than one instance is available, the last available will get used. You also have a `@returnable_here` instance variable to say whether any book instance is lent from this library.

So, for the view you have the @book, @sorted, @lendable_here, and @returnable_here instance variables to use for providing good information to both a Borrower and a Librarian. You do that like this:

```
<h1><%=@book.name%></h1>
<p><b>Authors:</b>
<ul>
  <% for author in @book.authors %>
    <li><%= author %></li>
  <% end %>
</ul></p>
<p><b>ISBN:</b> <%= @book.isbn %></p>
<p><b>Copies:</b>
  <% for id, instance in @sorted %>
    <li>At <u><%=instance[0]%></u>: <%= instance[1] %>
         <i>(<%= instance[2] %> available)</i></li>
  <% end %>
</ul></p>
<br/>
<% if @a_librarian %>
  <%= link_to 'Add instance', {:action => 'add_instance',
        :id => params[:id]}, :post => true %> |
  <%= link_to 'Remove instance', {:action => 'remove_instance',
        :id => @lendable_here, :bookid => params[:id]},
        :post => true if @lendable_here %>
  <%= 'Remove instance' unless @lendable_here %> |
  <%= link_to 'Remove this book', {:action => 'remove_description',
        :id => params[:id] }, :post => true if @sorted.empty? %>
  <%= 'Remove this book' unless @sorted.empty? %>
  <br/><br/>
<% end %>
<%= link_to 'Borrow this book', {:action => 'lend',
        :id => @lendable_here,
:bookid => params[:id]},
        :post => true if @lendable_here %>
<%= 'Borrow this book' unless @lendable_here %> |
<%= link_to 'Return this book', {:action => 'ret',
        :id => params[:id]}, :post => true if @returnable_here %>
<%= 'Return this book' unless @returnable_here %>
```

The first step is just to display all the easy information about title, ISBN, and authors. You then display which copies are available at which library by iterating over the @sorted hash, showing how many books each library has, and how many of these are available. After that information, if you are a Librarian you show some more links that are useful. The first link

adds a new instance for this book ID. The next one shows a "Remove instance" link if
@lendable_here is set. You cannot remove an instance from the system that isn't in the library.
You also just print the text "Remove instance" if the link isn't displayed; this makes the output
much more readable. You do the same thing for removing a book description, with the added
criteria that there can't be any instances available at any library for you to be able to remove a
book description.

After the links for Librarians, you provide a borrowing link, if any lendable copies are
available. Finally, you provide a return link, which is only displayed if this library has lent
books.

Taking a look at the operations in the Book controller that are available for Librarians,
you see that most are simple, because the basic operations map well against what the legacy
system provides. They are also similar to one another:

```
def add_instance
  LegacySystem::add_book_instance($CURRENT_LIBRARY_ID,
                          params[:id].to_i)
  flash[:notice] = "Book instance added"
  redirect_to :action => 'book', :id => params[:id]
end

def remove_instance
  LegacySystem::remove_book_instance(params[:id].to_i)
  flash[:notice] = "Book instance removed"
  redirect_to :action => 'book', :id => params[:bookid]
end

def remove_description
  LegacySystem::remove_book_description(params[:id].to_i)
  flash[:notice] = "Book removed"
  redirect_to :action => 'search'
end
```

The two operations we haven't looked at yet in the Book controller are lend and ret. They
follow mostly the same pattern, but they're a little more complicated because they need to
update the BorrowedBook models on a Borrower:

```
def lend
  @a_borrower.borrowed_books.create(:book_description_id =>
          params[:bookid], :library_id => $CURRENT_LIBRARY_ID,
          :book_instance_id => params[:id])
  LegacySystem::lend_book_instance(params[:id].to_i)
  flash[:notice] = "Book lended to you"
  redirect_to :action => 'book', :id => params[:bookid]
end
```

Lending a book entails using the @a_borrower instance variable and creating a new
BorrowedBook for the Borrower. This is easy. The next step is to use the LegacySystem to lend the
specific book instance, and finally flash information to the user and redirect back to the book
description you came from. Returning a book looks like this:

```
def ret
  bbook = @a_borrower.borrowed_books.detect {|bb|
    bb.book_description_id == params[:id].to_i &&
    bb.library_id == $CURRENT_LIBRARY_ID}
  if bbook
    LegacySystem.return_book_instance(bbook.book_instance_id.to_i)
    @a_borrower.borrowed_books.destroy(bbook)
    flash[:notice] = "Book returned from you"
  else
    flash[:error] = "You haven't loaned this book at this " +
            "library and can thus not return it"
  end
  redirect_to :action => 'book', :id => params[:id]
end
```

The thing that complicates returning books is the fact that you should only be able to return books that you yourself have lent. You use detect to find a BorrowedBook where the library ID of the borrowed book is the current library ID, and the book description is the same as the book you're looking for. If you find one, you return that book instance and destroy the BorrowedBooks instance. Otherwise, you give the Borrower an error message. In both cases, you redirect back to the book action for the book in question.

That's all there is to the book handling. Most of this will work, except for the parts that require the user to be logged in. That's what we'll cover now.

Authentication

You need to make one small addition to the Book controller for all your authentication needs to be satisfied there. The private authenticate_borrower method needs to be in place for the filters to function:

```
private
def authenticate_borrower
  unless session[:borrower_id] &&
    (@a_borrower = Borrower.find_by_id(session[:borrower_id]))
    redirect_to :controller=>'auth', :action=>'blogin',
                :into=>url_for(params)
  end
end
```

You just check if the person is already authenticated as a Borrower, and otherwise you redirect to the Auth controller, adding your regular technique of an into parameter. The Auth controller is a little complicated because you need to provide several more features in the login than in your other systems. Let's begin by looking at the two filters that are in place for blogin and llogin in AuthController:

```
before_filter :b_already_authenticated, :only => 'blogin'
before_filter :l_already_authenticated, :only => 'llogin'
```

The purpose of these filters is just to make sure that if you manually type in the address /auth/llogin, you will just be redirected to a useful place, instead of having to log in again:

```
private
def b_already_authenticated
  if session[:borrower_id]
    redirect_to params[:into] || {:controller => 'book',
                                   :action => 'index'}
  end
end
def l_already_authenticated
  if session[:librarian_id]
    redirect_to params[:into] || {:controller => 'librarians',
                                   :action => 'index'}
  end
end
```

These methods are also "into"-aware, which makes them a little smarter. The next step is to look at the logout action, which is simple:

```
def logout
  flash[:notice] = "You have been logged out"
  session[:borrower_id] = nil
  session[:librarian_id] = nil
  redirect_to :controller => 'book', :action => 'index'
end
```

You just remove the Borrower ID and Librarian ID from the session and redirect to the start page. The llogin action is less complicated than the blogin action, so we'll look at that one now:

```
def llogin
  if request.post?
    if auth = Authentication.find_by_username_and_password(
              params[:username],params[:password])
      if librarian = Librarian.find_by_authentication_id(auth.id)
        session[:librarian_id] = librarian.id
        flash[:notice] = "You have been logged in as a Librarian"
        redirect_to params[:into] || {:controller => 'librarians',
                                       :action => 'index'}
        return
      else
        flash[:error] = "You don't have a librarian account"
      end
    else
      flash[:error] = "Wrong username or password"
    end
  end
  @into = params[:into]
end
```

You only consider it a login try if it's a post, otherwise you just set the @into variable. If it's a post you try to find the authentication object with corresponding username and password, and then to find a librarian associated with this authentication. If you find this, the person gets logged in and redirected to the correct place; otherwise an appropriate error message is displayed.

The view for this action is straightforward (see Listing 14-5).

Listing 14-5. *app/views/auth/llogin.rhtml*

```
<h2>Please login with your username and password</h2>
<%= start_form_tag %>
<%= hidden_field_tag 'into', @into %>
<table>
  <tr>
    <td>Username:</td><td><%= text_field_tag 'username' %></td>
  </tr>
  <tr>
    <td>Password:</td><td><%= password_field_tag 'password' %></td>
  </tr>
  <tr>
    <td colspan="2" align="right"><%= submit_tag 'Login' %></td>
  </tr>
</table>
<%= end_form_tag %>
```

As mentioned earlier, the blogin action is complex. The main reason for that is the possibility that you have a borrower account at another library, and would like to import that into this library. This option is provided with a check box, which when marked will try to import user information with the specified username and password from other libraries using the Rails intercommunication library you built in the last chapter:

```
def blogin
  if request.post?
    if params[:other_library]
      data = ::LibLib::Communication::find_borrower(
                  params[:username],params[:password])
      unless data.blank?
        b = Borrower.new(data[:borrower])
        b.authentication = auth = Authentication.create(data[:auth])
        for bookinstanceid, bbook in data[:borrowed]
          b.borrowed_books << BorrowedBook.create(bbook)
        end
        b.save
      end
    end
    if auth = Authentication.find_by_username_and_password(
                          params[:username],params[:password])
      if borrower = Borrower.find_by_authentication_id(auth.id)
```

```
          session[:borrower_id] = borrower.id
          flash[:notice] = "You have been logged in as a Borrower"
          redirect_to params[:into] || {:controller => 'book',
                                          :action => 'index'}
          return
        else
          flash[:error] = "You don't have a borrowing account"
        end
      else
        flash[:error] = "Wrong username or password"
      end
    end
  @into = params[:into]
end
```

As with blogin, you only consider posts to be valid login tries. If the other_library parameter has been set you use the find_borrower method call to try to find borrower information
from other libraries. If you get data back, you'll create a new Borrower for it, and also add all
the information about that person's already borrowed books to the database. Finally the data
is saved. Note that this code doesn't check for clashes against current users, so if you're
unlucky, this Borrower can't import his or her account because he or she has the same username as someone already existing in this library.

The final login code is almost exactly the same as in llogin. You don't have to handle the
case of an imported Borrower any differently, for the simple reason that you just save his or her
data to the database, and the authentication lookups will find him or her. Of course, this also
works for already existing users doing a regular login.

The view for blogin looks like Listing 14-6.

Listing 14-6. *app/views/auth/blogin.rhtml*

```
<h2>Please login with your username and password</h2>
<%= start_form_tag %>
<%= hidden_field_tag 'into', @into %>
<table>
  <tr>
    <td>I have an account at another library (importing will
          take a few seconds):</td>
    <td><%= check_box_tag 'other_library' %></td>
  </tr>
  <tr>
    <td>Username:</td><td><%= text_field_tag 'username' %></td>
  </tr>
  <tr>
    <td>Password:</td><td><%= password_field_tag 'password' %></td>
  </tr>
  <tr>
    <td colspan="2" align="right"><%= submit_tag 'Login' %></td>
  </tr>
```

```
</table>
<%= end_form_tag %>
<%= link_to "I don't have a borrowers account",
        :controller => 'borrower', :action => 'new', :into => @into %>
```

This view provides the check box for other_library, and also adds a link to create a new Borrower account, if needed. That's all you need for authenticating Borrowers and Librarians, and also importing them from other libraries. Next, we should look at how Borrowers and Librarians come into existence.

Borrowers and Librarians

As you saw in the last section, you provide a link to the Borrower controller's action called new to let a Borrower create him or herself. The action looks like this:

```
def new
  @authentication = Authentication.new
  @borrower = Borrower.new
  @into = params[:into]
end
```

To create a new Borrower, you need to have an Authentication model, a Borrower model, and also the into information if there is any. The view for this action is almost a standard scaffolding view, except that the error information for both the Authentication model and Borrower model is displayed manually, to give you more control over the output (see Listing 14-7).

Listing 14-7. *app/views/borrower/new.rhtml*

```
<h2>Please submit your borrower information</h2>
<%= start_form_tag :action => 'create' %>
  <%= error_messages_for 'authentication' %>
  <%= error_messages_for 'borrower' %>
<%= hidden_field_tag 'into', @into %>
<table>
  <tr>
    <td>Name:</td><td><%= text_field_tag 'borrower[name]',
                @borrower.name %></td>
  </tr>
  <tr>
    <td>Username:</td><td>
    <%= text_field_tag 'authentication[username]',
                @authentication.username %></td>
  </tr>
  <tr>
    <td>Password:</td><td>
        <%= password_field_tag 'authentication[password]' %></td>
  </tr>
  <tr>
    <td colspan="2" align="right"><%= submit_tag 'Create' %></td>
```

```
      </tr>
    </table>
<%= end_form_tag %>
```

The create action looks like this:

```
def create
  @borrower = Borrower.new(params[:borrower])
  @authentication = Authentication.new(params[:authentication])
  unless @authentication.save
    @into = params[:into]
    flash[:error] = "Couldn't save authentication information"
    render :action => 'new'
    return
  end
  @borrower.authentication = @authentication
  if @borrower.save
    flash[:notice] = "You have been created " +
            "with username #{@authentication.username}"
    redirect_to params[:into]
  else
    @into = params[:into]
    flash[:error] = "Couldn't save borrower information"
    render :action => 'new'
  end
end
```

You need to handle the creation of a Borrower in two stages, because the creation of the Authentication model could fail or the creation of the Borrower model could fail. In both these cases you need to handle it correctly and redirect back to the new.rhtml view.

The rest of the BorrowerController is parts only a Librarian has access to. You control this by adding authentication filters for the actions in question:

```
before_filter :authenticate_librarian, :only =>
                [:list, :remove, :create_librarian]
```

The index action should redirect to the new action:

```
def index
  new
  render :action => 'new'
end
```

A Librarian should be able to list Borrowers:

```
def list
  @borrower_pages, @borrowers = paginate :borrowers, :per_page => 20
end
```

Because the information to display about a Borrower is small, you can have a pagination with 20 entries instead of the standard 10 (see Listing 14-8).

Listing 14-8. *app/views/borrower/list.rhtml*

```
<h1>Borrowers</h1>
<table width="600">
  <tr>
    <th align="left">Name</th>
    <th align="left">Username</th>
    <th></th>
    <th></th>
    <th></th>
  </tr>
<% for borrower in @borrowers %>
  <tr>
    <td><%=h borrower.name %></td>
    <td><%=h borrower.authentication.username %></td>
    <td></td>
    <td><%=link_to('Create librarian',
          {:action => 'create_librarian', :id => borrower},
          :post => true) unless borrower.is_librarian? %></td>
    <td><%=link_to('Remove',
          { :action => 'remove', :id => borrower },
          :confirm => 'Are you sure?', :post => true) %></td>
  </tr>
<% end %>
</table>
<%= link_to 'Previous page', {
      :page => @borrower_pages.current.previous } if
                    @borrower_pages.current.previous %>
<%= link_to 'Next page', {
      :page => @borrower_pages.current.next } if
                    @borrower_pages.current.next %>
```

The listing allows you to see the name and username of a Borrower, create a Librarian from the Borrower entry, and also remove a Borrower. The remove and create_librarian actions look like this:

```
def create_librarian
  b = Borrower.find(params[:id])
  l = Librarian.create(:name => b.name,
                    :authentication => b.authentication)
  flash[:notice] = "Borrower #{b.name} is now a librarian"
  list
  render :action => 'list'
end
def remove
  b = Borrower.find(params[:id])
  a = b.authentication
  a.destroy unless Librarian.find_by_authentication_id(a.id)
  b.destroy
  redirect_to :action => 'list'
end
```

When creating a Librarian from a Borrower, you just create a new Librarian model object with the same authentication object as the Borrower. You then go back to the list view.

Removing a Borrower includes removing that Borrower's authentication object, unless that object is also used by a Librarian.

The Librarian controller gives you access to most of the same operations, but should only be available to a Librarian. That's why the first entry in the class definition for the controller is this before_filter:

```
before_filter :authenticate_librarian
```

You view and list Librarians by using the index and list actions, which are almost exactly the same implementation as the corresponding Borrower actions:

```
def index
  list
  render :action => 'list'
end
def list
  @librarian_pages, @librarians = paginate :librarians, :per_page => 20
  @librarian = Librarian.new
  @authentication = Authentication.new
end
```

The main difference here is that you also include the parts needed from a new action inside of the list action, by creating empty Authentication and Librarian models. Listing 14-9 shows the list view.

Listing 14-9. *app/views/librarians/list.rhtml*

```
<h1>Librarians</h1>
<table width="600">
  <tr>
    <th align="left">Name</th>
    <th align="left">Username</th>
    <th></th>
    <th></th>
    <th></th>
  </tr>
<% for librarian in @librarians %>
  <tr>
    <td><%=h librarian.name %></td>
    <td><%=h librarian.authentication.username %></td>
    <td></td>
    <td><%=link_to('Create borrower', {
          :action => 'create_borrower', :id => librarian},
          :post => true) unless librarian.is_borrower? %></td>
    <td><%=link_to('Remove', {
          :action => 'remove', :id => librarian },
          :confirm => 'Are you sure?', :post => true) %></td>
```

```
    </tr>
<% end %>
</table>
<%= link_to 'Previous page', {
        :page => @librarian_pages.current.previous } if
        @librarian_pages.current.previous %>
<%= link_to 'Next page', {
        :page => @librarian_pages.current.next } if
        @librarian_pages.current.next %>
<% form_tag :action => 'add' do %>
  <%= error_messages_for 'authentication' %>
  <%= error_messages_for 'librarian' %>
  <p><label for="librarian_name">Name</label><br/>
  <%= text_field 'librarian', 'name'  %></p>
  <p><label for="authentication_username">Username</label><br/>
  <%= text_field 'authentication', 'username'  %></p>
  <p><label for="authentication_password">Password</label><br/>
  <%= password_field 'authentication', 'password'  %></p>
  <%= submit_tag "Create" %>
<% end %>
```

The listing of Librarians shows their name and username, and provides the possibility to create a Borrower from a Librarian, and also to remove a Librarian. The second part shows a form for creating a new Librarian, with help from the objects created in the list action.

Adding a new Librarian has the same problem as creating a new Borrower: you need to stagger the creation because you have two different objects to create, where the second depends on the first:

```
def add
  @librarian = Librarian.new(params[:librarian])
  @authentication = Authentication.new(params[:authentication])
  unless @authentication.save
    flash[:error] = "Couldn't save authentication information"
    @librarian_pages, @librarians = paginate :librarians,
                                        :per_page => 20
    render :action => 'list'
    return
  end
  @librarian.authentication = @authentication
  if @librarian.save
    flash[:notice] = "Librarian created successfully"
    redirect_to :action => 'list'
  else
    @librarian_pages, @librarians = paginate :librarians,
                                        :per_page => 20
    render :action => 'list'
  end
end
```

Creating a `Borrower` from a `Librarian` is easier, because the `authentication` object already exists:

```
def create_borrower
  l = Librarian.find(params[:id])
  b = Borrower.create(:name => l.name,
                      :authentication => l.authentication)
  list
  flash[:notice] = "Librarian #{l.name} is now a borrower"
  render :action => 'list'
end
```

Finally, removing a `Librarian` is done the same way as removing a `Borrower`:

```
def remove
  l = Librarian.find(params[:id])
  a = l.authentication
  a.destroy unless Borrower.find_by_authentication_id(a.id)
  l.destroy
  redirect_to :action => 'list'
end
```

You make sure not to remove the `authentication` object unless no `Borrower` references it.

Importing from Amazon.com

The last part of our application uses the library you created in Chapter 12, which lets you communicate with Amazon.com. The controller is the easiest part of the application; that's because most of the logic is in the library. The controller offers two possibilities: to search for books on Amazon.com, and to import a book description into the legacy system. You have a `before_filter` to make sure only `Librarians` use this code, and an `index` action that uses the search action:

```
before_filter :authenticate_librarian
def index
  search
  render :action => 'search'
end
def search
  if params[:searching]
    @search = params[:search]
    @results = BookService::find(@search)
  end
end
```

The `search` action itself just uses the `BookService` to find entries, and puts these in the `@results` instance variable. The dynamic nature of Ruby makes it easy to handle things like this. That's because you don't need to declare types, and if you follow logical conventions for the results, you don't need to know what actual types are in the result list. The `search` view to display results and the search box looks like this:

```
<h1>Amazon Book search</h1>
<p>Search for book:
<% form_tag({}, :method => :get) do %>
  <%= text_field_tag 'search', @search || '' %>
  <%= hidden_field_tag 'searching', 'true' %>
<% end %>
<% if @results %>
  <% if @results.empty? %>
    <p>No books found</p>
  <% else %>
    <p><%=pluralize @results.size, 'book'%> found</p>
    <table width="800">
    <%= render :partial => 'amazon_result', :collection => @results %>
    </table>
  <% end %>
<% end %>
```

You use a partial for each book entry, and you use the pluralize helper to display a count
of how many results were found.

The amazon_result partial looks like this:

```
<tr>
  <td><%= image_tag amazon_result.image_url %></td>
  <td>
    <table>
      <tr><td colspan="2"><h3><%=h amazon_result.name %></h3></td></tr>
      <tr><td><b>Publisher</b></td><td>
            <%=h amazon_result.publisher %></td></tr>
      <tr><td><b>ISBN</b></td><td><i>
            <%=h amazon_result.isbn %></i></td></tr>
      <tr><td><b>Price</b></td><td>
            <%=h amazon_result.price %></td></tr>
      <tr><td><b>Author(s)</b></td><td>
            <%=amazon_result.authors.map{|v|h v}.
                join("<br/>") %></td></tr>
    </table>
  </td>
  <td>
    <%= start_form_tag :action => 'import' %>
      <%= hidden_field_tag 'name', amazon_result.name %>
      <%= hidden_field_tag 'isbn', amazon_result.isbn %>
      <%= hidden_field_tag 'authors',
                      amazon_result.authors.join(";") %>
      <%= hidden_field_tag 'search', @search %>
      <%= submit_tag 'Import this book' %>
    <%= end_form_tag %>
  </td>
</tr>
```

Because the result includes an image URL, you display that image if you can, and also show the name, publisher, ISBN, price, and authors of the book. Each entry also gets a form that can be used to import this book. Instead of having to hit Amazon.com twice to import a book, you just provide all the information in the form that is needed to import the book. This approach also makes it easier to add other ways of importing a book. The `import` action looks like this:

```
def import
  bd = BookDescription.new(nil, params[:name],
                           params[:authors].split(';'), params[:isbn])
  LegacySystem::add_book_description(bd)
  flash[:notice] = "The book \"#{params[:name]}\" has been " +
      "imported. <br/><font size='small'>(<i>Remember to " +
      "actually create instances of it too.</i>)</font>"
  redirect_to :action => 'search', :searching => 'true',
              :search => params[:search]
end
```

It creates a new book description from the parameters, then uses the `LegacySystem` module to add the book description. It then redirects back to the search. It could be argued that the redirect should go to a display of the newly created book description instead. The display would be easy to add if that was needed.

Summary

In this chapter we created the LibLib Rails application more or less from scratch, but using the libraries developed in the last two chapters. We saw how to bundle together functionality from widely different data sources and provide operations through Java services that would be hard to add to a pure Ruby system.

We saw how to use JMS and web services to talk to legacy systems and interact with them in highly productive ways. The overall theme for these three chapters is that many strange technologies exist in the world, and at some point or another you'll need to create code that works together with these systems. By using JRuby to leverage Java libraries, you'll live in the best world imaginable.

This was the last project in this book; the four we developed should have shown you a large amount of what can be accomplished by using the strongest features of Java and Ruby together. In the next chapter we'll take a look at a few things we haven't discussed, and also at things that you can do yourself to improve the JRuby ecosystem. Because JRuby is a classic open source project, your contributions are not only valued, but necessary.

CHAPTER 15

■ ■ ■

Coda: Next Steps

We've created four different projects based on JRuby on Rails in this book. Most of what we've done can be generalized and put into real world usage with few changes. However, there are still many things left to try with JRuby. Because this book has focused on using JRuby in conjunction with Rails, there's a whole area of non-Rails applications and libraries to discover.

In this chapter I'll take a quick look at how you can contribute back to JRuby and the surrounding projects. I'll also give you a quick overview of the main projects living around JRuby in the JRuby-extras project. Finally, we'll take a look at three home projects you can try out if you feel like changing a substantial part of Rails to use more Java features.

I'll try to point you in several directions where you can go from here, expanding and intensifying your JRuby and Rails usage.

JRuby-extras

Most of the projects that provide support for JRuby in different ways live on RubyForge, inside a project called JRuby-extras. There has been talk about moving these projects to Codehaus, but so far it hasn't happened. JRuby-extras was created in conjunction with JRuby when JRuby first starting showing promise of running Rails and other larger applications. The point was to have a collection point for all utilities that are specifically for enabling JRuby in different ways. As such, it's been successful. Right now, 21 developers commit to projects, with 5 project administrators. There are 12 different subprojects within the project, which have had at least one release.

In fact, some of the projects have been incubated long enough, and there's talk about extracting some of the projects into their own file areas. That's also the main point about JRuby-extras: to provide a place where nice ideas can get started, incubate, get some help from all the available developers there, and finally grow up and be separate projects.

Contributing

It's easy to contribute to JRuby-extras. You should sign up on the mailing list. Once you've done that and you'd like to help out, just send a message to the list detailing how you'd like to contribute, and if your idea sounds reasonable you'll get commit access to the project. The main development happens through SVN, and much discussion usually happens on the mailing list. If you have an existing project you'd like to commit to JRuby-extras, follow the same procedure and add it to JRuby-extras.

Many of the existing projects could sorely use some more help; many of the current developers are stuck working hard on JRuby itself or on other projects, so if you see something in the following list that you think is important, don't hesitate to sign up for it.

Current Projects

As mentioned earlier, 12 different projects in JRuby-extras have had at least one release. I'll give a quick introduction to each of these here, to give you a feeling about what kind of things end up in the JRuby-extras project.

ActiveRecord-JDBC

AR-JDBC is probably the most important project in JRuby-extras, and something we've considered extracting from RubyForge for a long time. It's quite grown up, working fairly well. The current version is 0.5 and the core databases are supported well. That's not to say there's nothing you can do to help. In fact, AR-JDBC needs lots of help, because every database adapter needs someone to adopt it and make sure it runs correctly. Specifically, if you have access to a strange or nonstandard database, it would be appreciated if you helped out by writing a supported adapter for this database. I'll talk more about that in the section "Home Projects."

AntBuilder

Several projects in JRuby-extras are based on a good idea for which someone did a proof of concept that works well enough, and then no one has had time to commit more code to the project. AntBuilder is such a project. The idea is to create a JRuby DSL that can be used to build Ant configuration files without having to touch Ant XML. In fact, using the AntBuilder hides all invocations to Ant, and all the Ant XML. This makes it much easier to use your existing Ant tasks while having a nice Ruby way of writing the configuration files.

It could be argued that we should try to do away with Ant altogether, but if you're stuck with situations such as legacy code that uses important Ant tasks, this project makes Ant much easier to handle. When starting a new project, I'd recommend just going with Rake instead, even for your Java projects.

JRuby SwingConsole

The JRuby SwingConsole is a small project for creating a Windows console equivalent of IRB for JRuby. The project succeeded well enough that this console is now included in the JRuby core distribution. It's a small Swing program that runs IRB and provides good-looking completions, and also a few other features.

RMagick4J

RMagick4J is a typical example of the kinds of projects that are needed for JRuby to make it equivalent to Ruby in usage. RMagick is one of the most popular downloads for Ruby, and JRuby can't use it because it contains extensive C extensions. RMagick4J tries to rectify this by re-creating the API of RMagick, but using Java2D for the low-level operations. What's interesting with this approach is that in time this project should be more usable than RMagick. One of the major problems with RMagick is that it can be hard to install and get all the ImageMagick bindings set up correctly. Because many people want to use RMagick for graphs and so on, they still do so, but many man hours are lost in getting it working correctly.

RMagick4J uses Java2D, which is a part of every Java 1.4 platform existing, on any operating system you can imagine. So, the installation of this Gem is extremely simple, and everything will just work after it's been installed. The project originally started with the explicit goal of porting the RMagick Gem, but it soon got noticed because of the great portability features offered from it. This is a typical example of the Java platform coming into its own through JRuby.

GoldSpike

Still released under the name Rails-integration, GoldSpike is extremely important because it's currently the only way to make your Rails application interact with a standard J2EE web container. It's also currently understaffed. The code base isn't that large, but it's an important piece of code that's used for every request any Rails application will ever handle when running on JRuby. GoldSpike needs more eyeballs—people looking at the code and contributing back fixes. We would also appreciate people doing load testing and scalability tests to see where the current project's reliability and robustness is.

JavaSand

JavaSand is a small piece of code that is a port of the project Sandbox. What made Sandbox interesting for the regular Ruby distribution is that in most cases, you can't have more than one Ruby interpreter per process. If you wanted to embed Ruby or just not handle communication problems between processes, you were out of luck. Sandbox allows you to run several Ruby instances within the same process, and also gives you capabilities to handle security in a way that makes it safe to run any code you'd like in it. The user of the Sandbox library can describe which classes and operations should be available, and which shouldn't.

Because JRuby already provides for more than one runtime in the same process, Sandbox isn't that important for JRuby from that perspective. On the other hand, providing the same interface for creating more than one runtime, and also having the same interface for specifying security constraints was useful, which is why I put together JavaSand. The code is small and easy to understand, but uses many of the deeper features of the JRuby runtime to make everything go smoothly. It's a useful project for some specific domains.

JParseTree

JParseTree is another port of a project that's useful in some circumstances, called ParseTree. This project allows you to get a normalized AST from Ruby code. This allows you to implement code generation and decoration in a dynamic and powerful way. ParseTree was used to bootstrap rubinius, and the JRuby project is planning on using JParseTree to get rubinius working on JRuby. If you're interested in how Ruby parsing and compilation works, looking at the output of ParseTree and JParseTree is a good way to start.

JRuby-OpenSSL

One of the more ambitious projects in JRuby-extras, JRuby-OpenSSL was originally a part of JRuby, but was extracted due to export restrictions on heavy cryptography. The basic objective of the project is to port all the functionality of the Ruby OpenSSL library to Java, using Java's cryptographic extensions. This wasn't as easy as it sounds, but in most cases OpenSSL works with JRuby now. If you like cryptography, this is a project where you could help out and make a huge difference. The code base hasn't been touched in a long while due to resource conflicts.

AntWrap

AntWrap is also a wrapper around Ant, just like AntBuilder. The main difference is that AntWrap never generates Ant XML files, but uses Ant internally instead.

Stemmer4JR

Stemmer4JR is a port of the Stemmer4R project, using the Java package stemmer to implement stemming. This is used, among other projects, by the Hitta project on Google for implementing full text search on ActiveRecord model objects. The code is mostly just a wrapper around the stemmer Java library, and as such is a good example of a small JRuby extension implementation.

Mongrel-support

Mongrel uses two C extensions that are ported in the Mongrel-support project. At some point, these extensions will be merged with the Mongrel code base so that everything is collected in the same place. Mongrel-support contains an implementation of a ternary search tree, and also an HTTP parser implemented with Ragel.

Mongrel-JCluster

We talked about this plug-in in Chapter 11: JCluster allows you start up several Mongrel instances inside the same Java process, and also provides capabilities to control all instances with few commands. The code is mostly a port of the mongrel_cluster project.

Contributing to JRuby

JRuby is—and has always been—an open source project. As such, it is incredibly important that as many people as possible contribute and help out with everything in the project.

There are many ways of helping out. The first step is to join the mailing lists (you can find links to these in Appendix C). The user list is good, but most of the JRuby discussions happen on the dev list. Post to the user list in case you have a problem with getting something working, and post to the dev list if you want to know about something regarding the implementation. Someone is almost always available to answer your questions.

Using IRC is also a good way of getting questions answered. The #jruby channel almost always contains at least one of the core developers and several JRuby power users.

The main ways of contributing can be divided into three basic categories: reporting bugs (and ideally helping us pinpoint the cause for them), sending in patches, and providing documentation. For bug tracking, JRuby uses JIRA, where you can browse all current bugs and also see all bugs that have been resolved. We usually try to use JIRA for handling patches too, so go to the address listed in Appendix C and get an account so you can send in bug reports. When sending in a report, try to include as much information as possible about your environment and what you did. If possible, try to narrow down the problem and provide an actual Ruby script that exhibits it. If we have test cases to look at, it's much easier to provide solutions.

When sending in a patch for a bug, you should use the `svn diff` command to generate patches. Then, attach them to the bug in JIRA, and also write a small log about what you did to fix the bug, and what the actual problem in the bug was.

In most cases, patches should provide documentation in the code base. If there are no bugs for it in JIRA, you can create a new documentation bug, with a subject such as "RubyKernel needs more JavaDoc," and then send your patches to that bug. Filing everything in JIRA makes it easy for the developers to keep track of what status everything has and if someone is working on it. Developers can also keep track of all the versions of patches sent in, and conversations pertaining to the bug in question.

Home Projects

A large part of contributing to open source projects is working on already existing code. However, you can also start out by creating something totally new. Currently there are a few areas where it would be interesting to see some development, and these areas can also be a good way of getting into direct development with JRuby. You can implement all the projects suggested here in pure Ruby, but there are also areas where using Java and integrating directly with the JRuby runtime can make the code easier.

I'll introduce three suggestions of home projects that you can use as a starting point for your own JRuby work; these projects would all be highly useful, and I would love to see someone contribute these back to JRuby-extras.

Database Indexing with Lucene

One of the best open source tools for handling text indexing and search is called Lucene. A Ruby port for Lucene exists called Ferret; it's good and provides some nice features. In addition, it has good performance because it's implemented in C. At the moment, if you need searching for JRuby, you can use a pure Ruby project such as Hitta, or you can use Lucene through the Java interface. However, it would be nice to take a project using Ferret and continue to use the Ferret interface in the same way, only implement the operations using Lucene instead. It wouldn't be a big project, because Ferret's API is based on Lucene's, but it would be highly useful.

Several smaller projects are also based on Ferret. For example, an acts_as_ferret plug-in for Rails exists, which handles indexing and searching of ActiveRecord models almost transparently. By enabling Ferret to run on JRuby, all these smaller projects would also work without a hitch.

To get started on this project, you'd first have to learn Lucene and then read through the Ferret code and see which parts are implemented in C. In all cases where Ferret uses C code, you'd need to figure out a way of replacing that operation with the corresponding Lucene call. After that's done, you'd need to package everything up inside a Gem and publish it somewhere so people could use it.

Replacing ActiveRecord with Hibernate

ActiveRecord has some good points. First of all, convention over configuration makes it incredibly productive and useful, at least when starting out using it. There are a few problems with the current approach used, though. For example. it's almost impossible to get ActiveRecord and prepared statements to work together, due to the incredibly dynamic nature of ActiveRecord. This means performance won't necessarily be the best, and some databases won't be too fond of this approach. ActiveRecord is also a simple implementation, meaning it doesn't support everything an OR mapping framework can support. Composite primary keys are one of these areas, but ActiveRecord doesn't do several other things well.

Hibernate is generally considered one of the best OR frameworks on the Java platform, both because it's fast, and because the XML configuration is quite usable. It also provides about all the features you'd ever need from a database connecting library.

There has been some discussion on the Internet about implementing an ActiveRecord replacement using Hibernate. This would bring many of the benefits of Hibernate to Rails, and could potentially improve performance and make Rails much more interesting for many types of businesses where ActiveRecord doesn't provide enough power.

Doing an ActiveHibernate would require some work, though. The first step is to decide what the API should look like and what features of ActiveRecord should be retained. Some of the things I like about ActiveRecord and would like to see in ActiveHibernate, too, would be a good validation framework. Also, it should be possible to create a much better configuration format based on a Ruby DSL instead of XML. The hardest part of the project, but also probably the most interesting, would involve creating a custom Hibernate type handler that can set and get properties on Ruby objects. That would allow Hibernate to do OR mapping on Ruby objects, and not just Java objects.

The actual implementation shouldn't be too complicated, though. The hard part is deciding what the API should look like, making a good compromise between power and ease of configuration.

Creating a New ActiveRecord-JDBC Adapter

AR-JDBC supports many of the most important databases out of the box, but because Java has access to just about every database in the world, there will always be JDBC drivers that need to be supported. There was a quick introduction in Chapter 5 about how you start creating support for a new database. In most cases there are two or three areas where you need to customize how AR-JDBC works. It's important that you have a good reference to the SQL dialect used when trying to implement support such as this.

Provided you've gotten to the stage where the basic support loads and you've followed the instructions in Chapter 5, the most likely areas where you'll need to customize how everything works are DDLs, custom types, and quoting.

AR-JDBC tries hard to figure out the correct database types to use for the simplified types that Rails provides. In most cases you'll need to customize the values a little, because AR-JDBC doesn't necessarily choose the right one. The way to do this is to override the `modify_types` method; typical code for doing that can look like this:

```
def modify_types(types)
  types[:primary_key] = "NUMBER(38) NOT NULL PRIMARY KEY"
  types[:datetime] = { :name => "DATE" }
```

```
    types[:timestamp] = { :name => "DATE" }
    types[:time] = { :name => "DATE" }
    types[:date] = { :name => "DATE" }
    types
end
```

This is code from the Oracle database adapter, and also shows areas you most often need to work with: the primary key type and date and time types.

The second area that usually needs work is handling the quoting of values. Most databases have different ways to handle how values will be represented, and that code is database specific. The quoting code for Oracle looks like this:

```
def quote_string(string) #:nodoc:
  string.gsub(/'/, "''")
end


def quote(value, column = nil) #:nodoc:
  if column && column.type == :binary
    if /(.*?)\(([0-9]+\))/ =~ column.sql_type
      %Q{empty_#{ $1 }()}
    else
      %Q{empty_#{ column.sql_type rescue 'blob' }()}
    end
  else
    if column && column.type == :primary_key
      return value.to_s
    end
    case value
    when String      : %Q{'#{quote_string(value)}'}
    when NilClass    : 'null'
    when TrueClass   : '1'
    when FalseClass  : '0'
    when Numeric     : value.to_s
    when Date, Time  : %Q{TIMESTAMP'#{
                 value.strftime("%Y-%m-%d %H:%M:%S")}'}
    else              %Q{'#{quote_string(value.to_yaml)}'}
    end
  end
end
```

There are two interesting methods here: quote_string and quote. quote_string quotes all values in the string sent in to it, to make sure that the database interprets the values correctly. A typical example is how quoting of the single quote works. In some databases you should write two single quotes, and in other cases use a backslash.

The quote method takes the value to quote and a column definition if available, and tries to guess the best representation of the value based on this information. The parts that are most important to get right are usually binary values and date and time values, because these have a tendency to vary wildly between database implementations.

The final part that causes trouble for AR-JDBC is the DDL code, which allows you to do migrations such as creating tables. In some cases, the default implementations work, but it usually breaks down for nonstandard operations such as renaming tables, adding columns, changing column types, and so on. In the case of Oracle, the default implementation is not enough, because we need to create sequences for primary key values. A few typical implementations can look like this:

```ruby
def create_table(name, options = {}) #:nodoc:
  super(name, options)
  execute "CREATE SEQUENCE #{name
          }_seq START WITH 10000" unless options[:id] == false
end


def rename_table(name, new_name) #:nodoc:
  execute "RENAME #{name} TO #{new_name}"
  execute "RENAME #{name}_seq TO #{new_name}_seq" rescue nil
end

def remove_index(table_name, options = {}) #:nodoc:
  execute "DROP INDEX #{index_name(table_name, options)}"
end

def change_column_default(table_name, column_name, default) #:nodoc:
  execute "ALTER TABLE #{table_name} MODIFY #{column_name
          } DEFAULT #{quote(default)}"
end

def change_column(table_name, column_name, type, options = {}) #:nodoc:
  change_column_sql = "ALTER TABLE #{table_name} MODIFY #{
          column_name} #{type_to_sql(type, options[:limit])}"
  add_column_options!(change_column_sql, options)
  execute(change_column_sql)
end

def rename_column(table_name, column_name, new_column_name) #:nodoc:
  execute "ALTER TABLE #{table_name} RENAME COLUMN #{
          column_name} to #{new_column_name}"
end

def remove_column(table_name, column_name) #:nodoc:
  execute "ALTER TABLE #{table_name} DROP COLUMN #{column_name}"
end
```

The best way to start implementing a new database adapter is usually to create a simple Rails application and try to get it working, using the logs to figure out which parts of the adapter don't work. Get a basic migration working so you can create a table or two, and then add a new model, some more advanced features, and so on until you feel it works well enough for standard usage. At that point the best way to proceed is to get the database adapter running with Rails' own test suites. They test many, many areas of Rails and will find all issues that can be problematic with your AR-JDBC code. How to do this can be a little tricky, but you can get good help from the AR-JDBC mailing list.

If you create a new database adapter, don't hesitate: try to get it included in the default AR-JDBC distribution. As mentioned in the section about contributing, we would love for people to own their database implementations and have them be part of AR-JDBC.

Summary

You've now seen the possibilities JRuby on Rails can offer you. Now is the time to head out in the world, create your first application that uses it, and get it into production. Most of the information needed is somewhere within this book, and I hope this book has given you inspiration and some ideas of how to use these capabilities in your work.

The ecosystem for Ruby implementations is changing fast, and JRuby provides an exciting new opportunity for use in places where the regular Ruby implementation will never get traction. But JRuby isn't only for those cases; JRuby also tries to be a great Ruby implementation regardless of platform. Running Ruby on the Java platform is natural for some and unnatural for others, but it can be highly useful and gives you power that would be hard to apply on another implementation.

Go out, write applications, and contribute code back to the community. Tell people what you're doing, what you find good and bad with the current implementation, and create documentation to help other people get started. JRuby is the way forward, and right now you can help.

APPENDIX A

■ ■ ■

Ruby for Java Programmers

This appendix is not supposed to be a full reference to the Ruby language. Instead, the point is to give an introduction based on what you already know from Java, noting some differences and things that are useful to know. With the help of this appendix, you should be able to understand almost all the code in this book.

If you want to learn Ruby from scratch and in more depth, several good books, both published and online, can help. Appendix C details some of the best.

If you're a Java programmer coming to Ruby, it's important to keep in mind that Ruby is quite different from Java. You can write Ruby code in the style of Java if you want, but you'll lose some of the benefits. The style of Ruby can be widely different from Java, and Ruby readily incorporates metaprogramming features in most tasks. It's also important to try to understand the functional aspects of Ruby, because you can make code concise and readable by good usage of blocks and closures.

Core Ruby

Some concepts are important to know before you start looking at Ruby at all. First of all, Ruby is executed sequentially, top down. Even class definitions are just executions of code, one line after another. Because Ruby doesn't have a compilation step that collects all code and reorganizes it, this means you can do some interesting things in class definitions that aren't possible in Java.

Naming

Ruby uses naming to determine what kind of variable you're referencing. This can be useful because it gives you a visual cue about what is happening. You can use five different types of names. What's common for all of them is that they spring into being the first time you give a value to them.

Globals

Any name starting with the dollar sign is a global variable and will have the same value no matter from where you reference it. The value of a global can be changed, and that change will be seen in all code running after that.

```
$foobar = "Hello World"

def print_foobar
  print $foobar
end

print_foobar
```

Constants

All names beginning with a capital letter are constants. A constant belongs to a certain scope, and constants can be nested inside modules and classes. Class names and module names are almost always constants, but that doesn't mean a constant can't contain another value. Typical class constants are String, Hash, and Array. You can set other constants like this:

```
Value = 1
VALUE_NO_2 = 2

module Mod
  VALUE_3 = 3
end

puts Value
puts VALUE_NO_2
puts Mod::VALUE_3
```

Notice that you reference a constant inside a module using ::. You can reset constants to another value, but that causes a warning message to be printed. If you reference a constant that doesn't exist, an error will be raised. You can change that behavior using the const_missing hook method, which we'll look at later.

Instance Variables

Instance variables begin with an @ sign, and act like member variables in Java. The difference is that they don't have to be defined in any way. As with the other names, the first time you set a value, the instance variable will exist:

```
@hello = "Hello"
puts @hello
```

Class Variables

Class variables begin with two @ signs and are mostly like static member variables in Java. They are shared between instances of the same class, and it's also possible to access them from class methods. There are a few subtle points in the sharing of class variables; you can look up or just experiment with that information.

```
@@counter = 1
@@counter += 1
puts @@counter
```

Local Variables and Method Names

Local variables always begins with either an underscore or a lowercase letter. A method name is usually named the same way, but it's possible to create methods that are named more creatively.

Core Types

The core Ruby library contains many classes for all kinds of different purposes. Some of the most central classes also have custom ways of creating instances for them.

Object

Object is the superclass for all classes in Ruby. In fact, most of the methods available on the Object class are mixed in from the Kernel module, but that distinction isn't important. If you want to add global functionality to Ruby, you should put it in the Object class.

There are several important methods on Object; following are the most used of these:

- ==
- class
- clone
- dup
- equal?
- hash
- inspect
- send
- to_s

You can use the methods equal? and == to compare objects. clone and dup allow you to make copies of an object. The class method returns the type of the object in question. hash returns a hash code. inspect returns a String describing the object in detail, while to_s returns a String representation that doesn't contain all detail about the object. send allows you to call a named method on the object.

String

Strings are very useful and arguably the type most often used in Ruby. There are several ways to create new String instances. Double quotes and single quotes are most common, but there are also other versions. The difference mostly involves what kind of quoting is available inside the String. With double quotes and %Q(), all quotes available in C Strings work, and you can also interpolate any Ruby value. Single quotes and %q() only allow quoting backslash and the single quote or end parenthesis, respectively.

In a double quoted string, you can use the syntax #{} to interpolate any Ruby value you want; you can also nest these statements and execute any Ruby code you want inside them:

```
"Hello, #{"world"}"
```

```
"Hello, number #{1+1}"
```

```
'Here, this: #{asdafgsd} doesn\'t do anything'
```

```
%Q(Interpolation, "is really good", he quipped #{'twice'})
```

```
%[Percent followed by parentheses, braces or brackets work like %Q]
```

```
%q(I can use any quote I want in here, like this: ', or this: ".
 But I need to
```

```
quote the right parenthesis: \) ... )
```

String contains many highly useful methods. Refer to http://ruby-doc.org for an extensive listing of everything you can do with String.

Symbol

Symbols are mostly like Strings, except that they are immutable and one Symbol will always be the same as any other symbol with the same name. Symbols are used to identify names of different kinds, and they make it more explicit when you're dealing with a specific value. This is a huge difference compared to Java, where Strings are usually interned (meaning that different String literals with the same content will refer to the same String instance), and can never be modified. In Ruby, Symbols are closer to interned Java Strings, and Ruby Strings look like Java StringBuffers.

You prefix a Symbol with a colon:

```
:hello_world
```

You can use double quotes around the name of a Symbol, if it contains things that wouldn't parse otherwise:

```
:"this is one symbol"
```

You can create a Symbol with an interpolated name because they're double quotes:

```
:"this is symbol ##{13*13}"
```

Fixnum and Bignum

Ruby integer numbers are represented with the classes Fixnum and Bignum. In most cases it's transparent to the programmer what class is actually used. Fixnums will turn themselves into Bignums when the result of an operation gets too big for Fixnum. Both support the same operations, and you can do all mathematics you would expect to be able to by using Java primitives.

One of the things that can make Ruby code more readable is the ability to include arbitrary amounts of underscores in a numeric literal:

```
num = 1_000_000_000
```

The variable num will contain the number one billion, and the underscores will be stripped away, but the code is much more readable in this way.

You can also represent numbers in hexadecimal, octal, and binary notation:

```
0b0101010    # => binary for 42
0700         # => octal for 448
0xFE_FE      # => hex for 65278
```

Float

The Ruby Float class is internally represented as a Java double, and it also works in mostly the same way as Java doubles. You can use all the regular numeric operations on Floats, and you can define the literal values like this:

```
0.0002323
23234.233
-0.42e3
1E-132
```

Array

One of the most important types in Ruby, an Array contains the equivalent of java.util.List, and some more useful operations too. A Ruby Array can contain any values you want, and nothing stops you from mixing and matching. The Ruby Array is zero indexed, and you can use numbers and ranges to get and set information in it. If you try to get a value from a larger index than the size of the Array, it will return nil. If you set a value at a higher index, the Array will expand to that point, and will insert nil values at the intermediate points.

The literal syntax uses square brackets:

```
[:abc, "foo", 123, bar]
```

There is a shortcut for the case of creating an array of strings, where each string is one word:

```
%w(hello there my friend)
```

The preceding code is the same as this:

```
['hello', 'there', 'my', 'friend']
```

Ruby Arrays can be recursive:

```
a = []
a[0] = a
```

You use square brackets to retrieve and set values in an Array:

```
a = [1, 2, 4, 8, 16, 234]

puts a[1]

puts a[1..3]
puts a[1, 2]

a[423] = 13
a[2..3] = nil

a[15..28] = [1,2,3]
```

By using Ranges as indexes you can change the size of the array dynamically. By setting an area of an Array to nil, you remove those values. You can also splice a new array into a range of indexes like the last example shows.

Hash

The Ruby Hash class is almost exactly the same as the Java HashMap, but just like with Array, Ruby adds several practical methods and a literal syntax that makes it easier to create. To create a new Hash, you can use the curly brackets:

```
{1 => 2, 3 => 4}
```

It's also possible just to separate the keys and the values with commas:

```
{1, 2, 3, 4}
```

Just as with Java, you can put whatever you want in a Hash, but the keys should probably return something useful from the hash code. Also like Java, the iteration order is undefined.

You can set or put a value using the same syntax as for Array:

```
h = {1 => 2, 3 => 4}
h[5] = 18
```

Do this to fetch values:

```
h = {1 => 2, 3 => 4}
puts h[1]
```

You can't use Ranges to get more than one value, but you can use another method, called values_at:

```
h = {1 => 2, 3 => 4, 5 => 6, 7 => 8}
puts h.values_at([1,5,7,1])
```

This returns an Array of the corresponding values.

Ruby hashes have a default value or a default block. The default value is nil, but you can provide another one by creating a new Hash explicitly using this constructor:

```
h = Hash.new(0)
p h[36]
```

This prints 0 instead of nil.

Regexp

One visible heritage from Perl and the Unix tradition is Ruby's strong support for regular expressions. Ruby supports much of what you would expect from such an engine, including many Portable Operating System Interface (POSIX) features, escape sequences, and also both greedy and lazy matching. A slash delimits the syntax for a literal regular expression, but you can also use %r and any choice of start and end delimiter:

```
/abc/
%r(foo)
%r!^bar$!
```

You can interpolate values into a regular expression the same way you do with a String:

```
/a#{1+32}c/
```

To match a regular expression against a String, use either =~ or ===. The triple equal method will return true if the regular expression matches, and otherwise false. Using the =~ method to match will return the index where the expression first matched.

You can use several implicit variables to get hold of information about a matching. If you captured groups inside the expression, you can get at them using the globals $1 to $9, where each group is numbered sequentially.

Range

A range represents a start and an end, and everything in between. A range can be either inclusive or exclusive, meaning that the end is either part of the range or not. The most common usage of ranges is for representing numbers, but you can also do ranges of Strings and other types:

```
1..9          #inclusive
1...34        #exclusive
'aaa'..'zzz'  #lowercase letter combinations of length 3
```

nil, true, and false

nil is the Ruby equivalent of null, but nil is slightly different from null. In Ruby all values are considered true unless they are nil or false. There exists an explicit true value too, though. What makes it more interesting is that nil, true, and false are all instances of classes, and are objects in their own right. That means you can add new methods to them if you want. nil is the only instance of the class NilClass, true is the only instance of TrueClass, and false is the only instance of FalseClass.

Classes and Modules

Ruby is a pure object-oriented language. That means that everything is an instance of a class. All classes are also modules, but modules can exist on their own. There are two main usages for modules: they act as namespaces and they allow you to mix behavior into classes. That second feature is the reason why Ruby can be single inheritance and not need interfaces.

Use this code to define a new module:

```
module Foo
end
```

Do this to define a new class:

```
class Bar
end
```

Use this code to define a class with a superclass:

```
class MyString < String
end
```

To define a class inside the namespace of a module, open up that module and define the class in it:

```
module Foo
 class MyString
 end
end
```

To refer to that class, use the double-colon syntax mentioned earlier:

```
Foo::MyString.new
```

Defining Methods

All methods must exist within either a module or class. If you define a method at the top level, you will in fact define it on the Singleton class of the top-level object.

To define a new method, use the keyword def:

```
class Foo
 def hello
 end
end
```

Do this to define a method that takes arguments:

```
def hello(arg1, arg2)
end
```

Use this code to define a method that takes optional arguments:

```
def hello(arg1, arg2 = "foo")
end
```

An optional argument needs to have a default value. This default value can be any valid Ruby expression, but default values are almost always simple values. A method can have more than one optional argument. A method can also take a rest argument. A rest argument collects all the arguments sent to the method that didn't have any other place, and puts them in an array:

```
def hello(arg1, *rest)
end
```

If you call the method hello with the arguments 1, 2, and 3, arg1 will contain 1, and rest will contain [2, 3]. The rest argument always needs to be the last argument provided, except if you have a block argument.

When invoking a method, you can provide hash values to it. If there is no bad interaction with the rest of the method call, you don't need to provide the curly brackets around the hash literal, as long as Ruby can understand what you mean. Say you have a method defined like this:

```
def hello(arg, options = nil)
end
```

You can call it like this, and options will contain a Hash with the values 1=>2 and 3=>4:

```
hello :foo, 1=>2, 3=>4
```

You can also use the star when calling a method for unpacking an Array into separate arguments. That is an advanced feature that can also be confusing. In most Ruby literature it's called *splatting*.

You can define the equivalent of static methods on a class in Ruby using several methods:

```
class Foo
 def self.hello
 end
end

class <<Foo
 def hello
 end
end

class Foo
 class <<self
  def hello
  end
 end
end
```

These three definitions all define a method called hello on the Foo class object, which can be invoked by calling Foo.hello. You can find more information on why this works in the section "The Singleton Class."

Including and Extending

You can define methods on a module in two ways:

```
module Foo
 def self.hello
 end
end
```

```
module Foo
 def hello
 end
end
```

The first version does the same thing as the equivalent for classes, meaning you can invoke Foo.hello on that module. The second version is more tricky. Because Foo is a module, it cannot be instantiated, meaning there is no way to call instance methods on it. However, we can use this method by including it in another class:

```
class ARealClass
 include Foo
end
```

```
ARealClass.new.hello
```

All instance methods on the module Foo are now callable on instances of ARealClass. Also, if I add a new method to Foo, that method will also be callable on instances of ARealClass. This is called a mixin, and many features in the Ruby library are created in this way. Many of the most interesting parts of Hash and Array come from the module Enumerable.

You can call include on any module and class, and that includes the instance variables of the included module into the dispatch chain for instances of that class. You can also do the same thing on a specific instance of an object by using extend:

```
a = Object.new
a.extend Foo
a.hello
```

The Singleton Class

When discussing the Ruby object system, the most hard part to explain is the singleton class. However, it is also the part that's the most important for the flexibility of Ruby. As mentioned earlier, everything in Ruby is an instance of a Class. Every Ruby object has a series of ancestors. The singleton class is an anonymous class specific to an instance. That means that ultimately, every instance in a Ruby system could have its own singleton class. That's also what allows us to do something like this:

```
a = Object.new
def a.hello
 puts "Hello"
end
```

```
a.hello
```

The `hello` method is defined on the singleton class of the instance called a. No other class or object in Ruby has this method. But what is interesting about the singleton class is that classes in Ruby also can have a singleton class, because they are regular instances. Now, a class such as `String` is an instance of `Class`. However, you can define new methods on the `String` object, which isn't available on the `Class` class. These methods are available on the singleton class of the `String` object. If you think about it, that's what allows you to create something similar to static methods in Java like this:

```
class String
 def self.hello
  puts "Hello from the String singleton class"
 end
end
```

```
String.hello
```

The difference is, in Ruby there's only one single type of method. There's nothing strange or static about these methods; they're just defined on the singleton class instead of on a regular class. If you need to get a reference to the singleton class of an object, this code will achieve it for you:

```
class Object
 def singleton_class
  (class <<self; self; end)
 end
end
```

Now you can invoke the method `singleton_class` on any object in Ruby and get back a reference to that class. This is more useful than you can imagine.

Blocks

One of the more distinctive features of Ruby is the block mechanism. Ruby blocks are closures and don't have a good counterpart in Java. They allow you to encapsulate code and send it to a method for any kind of usage that method wants to use it for. Any method call in Ruby can have a block attached to it. There are two syntaxes for blocks: one using curly braces and one using the keywords do followed by end. They are almost equivalent, only different in precedence:

```
2.times { puts "Hello" }
2.times do
  puts "Hello"
end
```

A block can take arguments—either regular named arguments or `rest` arguments. The current version doesn't support optional arguments and block arguments. The arguments to a block are defined within pipes:

```
[1, 2, 3].each do |n|
  puts n*2
end
```

```
foo { |*args| p args }
```

You can do some other things with block arguments, but most of them are bad style and you won't find them in most code.

If you write a method where it makes sense to use a block, you can invoke it using the `yield` call. You can also see if a block has been given by using `block_given?`:

```
def foo
  yield 1
  yield 2
  yield 4
end
```

```
def bar
  if block_given?
    yield 1,2,3
    yield 4,5,6
  else
    puts "NO BLOCK"
  end
end
```

You can call `yield` however many times you like, but it will raise an exception if no block has been given.

In most cases, blocks are used in the method they are sent to, but in some circumstances it can be useful to save a block away and use it later on. You can do that by defining a method that takes a block argument. The block argument must be the last defined, even after `rest` arguments:

```
def foo &blk
  @block = blk
end
```

```
foo { puts "Hello" }
```

This sequence won't invoke the block at all, but will instead turn it into an instance of the class `Proc`, and save that away in the instance variable named @block. You can later invoke the block by calling `call` on it and also by providing arguments as usual:

```
@block.call
```

If you have a `Proc` instance, you can turn that back into a real block using the same syntax when calling the method that requires a real block:

```
10.times &@block
```

You can use three method calls in the standard library to turn a block into a `Proc` instance:

```
lambda { puts "hello" }
proc { puts "hello" }
Proc.new { puts "Hello" }
```

`lambda` and `proc` are aliases of each other, and `Proc.new` just creates a new `proc` instance with the provided block. There are some differences between them, regarding what happens when you call `return` from inside the block and so on, but we won't use this in this book.

Metaprogramming

Ruby is probably most famous for its metaprogramming features. In Ruby, you can do some amazing things dynamically; many aspects of the language make it easy to create incredibly succinct and readable code. Of course, you can use those same features to create a totally unreadable mess. However, used in the right way, metaprogramming can be very useful.

I'll quickly walk through some of the more common aspects of metaprogramming that allow you to do things in Ruby that cannot easily be done in Java. Some of the metaprogramming capabilities are available because you can always open up a class and change the methods in it after the fact.

Introspection

You can find out almost everything about a Ruby object dynamically using its introspection features. I'll show most of them here. I'll also show some method calls that aren't really introspection in the strictest sense, but that still make sense to show here.

Methods

You can find out much information about the methods available on any object instance by using the `method` methods:

```
Object.new.methods
```

This call returns an array containing the names of all publicly accessible methods available on the object it's called on. The methods returned include all ancestor methods too. In the same manner, you can find out the private, protected, public, and singleton methods by calling `private_methods`, `protected_methods`, `public_methods`, and `singleton_methods`.

If you have a `Class` or `Module` object, you can use the same methods to find the static methods, but you can also use `instance_methods` to find the methods you can call on an instance of that class. There are also versions for public, protected, and private instance methods: `public_instance_methods`, `protected_instance_methods`, and `private_instance_methods`. It doesn't make sense to be able to check the singleton methods of instances, because by definition a class cannot know the singleton methods that might be available on instances of that class.

You can also ask an object if it responds to a specific method call. For example, do this to see if you can call the method foo on the object a:

```
a.respond_to? :foo
```

Instance Variables

You can dynamically find out the instance variables defined on an object by calling instance_variables. This returns an array of strings with the names of instance variables that are set on that object at that time. You can use instance_variable_set and instance_variable_get to set and get instance variables:

```
a = "foo"
a.instance_variables      # will return []
a.instance_variable_set "@foo", 42
a.instance_variables      # will return ["@foo"]
a.instance_variable_get "@foo"
```

Constants

You can ask any class or module for which constants it has defined in it:

```
File.constants
```

You can use const_get and const_set to get the values of constants dynamically and also set them. This works in the same way as instance_variable_get and instance_variable_set. Make sure that you get the naming right; otherwise, an exception will be raised.

send

In many situations it can be highly useful to be able to call a method that you won't know the name of until runtime. send allows you to call any method on any object based on the name of the method. Rails uses this extensively; for example, to invoke a method on a controller based on the action name. To use send, just call send with the first argument as the name of the method to call, and the rest of the arguments in the same way as a regular method call:

```
a = (rand(2) == 0) ? '+' : '-'
123.send a, 50
```

In 50 percent of all cases, the preceding routine will add 123 and 50, and the rest of the time it will subtract 50 from 123.

method_missing, const_missing

While send allows you to call anything you'd like dynamically, method_missing is a callback hook that makes it easy to change the behavior in case a method is called on an object that doesn't respond to that method. This allows much flexibility, and gives you the possibility to create message recording, delegators, and distributed systems easily.

To use method_missing, just define it on a class:

```ruby
class Foo
  def method_missing(name, *args, &block)
    puts "Method #{name} called"
  end
end


Foo.new.hello_world
Foo.new.adgsdfgsdfgsdfgsdfgsdfgertgsertg
```

In this case, no method call on a Foo instance raises an exception, because you've changed the behavior of method_missing just to print the name of the method invoked. A more useful scenario is probably to look for a specific format of the method names provided and fall back on the regular method_missing behavior otherwise:

```ruby
class Finder
  def find(name); end

  def method_missing(name, *args)
    if /^find_(.*)/ =~ name
      return find($1)
    end
    super
  end
end
```

When using an instance of this finder, and you call anything that begins with find_, that method call will be forwarded to the find method. The argument will be the rest of the method name, after find_. Otherwise, call super. Note that calling super without any arguments and parentheses forwards the original arguments to the currently executing method, so it's a shorthand for just providing all arguments explicitly.

The hook const_missing allows you to do exactly the same thing as method_missing, except it's for constants instead of methods.

define_method

Using define_method, you can create new methods from scratch at runtime. You can use eval for this too, but the nice thing about define_method is that it can take a block and have that be the body of the method. That means that it's possible to implement a method based on a block someone saved earlier. You can also decide the name of the method at runtime. The only current limitation of define_method is that methods defined in that way cannot take block arguments.

```ruby
define_method :hello do |arg1, arg2|
  puts "I got #{arg1} and #{arg2}"
end


hello(1, 13)
```

Class.new and Module.new

Not only can you create new methods dynamically, it's also possible to create new anonymous classes and modules at runtime using Class.new and Module.new. In the case of Class.new, you can dynamically create subclasses of existing classes if you want. As soon as you have a reference to the newly created object you can do anything you want with it, because it's just a regular Ruby instance. Both Class.new and Module.new can take a block where you can define methods and execute mostly anything you could in a regular module or class definition:

```ruby
mod = Module.new do
  def self.hello_world
  end
end

my_string = Class.new(String)
p my_string.new("ABC")
```

eval and Friends

If all else fails, Ruby allows you to interpret arbitrary Ruby code using eval. However, in most cases you don't need that; it's usually enough to use either instance_eval or module_eval/class_eval. eval takes a String containing the code to execute, while instance_eval and module_eval take a block. That block will be executed in a different context depending on which you use. If you run instance_eval, you can access instance_variables and private methods of the instance executing within. If you use module_eval or class_eval, you can define new methods using the def syntax.

```ruby
1.instance_eval do
  puts self
  @foo = 42
end

String.module_eval do
  def hello_world
  end
end
```

As a last shot, you can always use eval:

```ruby
ret = eval("1 + 42")
```

You can define new methods and classes based on strings:

```ruby
method_name = 'do_it'
eval("def #{method_name}; puts 'hello'; end")
do_it
```

The Symbol to_proc Trick

A useful trick is extensively used in much of the Rails code, based on what happens when you use & to turn a `Proc` instance into a block to a method call. I'll show it to you in a bit, but first look at this:

```
a = ["one", "two", 1..3]
p a.map { |arg| arg.inspect }
```

This prints

```
["one", "two", 1..3]
```

That's because the `map` method call returns an array containing the result of running the provided block on each value of itself. Now, it's common to call a method with no arguments when using a block. The `Symbol to_proc` trick makes it possible to write the preceding code like this instead:

```
a = ["one", "two", 1..3]
p a.map &:inspect
```

There's not a huge difference, but it matters more when chaining block method calls together. Now, what happens is this: we have the symbol `:inspect`. When the Ruby interpreter finds an ampersand, it will check if the value after the ampersand is a `Proc`. If it isn't, Ruby will try to call a special hook method called `to_proc` on the value it finds there, and if it succeeds will turn the resulting `Proc` object into a block to the method call. So far all is good. What's missing is the `to_proc` method on `Symbol`, which should look like this:

```
class Symbol
  def to_proc
    proc { |obj| obj.send self }
  end
end
```

Remember that the `Proc` returned is turned into a block, and that block is invoked with one argument for each object in the collection. That argument is the `obj` argument to the block. We use `send` to call a method dynamically, and we send in `self` to the `send` call. Remember, `self` is the same as `this` in Java, and `self` is a `Symbol` in this case—in fact, the `Symbol` that names the method to be called.

The end result is that the symbol `:inspect` will be turned into a `Proc`, which is then turned into a block, which will call the method `inspect` on the object sent in as an argument to the block.

APPENDIX B

■ ■ ■

JRuby Reference

This appendix will serve as a reference when using pure JRuby features. All these features (except for the JRuby module) are only available after executing this:

```
require 'java'
```

This happens automatically if you reference the module named Java, though. Chapter 6 also covers the information in this appendix, with much more information and detail, when that is needed.

Classes and Interfaces

It's easy to use Java classes and interfaces from JRuby, as we've seen through the book.

Referencing a Java Class or Java Interface

To reference a Java class in the java, javax, com, and org packages, you can use top-level references:

```
com.foo.Bar
java.util.HashMap
org.jruby.Main
```

When working with a class in another package, use the Java module:

```
Java::se.ki.HelloWorld
Java::net.hello.World
```

There are three ways to include a class into the current context. First, you can assign a constant:

```
Runtime = java.lang.Runtime
TestClass = Java::se.ki.HelloWorld
```

The most intuitive way for Java programmers is probably the import command:

```
import java.lang.Runtime
```

This does exactly the same thing as assigning the constant `Runtime` to the value of `java.lang.Runtime`.

When the class you need to use doesn't follow the standard Java naming conventions, none of these variations will work in all cases. To reference a class or interface in these circumstances, you can use `include_class`. There is also an equivalent command called `import_package`, but you should consider that deprecated, and it won't be described here.

Here's how to include a class into the current namespace giving it the same class name as the `Java` equivalent:

```
include_class 'java.lang.Runtime'
```

You can also use this version with an array of class names to include:

```
include_class ['java.lang.Runtime', 'java.util.HashMap']
```

You can also give the classes new names by generating a new name in a block sent to `include_class`:

```
include_class 'java.lang.Runtime' do |package, class_name|
 "J#{class_name}"
end
```

The block is invoked once for each class name given to `include_class`, and receives the package name and the class name as arguments. It should return a string containing the name of the constant to set with the value of the Java class.

Using Classes

Once you've gotten hold of a Java class, you can do all the things you could do to a Ruby class with it. You can invoke methods, alias, add and remove methods, and so forth.

You can create a new Java instance by calling `new` on a Java class. The argument matching proceeds in the same way invocation of all Java method invocations happens. Chapter 6 details these more. The correct constructor is matched and called.

```
java.util.HashMap.new
java.util.HashMap.new {"a"=>"b", "c"=>"d"}
```

Note that Ruby `Hashes` are instances of `java.util.Map`, meaning that you can initialize a `HashMap` with them.

Invocation of Java methods works in the same way as regular Ruby invocation. However, to make sure that you can write code that looks like Ruby, most Java methods have aliases that use Ruby naming conventions. So, for example, you can invoke the Java method `printAndWait` as `print_and_wait` from JRuby. A special case is JavaBean setters and getters, which are transformed into `attr_accessor` conventions:

```
foo.setState(13)
foo.state = 13
print foo.getState
print foo.state
```

Both versions work, but it usually makes the Ruby code clearer not to mix naming conventions.

Extension and Implementation

Ruby classes can extend a Java class and override abstract and concrete methods, and those overridden versions will be visible on the object when sent back into Java code. Java cannot in any way see completely new methods, nor methods changed or added on final classes. That means you can override methods on java.lang.String, and the changes will be seen inside JRuby, but not by Java code.

The syntax for extending a Java class is the same as for a Ruby class:

```
class MyOS < java.io.OutputStream
  def write(b)
  end
end
```

When overriding overloaded methods, it's important to note that your Ruby method will be responsible for handling all method invocations with the same name, regardless of argument count.

To implement one or more interfaces, use the include method call:

```
class Foo
  include java.lang.Runnable
  include java.lang.Comparable
end
```

Make sure only to do these include statements the first time you create a class. You cannot include a Java interface in a class that already implements interfaces from another definition.

Primitive Arrays

Because Ruby doesn't have a concept of primitive arrays, you usually need to convert back and forth. The easiest way to create a Java primitive array is from an existing Ruby array, using to_java:

```
[1, 2, 3].to_java :byte
```

The argument to the to_java method can be any Java class instance, or any of the following symbols:

- :boolean

- :byte

- :char

- :short

- :int

- :long

- :float

- `:double`

- `:decimal`

- `:big_decimal`

- `:big_int`

- `:big_integer`

- `:object`

- `:string`

To turn a Java array into a Ruby array, just use `to_a`:

```
[1, 2, 3].to_java(:byte).to_a
```

An existing Java array allows you to use `[ ]` and `[ ]=` just as you would be able to using a regular Ruby Array. The only restriction is that you can only provide simple integer indexes when setting.

```
arr = [1, 2, 3, 4, 5].to_java :byte
p arr[1..3]
arr[1] = 15
```

Several variations are possible for creating new Java arrays. All of them depend on you using class objects. To get at the primitive class objects, you can use the `Java::byte`, `Java::char`, and `Java::boolean` type of references. All other classes are accessible as usual.

Do this to create a new array with one dimension:

```
java.lang.String[10].new
```

This returns a primitive Java array of length 10. Use this code to create multidimensional arrays:

```
java.lang.String[10][2].new
```

You can find the other versions available for creating arrays in Chapter 6.

Extensions to Java Classes

To make life easier when using Java classes from Ruby, JRuby has added several extensions so that some things that make sense from a Ruby perspective are available on the Java classes.

java.lang.Runnable

The `java.lang.Runnable` interface has the method `to_proc` added to it, which means that if you have an instance of `Runnable`, you can use the block syntax to turn it into a real block:

```
10.times &a_runnable
```

java.util.Map

The methods added to Map generally serve the purpose of making it look more like a Ruby Hash:

- each

- include Enumerable

- []

- []=

java.lang.Comparable

The Java Comparable interface needs to have the "spaceship operator" and include the Ruby Comparable Module to be able to handle sorting and comparisons correctly in the Ruby world.

- <=>

- include Comparable

java.util.Collection

Every instance of Collection provides many useful methods, most of them originally from Array:

- each

- include Enumerable

- <<

- +

- -

- length

java.util.List

In addition to the methods from java.util.Collection, List adds some more useful things:

- []

- []=

- sort

- sort!

The JRuby Module

If you execute this code, you'll get access to the module called JRuby:

```
require 'jruby'
```

Currently, this module only contains two utility methods, but you can expect that to expand so that you can get easy access later on to everything in the JRuby runtime. In fact, one of the methods gives you the current runtime. Through it you can do mostly anything, but it can be a little cumbersome. The hope is that some easier ways will be provided.

runtime

The runtime method call returns the current JRuby runtime by executing this:

```
JRuby.runtime
```

Of course, having access to the current runtime gives you possibilities to do more or less anything you can imagine, because you can work with the internals of JRuby directly. The possibilities are endless. You'll have to look at the JavaDoc for org.jruby.Ruby to see what kinds of things you can achieve with it easily.

parse

You can also dynamically parse code using the JRuby module. The parse method takes three arguments: the first is the string to parse, the second is the string describing the source of the code (used for stack traces), and the third argument is a Boolean that controls whether the parsing should be done with extensive parse information or not:

```
JRuby.parse "puts 'hello'", '-', false
```

The parse call will either raise a SyntaxError if the code is invalid in some way, or will return a JRuby AST root node, which you can inspect in whatever way you want. If you felt the inclination, one thing you could do with the help of the JRuby module would be first to parse some code, then change the AST returned, and finally execute the AST using one of the evaluation methods on the runtime object. In this way, it would be possible to implement a cumbersome variation of macros for Ruby.

compile

Later versions of JRuby have added the support to compile Ruby code into Java bytecode. If you want to see the result of a specific compilation without actually loading the class generated, you can do that with the compile method, and call inspect_bytecode on the result:

```
puts JRuby.compile("puts 'hello'").inspect_bytecode
```

This code prints the bytecode of a fully compiled Ruby snippet.

reference

In some cases it can be useful to get hold of the Java implementation of a Ruby core class. You can do several interesting things with this capability. (A Ruby library for MRI called evil.rb provides mostly the same kinds of interesting features.)

For example, say you want to unfreeze a Ruby object. That's impossible within the regular Ruby language, but the reference method provides a way around it:

```
str = "foo"
str.freeze
JRuby.reference(str).frozen = false
```

This can be very dangerous, and is not encouraged in production code. The best usage for it would probably be to learn more about the JRuby internals.

require

In almost all cases, the JRuby require works exactly like regular Ruby. There are two places where it's a little different, though. First, you can prefix a require with jar:. In that case, you want to require a JAR file resource, using a standard Java JAR Uniform Resource Identifier (URI). That isn't too common.

The other interesting part about JRuby's require is that you can use it to explicitly put a JAR file on the CLASSPATH for your program. Say I have a JAR file in the current directory called foobar.jar, containing com.foo.Bar:

```
require 'java'
require 'foobar.jar'
com.foo.Bar.methods
```

This works as expected. Doing an explicit require of a JAR file puts it on the CLASSPATH. This doesn't work in all cases, though, because Java's class loader semantics are a little tricky. For example, it doesn't work for JDBC database drivers, and not for XML drivers either. In most cases, things that are found by some kind of service provider interface won't work in this way. However, all other classes should be fine.

Resources

This chapter will give you a long list of helpful links, and pointers to a few useful books. I've tried to categorize the books by main subject, and I hope most of the addresses are still valid when you read this. Remember that the absolutely best resource when starting out with Ruby is your local Ruby User Group (RUG). Many cities in both the United States and Europe have a group that meets up once or twice a month, where members share information and help one another with problems. You should search the Internet for the closest RUG to you; it can be invaluable.

Ruby and Rails

These links are specifically about Ruby or Rails.

The Ruby Programming Language

`http://www.ruby-lang.org`

This is the main Ruby language home page. Go here first to find information about Ruby. This home page also contains lots of pointers to other resources not covered here.

Ruby-talk Mailing List

This mailing list is the main mailing list for everything related to Ruby. It's a high-volume mailing list, but you can usually get answers to questions related to Ruby here. You subscribe from the Ruby-lang home page.

Ruby-core Mailing List

If you're interested in the implementation of Ruby, or what will happen with the language in the future, Ruby-core is the mailing list to subscribe to. It is here that Matz, Koichi, and all the other Ruby core developers discuss the implementation.

Ruby on Rails

http://www.rubyonrails.com

The main home page for Ruby on Rails. Here you can find much documentation about Rails, you can see the introductory web casts, and the Rails wiki contains lots of information that is useful when you have any kind of problem with Rails.

Rails-talk Mailing List

The Rails counterpart to Ruby-talk, this list has even more posts than the Ruby-talk one. As with Ruby-talk, it's a good place to get questions answered. You can subscribe by visiting http://groups.google.com/group/rubyonrails-talk.

Rails-core Mailing List

Discussion related to the implementation of Rails is usually found on the Rails-core list. You can subscribe at http://groups.google.com/group/rubyonrails-core.

Matz Blog

http://www.rubyist.net/~matz

This is the blog of Yukihiro "Matz" Matsumoto, the creator of Ruby. It's in Japanese, so a little hard for non-Japanese speakers to digest, but Google Translate does a passable job on some of the blog posts, at least.

O'Reilly Ruby

http://oreillynet.com/ruby

The O'Reilly Ruby corner usually has some interesting articles posted on advanced issues in the Ruby world.

RubyInside

http://rubyinside.com

This is a nice site that collects the most interesting Ruby articles and blog posts—worth visiting.

On Ruby

http://on-ruby.blogspot.com

Pat Eyler writes the blog On Ruby, which contains news about Ruby, book reviews, and various other information.

Loud Thinking

http://www.loudthinking.com

Loud Thinking is the blog of David Heinemeier Hansson, the creator of Rails. The articles posted here are usually interesting and often controversial.

Riding Rails

http://weblog.rubyonrails.org

This is the collective blog of the Rails core team. Read here for updates on anything important regarding Rails.

Eigenclass

http://eigenclass.org

The Eigenclass blog concentrates on "singular Ruby resources and code." When new posts appear on Eigenclass I'm usually delighted, because the use of metaprogramming and other advanced features of Ruby gets a large place in them.

Polishing Ruby

http://blog.zenspider.com

Ryan Davis is the person behind the name zenspider; he has created some useful projects together with Seattle.rb (the Seattle Ruby brigade). His blog contains useful bits of information about testing, Ruby code, and Emacs usage—all very interesting.

Programming Ruby, Second Edition

The Pick-Axe: the original book for learning about Ruby, by Dave Thomas, Chad Fowler, and Andy Hunt (Pragmatic Bookshelf, 2004). It's still one of the only books necessary as a reference to the language.

The Ruby Way, Second Edition

This book, by Hal Fulton (Addison-Wesley, 2006) is a useful companion to the Pick-Axe. I find I often use it to look up how to do everyday things.

Agile Web Development with Rails, Second Edition

This is the main reference to the Rails framework, by Dave Thomas, David Hansson, Leon Breedt, and Mike Clark (Pragmatic Bookshelf, 2006). If you're serious about Rails development, you need this book, because it provides a reference for almost all parts of the framework.

JRuby

Here's a list of links and blogs about JRuby. If a blog or link is both about Ruby and JRuby, where I put them is based on the main focus.

The JRuby Home Page

`http://www.jruby.org`

This is where you download JRuby and see news about JRuby development.

The JRuby Dev Mailing List

The developers hang out on this mailing list, discussing the future of JRuby and also discussing bugs and problems with the current implementation. You can find links to subscribing on the JRuby home page.

The JRuby User Mailing List

If you're starting out with JRuby and have a problem, this mailing list is the best one to ask for help on. Most of the discussions related to using JRuby will happen here. You can subscribe on the JRuby home page.

The #jruby IRC Channel

The #jruby IRC channel almost always has at least one of the core developers online, and usually more than one. There are also other people versed in JRuby available here; if you need a quick answer, visiting IRC is the best way to accomplish that.

The JRuby-extras Project

`http://rubyforge.org/projects/jruby-extras`

This is the place where almost all surrounding projects for JRuby live. You can subscribe to mailing lists and download the different projects here. It's almost as important as the main JRuby home page.

JRuby JIRA

`http://jira.codehaus.org/browse/JRUBY`

JIRA is the bug tracker for JRuby, and if you experience problems and want to report them, the JRuby JIRA is the place to go. Report bugs here, or see if someone has had the same problem before you. This is also an important place if you want to contribute fixes.

JRubyInside

`http://jrubyinside.com`

A sister site to RubyInside, JRubyInside collects lots of interesting information relating to JRuby, and also aggregates some of the more widely read JRuby blogs.

Headius

`http://headius.blogspot.com`

This is the blog of Charles O. Nutter, one of the JRuby core developers. Charles writes about everything related to JRuby—often about his compiler and interpreter work.

Tom's Ruminations

`http://www.bloglines.com/blog/ThomasEEnebo`

Thomas Enebo is the core developer who has been with JRuby for the longest time. He posts updates about JRuby.

Ola Bini

`http://ola-bini.blogspot.com`

This is my own blog about everything related to JRuby, Ruby, and Java.

Nick Sieger

`http://blog.nicksieger.com`

Nick Sieger is one of the core developers and also writes about JRuby and Ruby.

Other

Here are links to other resources that are useful when reading this book.

MySQL

`http://mysql.com`

You can download the most commonly used database for developing Rails applications from the MySQL home page. The MySQL manual is also very useful.

ActiveMessaging

http://code.google.com/p/activemessaging

This is the home page for the ActiveMessaging project, which aims to provide MOM features for Ruby.

Hitta

http://code.google.com/p/hitta

This is one of the better Rails plug-ins for full-text search. It works fine with JRuby thanks to the stemmer4j extension.

Ferret

http://ferret.davebalmain.com/trac

Ferret is the Ruby version of Lucene, a highly useful library for indexing and searching.

GlassFish

http://glassfish.dev.java.net

GlassFish is one of the better Java application servers out there. It's open source and supports the next generation Java EE 5 specification.

Index

forums.apress.com

FOR PROFESSIONALS BY PROFESSIONALS™

JOIN THE APRESS FORUMS AND BE PART OF OUR COMMUNITY. You'll find discussions that cover topics of interest to IT professionals, programmers, and enthusiasts just like you. If you post a query to one of our forums, you can expect that some of the best minds in the business—especially Apress authors, who all write with *The Expert's Voice*™—will chime in to help you. Why not aim to become one of our most valuable participants (MVPs) and win cool stuff? Here's a sampling of what you'll find:

DATABASES

Data drives everything.

Share information, exchange ideas, and discuss any database programming or administration issues.

INTERNET TECHNOLOGIES AND NETWORKING

Try living without plumbing (and eventually IPv6).

Talk about networking topics including protocols, design, administration, wireless, wired, storage, backup, certifications, trends, and new technologies.

JAVA

We've come a long way from the old Oak tree.

Hang out and discuss Java in whatever flavor you choose: J2SE, J2EE, J2ME, Jakarta, and so on.

MAC OS X

All about the Zen of OS X.

OS X is both the present and the future for Mac apps. Make suggestions, offer up ideas, or boast about your new hardware.

OPEN SOURCE

Source code is good; understanding (open) source is better.

Discuss open source technologies and related topics such as PHP, MySQL, Linux, Perl, Apache, Python, and more.

PROGRAMMING/BUSINESS

Unfortunately, it is.

Talk about the Apress line of books that cover software methodology, best practices, and how programmers interact with the "suits."

WEB DEVELOPMENT/DESIGN

Ugly doesn't cut it anymore, and CGI is absurd.

Help is in sight for your site. Find design solutions for your projects and get ideas for building an interactive Web site.

SECURITY

Lots of bad guys out there—the good guys need help.

Discuss computer and network security issues here. Just don't let anyone else know the answers!

TECHNOLOGY IN ACTION

Cool things. Fun things.

It's after hours. It's time to play. Whether you're into LEGO® MINDSTORMS™ or turning an old PC into a DVR, this is where technology turns into fun.

WINDOWS

No defenestration here.

Ask questions about all aspects of Windows programming, get help on Microsoft technologies covered in Apress books, or provide feedback on any Apress Windows book.

HOW TO PARTICIPATE:

Go to the Apress Forums site at **http://forums.apress.com/**.
Click the New User link.

You Need the Companion eBook

Your purchase of this book entitles you to buy the companion PDF-version eBook for only $10. Take the weightless companion with you anywhere.

We believe this Apress title will prove so indispensable that you'll want to carry it with you everywhere, which is why we are offering the companion eBook (in PDF format) for $10 to customers who purchase this book now. Convenient and fully searchable, the PDF version of any content-rich, page-heavy Apress book makes a valuable addition to your programming library. You can easily find and copy code — or perform examples by quickly toggling between instructions and the application. Even simultaneously tackling a donut, diet soda, and complex code becomes simplified with hands-free eBooks!

Once you purchase your book, getting the $10 companion eBook is simple:

❶ Visit **www.apress.com/promo/tendollars/**.

❷ Complete a basic registration form to receive a randomly generated question about this title.

❸ Answer the question correctly in 60 seconds, and you will receive a promotional code to redeem for the $10.00 eBook.

THE EXPERT'S VOICE™

2855 TELEGRAPH AVENUE | SUITE 600 | BERKELEY, CA 94705

Offer valid through 3/08.